The Chatto Book of

CABBAGES AND
KINGS

Lists in Literature

The Chatto Book of
CABBAGES AND KINGS

Lists in Literature

Edited, with an Introduction, by
FRANCIS SPUFFORD

Chatto & Windus
LONDON

Published in 1989 by
Chatto & Windus Ltd
30 Bedford Square
London WC1B 3SG

A CIP catalogue record for this book is available
from the British Library

ISBN 0 7011 3487 9

Introduction and selection © Francis Spufford 1989

Typography by Humphrey Stone
Photoset by Rowland Phototypesetting Ltd
Bury St Edmunds, Suffolk
Printed in Great Britain by Mackays of Chatham plc
Chatham, Kent

Contents

I have made a great heap of all that I found.

NENNIUS

Introduction

Lists of writers with wooden legs, or unusual preferences at bedtime, are a familiar feature of books of literary trivia. This, however, is an anthology of lists as they are used by writers in their work. It may seem a strange idea. Promising lists that are epic, lists that are comic, and lists that are romantic may not seem any less odd.

Language usually puts the signs that represent things into definite relationships with each other. Syntax joins: *I want to be loved by you*, or *the sky is falling*, or *Mr Murdoch has bought The Times*. Lists, however, divide, or leave divided, the things they include. They offer only the relationship of accumulation: *I, you, love, sky, fall, purchase, Mr Murdoch, The Times*. Lists refuse the connecting powers of language, in favour of a sequence of disconnected elements. In a list, almost everything that makes writing interesting to read seems inevitably to be excluded.

'I had some cause,' wrote Pope in the long note that follows the enumeration of the Greek ships and troops in his translation of the second book of *The Iliad*, 'to fear that this Catalogue which contributed so much to the Success of the Author, should ruin that of the Translator. A meer heap of Proper Names tho' but for a few Lines together, could afford little Entertainment to an *English* Reader, who probably could not be appriz'd either of the Necessity or Beauty of this Part of the Poem.' Pope, of course, wrote that with his customary confidence in his own skills. He had done his best, over the two thousand or so previous words of the note, to demonstrate the practical usefulness of the 'meer heap' ('. . . there have been Laws in some Nations for the Youth to learn it by heart . . .'), as well as claiming for it – among other aesthetic virtues – mellifluousness, nobility, and fine dramatic placing. But his parade of argument and scholarship only claims compensations for something he assumes to be, at root, inexplicably dull. For lists are 'merely' many things: merely sequences, articulated in the least sophisticated of ways; merely juxtapositions, unconstrained by the ordered associations between this thing and that thing that constitute taste; merely dances-on-the-spot, when the reader may expect the interesting forward movement of a narrative or a line of reflection. Finally – and worst of all, for a writer like Pope, unacclimatised by the literary theory of his time to an appreciation of the effects 'low' material can

[1]

give – lists are 'merely' ordinary. They are only by extension a literary form at all.

Most of their life, as one of the most basically useful ways of ordering the world in language, happens outside literature. No one scribbles down a helpful sonnet before going shopping. Everyone uses lists. So finding a list in a book or a poem is an immediate reminder of the most obvious difference between literature and every other kind of non-performing art: literature is made out of something, language, that is an everyday stuff. Statues and paintings declare a distance from common life by the intrinsic specialness of their materials. Literature must declare its special intentions by a special use of words that are in all our mouths, all of the time. There may be glorious and rare words that offer a sort of equivalent to marble or gold-leaf, but language itself is chewed and familiar and quotidian, and to make it appear anything else requires a writer to organise a systematic illusion. Pope must have feared with some degree of seriousness, then, that his readers would see in the 'meer heap of Proper Names' a vulgar, illusion-busting similarity to the horde of non-literary lists they would have been acquainted with in the form of wills, censuses, medical compendiums and rotas. Furthermore, all the names were in Greek, and many had no resonance whatsoever even for the classically literate. The (supposed) inexpressiveness of lists is a long-standing literary joke. Lady Mary Wortley Montagu assured a correspondent that she wouldn't bore her with an enumeration of the relics she saw in Germany. Virginia Woolf breaks off an inventory of the things Orlando has bought for his/her mansion: 'Already – it is an effect lists have upon us – we are beginning to yawn.' A skit by Woody Allen calibrates the state of mind of a Great Writer against the number of socks he sends to the wash.

Yet lists are not always so intrinsically dull, so insistently mundane that 'English Readers' have to be bribed with promises of usefulness in order to struggle through them. To begin at the barest and apparently least promising end of the scale of those lists that are interesting, historians are used to finding, in documents that seem only to itemise property, evidence of character emerging, not because of any self-descriptive intention, but by a minute process of agglomeration, as language reaches out in the simplest way to the group of objects to which the list-maker stands in the revealing relation of ownership. The playwright and ex-historian Alan Bennett records his mother's surprising accidental recapitulation of the phenomenon:

> My mother's description of her clothes:
> My other shoes
> My warm boots
> My tweedy coat

That greeny coat of mine
That fuzzy blue coat I have
My coat with the round buttons
Like the inventory of a medieval will.

Thus have thousands upon thousands of testators set out, casually, frag-
mentarily, the invisible and characteristic hierarchies and affinities (which
are just about to cease to exist, when they die) among their possessions.
Some of them even give precise incidental information about their theo-
logies in their choices of words for the most important bequest of all – of
their souls to God. Of course the intention behind these kinds of list is
wholly unliterary. As repositories for scraps and scrapes of fact, they are
haphazard, which lists, though shapeless according to some definitions,
need not be. Their effect can hardly be said to be literary either, except in the
sense that someone the historian thought to be irrecoverable makes in them
a fractional entrance into a sphere of consideration, an area of individuality,
which adjoins that of, say, the novel. The person whose boots are warm (or
not), or whose soul comes with Anabaptist instructions, has a self in which
it is just possible to imagine that 'the lights and shadows must always
fall with a certain difference', as George Eliot put it. Such a person at least
inhabits the same order of being as a Mr Knightley or an Anna Karenina.

Rather richer, and a step closer to the complex intentions and complex
effects of literature proper, are the catalogues of some sorts of collections.
(If architecture is frozen music, museums are frozen lists.) So long as the
conventions by which the world's contents are classified have not been
completely established for the class of things that compose the collection,
the arrangement of the things can represent an understanding of the world
that is not yet conventional. The nineteenth-century anthropologist
Colonel Pitt-Rivers, theorising and collecting while the new science was
still in flux, decided that its governing principle must be the transmission of
similar forms of object across all cultures and all periods: 'Progress is like a
game of dominoes – like fits onto like.' The museum he founded in Oxford
follows his principle. The 'religious' section puts together pectoral crosses,
small idols and feathered fetishes, stubbornly ignoring what they don't
have in common in favour of the single feature that they do, and creating a
now-notorious effect of bizarre juxtaposition. Four-square in his ordinary
prose, Colonel Pitt-Rivers produced a teeming mélange for a catalogue
(though, sadly, he does not seem to have got around to the religious
section). You can read it – or 'read' it, if you are there – as a kind of copious,
intriguingly dulled, methodical version of one of the French Romantics'
purposefully exotic poems of abroad; including, because of the anthropo-
logical importance of weaponry, their brutality.

This would not be the kind of scavenging reading necessary to glean

[3]

interest from the facts of a medieval inventory. A catalogue of a collection describes its objects so that they can be imagined as nearly as possible in the absence of the objects themselves, for a practical purpose; by doing so it offers them to multiple interpretations, to impractical delight in what goes next to what. Ironies, telling absences and delicate presences are all possible; and objects colour each other, in an accidental concrete parody of imaginative writing. Something expressive and strangely articulated can be discovered, against the functional grain of the catalogue perhaps, yet without eccentricity or opportunism.

Both these ways of reading non-literary lists determinedly hint at means of extracting pleasure from Pope's enormous gathering of proper names. They also suggest a reason why imaginative writers, who have no immediate and practical need to record a set of objects, should sometimes want to use a list when they don't have to; when it might be reasonable to expect that, sensibly preferring banquets to crumbs, they would always choose to articulate what lists can only hint at. Why have fragments of self-revelation, when you can have an articulated self-portrait? Why have the intriguing suggestion of a poetic atmosphere, when you can have the poem itself? Because, from the writer's point of view, 'having' articulation or 'having' the poem – achieving writing as something finished – can require tools very like the search for clues that must be brought to an inventory, or the sensitivity to separate specific atmospheres needed to read a collection.

There is a stage in composition when the elements of the subject that is waiting to be articulated seem to lie higgledy-piggledy. The poet Elizabeth Bishop, digesting Florida, noted: 'I have that continuous uncomfortable feeling of "things" in the head, like icebergs or rocks or awkwardly shaped pieces of furniture – it's as if all the nouns were there but the verbs were lacking – if you know what I mean.' Imagined thus, it is the stage just before language changes its status by becoming imaginative, ceasing to be a simple denotation for objects and becoming a body in itself with its own self-sufficient rules. It is also a point of divergence. What most often happens next is a struggle for the lacking verbs, with the tools of list-reading applied to a collection of perceptions to discover affinities and contrasts that can then become syntax. Sometimes, however, it can seem appropriate for the original collection of stuffs to remain a collection, as a form of articulation in itself, equally reshaped by imagination yet with the artistry concealed in a deliberate choice to use the elementary tools of list-reading as the only ones. Crumbs should not be scorned: from time to time they have been made into very satisfactory banquets in themselves.

So, if lists do play a role in writing, it should not be surprising that when we turn as readers to fully-fledged literature, almost everyone can recall lists they have enjoyed and found expressive, lists whose distance from the tedium of the telephone book is immediately obvious. When the Walrus and the Carpenter talk of many things to the unsuspecting oysters, 'Of shoes and ships and sealing-wax/Of cabbages and kings', the effect is memorable because it is artful. Carroll has made a thumbnail sketch of *everything*, his five listed elements representing the idea of profusion in the same way that the single word 'crown' stands for the full meaning of monarchy, but also pulling apart from each other as if you were holding the strings of five balloons in your hand. He has used, though, the same fundamental method as a shopping list: it seems that in free, attentive hands an accumulation is a subtler, more flexible thing than first appears. The trick lies not only in the manipulation of texture – here, the selection of five words from different categories of concrete noun, which then alliterate as if they sat together by natural dispensation of sound, in a form whose practical origins emphasise orderly classification – but also in the paradox of authority and order that a list always raises. The paradox stems from the absence of any straightforward authorial presence inside a list (where would there be room for one, between element and element?). It is that a list is at the same time the most actively constructing and passively recording of representations. The duality is nicely caught in the reaction of James Joyce's father when told by Joyce's teacher at Clongowes school that the boy's letters home, filled with demands for good things, sounded like grocer's lists. John Joyce disagreed: 'If that fellow was dropped in the middle of the Sahara, he'd sit, be God, and make a map of it.' God or grocer? Lists *mix* God and grocer; they are divinely grocerly and grocerly divine, in variable proportions.

All this means for Carroll, who has only a brief comic effect in mind, is that the set of nouns he has come up with have the residual authority of a record; but the implications are much wider, the literary possibilities of the paradox much larger. When list-makers construe the world in listable fragments, are they fragmenting the world, actively, or collecting it, passively? Sundering, or assembling? When a list goes on and on, are we looking at an abdication of control over a torrent of separate pieces of data, or at the equivalent of a strongman's display of strength with more and more weights? Are the elements of a list, whether they are places or things or food or memories or lovers or heroes, held in place like the stones of an arch, or – to choose from the many spatial metaphors that naturally fit lists – do they cohere like a cloud? Lists congregate in the kinds of writing that exemplify one or other of the two poles of activity and passivity straightfor-wardly, in highly-determined works and in delicately impressionistic ones, in works organised by a compulsion to invent boldly and in works organised by a compulsion to note minutely. They are also particularly attractive to writers who feel the doubleness of destruction and construction – they have a structural affinity, for example, with modernism, and with some other renovating movements which see the reinvention of forms as both compelling and compelled by new kinds of observation. 'These fragments have I shored against my ruins' does not fall accidentally into the history of lists and list-making. But the paradox is most fruitful in the ambiguity of role it offers *any* writer who sets out to encompass the dizzying contents of the world in a list.

Writers who list may be impresarios of matter, commanding spoons, haystacks and Italian scooters to dance together; they may be mock-collectors, importing the methodology of a museum to set together the imaginary, the real, and the parodic; they may be demiurges, summoning things up out of darkness and naming them; they may be chroniclers sure that a hundred splendid names or battles are a hundred times more valuable than one; they may be connoisseurs of the mixed, the mingled, and the confused; they may be Saint Sebastians, variously pierced by flights of sharp experiences; they may be melancholy brooders over fragmentation; they may be rhetorical thunderers, raining down (as Virginia Woolf said of Swift) 'an iron pelt of words'; they may be observers of everyday life, convinced they are reporting a naturalistic absence of connectedness; they may be treasure-hunters, more eager for profusions of pearls than for stories or histories. They may be exhilaratingly arrogant in their dispensation with the usual ways of telling, or be witty so doing, or intriguingly mute and mysterious, or more expansive than connected narration can withstand, or open in their invitation to the reader to piece matters together in whatever way seems right.

Not surprisingly, the first response to a good list is often one of undifferentiated delight at the apparently universal reach displayed, at the purely pyrotechnical aspect of a device that can marshal so much so concentratedly. Keats (a fair lister himself) wrote out a list that had just taken him this way as a present for his brother and sister-in-law in America: 'I have been reading lately Burton's Anatomy of Melancholy; and I think you will be very much amused with a page I here coppy for you. I call it a Feu de joie round the batteries of Fort St Hyphen-de-Phrase on the birthday of the Digamma. The whole alphabet was drawn up in a Phalanx on the cover of an old Dictionary. Band playing "Amo, Amas, Amat &c."' The Burton list in question is a misogynistic extravaganza on the subject of blind love. It does indeed read as if all language's hoarded resources had been blown on one enormous party. Usually, though, something less universal is intended, something that, if not quite parsimonious, at any rate lays out its credit of words more economically, because the stances a writer who lists may take are to a great extent mutually exclusive.

[6]

Each use, each possibility, changes or adjusts the nature of the elements in the list, assigns them a particular way of being parts of a whole. A list of symptoms is different from a list of examples, which differs from a list of items. Elements may 'colour' other elements: but some sorts of list deliberately prevent such seepage. Their elements are in sealed compartments, their commas hermetic barriers. There may be a subtle dissonance of categories in adjacent elements (Georges Perec imagined a film called *Love, Maracas, and Salami*): yet some lists mine uniform seams of material. Lists may indeed offer the reader a brief intimation of everything: they can equally well be fierce flirtations with nothingness, on the simple principle that quite as many things aren't in any one spot as may be imagined to be there. The elements of lists can be balloon-like, tugging in different directions towards the areas of language or meaning that they came from; but they may sometimes be more like a file of stunned cattle, making their docile way towards the killing-floor.

Plainly a survey of what different writers have actually done with lists is likelier to be useful (and likelier to be pleasing) than any attempt to encompass the subject in a theoretical grand design. First, though, the separateness of the extraordinary variety of ways of using lists inevitably raises an uncomfortable question – whether 'lists' are at all a unified category of literary endeavour or whether 'a list' is only a name for something completely determined by what is put in it, like a paragraph. Are lists just too various to have a character? A device that can contain anything comes perilously close to being a device that is nothing in itself. Certainly, for all I've said about the specific possibilities lists offer, and the role of sensitivity to lists at one stage in the process of writing, the context when writers start a list often makes it clear that they see themselves as availing themselves of an accessible resource rather than working within a form. Any claim that a list *is* a form with rules in the same way that a verse-form is, for example, falls down at once upon consideration of a list's single rule of brute sequence – which provides an expanse to fill, rather than an architecture to work with. Besides, many lists are *in* sonnets or ottava rima stanzas, their rule of sequence overlaid, as its simple remit allows, by other and more rigorous rules.

And yet, and yet. The variety of lists also provides arguments for their distinctiveness, if not exactly as a 'form'. Too much of their flexibility springs from the paradox they have brought with them across the frontier from their non-literary origins for them to be dismissed as lacking in intrinsic character. They are too recognisable, whatever use they are put to, for it to be possible to claim that they are wholly subordinated to the medium they are found in. They have gathered to them a vocabulary, sometimes affectionate, sometimes contemptuous, that describes their suspension of the relationships by which syntax orders words and sense: hotch-potch, gallimaufry, omnium gatherum, medley, motley, mosaic, 'meer heap'. Above all, they too consistently interrupt the connected movement of thought into which they are inserted to be a device wholly transparent to that thought. My own inclination is to think of them as a rhetorical figure – like hyperbole, say, or zeugma – an essentially humble figure that can be extended indefinitely and still flavour what it is applied to.

2

Lists probably found their first particular use in epics. Epics are authoritat-ive, authority-filled works. Their size reflects a communal confidence in the value of the noble events and people they portray; their authors in turn are lent authority over their subject-matter by a consensus that the subject-matter is itself authoritative and central to some sort of collective self-definition – as in 'the Matter of Britain', for example. Certainty of this kind, combined with a relatively small (though not unsophisticated) palette of narrative effects, throws into prominence the subtle ways that noble matter can be organised spatially rather than developed: epics are full of arrays of names, corresponding to social structure. You could imagine epic without too much distortion as the kind of literature that exists when the functions of literature and the functions of Burke's *Peerage* have not yet separated. Lists of names are in themselves communicative when the names are agreed to speak for themselves, offering encapsulations of family and prowess in each element, and demonstrating orders of power and precedence. Malory's great catalogue of the Round Table, in the scene of the *Morte d'Arthur* where all the knights in turn lay their hands on the cursed Sir Urry to try to heal him, enacts in concrete terms the 'felyship' the King calls for in the scene; and when Lancelot, protesting his unworthiness but pushed into trying by good-fellowship, succeeds in healing Sir Urry, it proclaims a cathartic model for the proper relationship of group and individual hero, a definition of 'the best knight on earth' made out of a list. Epic lists could also speak of, and act on, the loyalties of an audience, the names counters or containers for regional and local and private alignments of faith, lovingly contextualised. Perhaps Homer's catalogue of ships, running through all the homes and varieties of the Greeks and giving them representative heroes, worked a little bit like a comic in a Northern club warming up an audience. 'Is there anyone here from Doncaster tonight?' – cheers from one corner of the hall. The language within which the names were embedded had to be studiously unremarkable, so as not to oppose the progress from importance to importance. In any case, stock connective phrases and conventional epithets ensured a smooth familiarity.

When returned to in search of effects – rather than used with the original confidence – epic and epic listing offered different attractions according to the taste of the re-user. Spenser, willing a British mythology into creation in *The Faerie Queene* for patriotic reasons, found a mode of decoration, an arrangement of euphonious beauties. His catalogues of the rivers of England and Ireland, and his roll-call of water-nymphs, heap up the signs of a new-minted authenticity. Chapman made his translation of Homer's catalogue an exercise in variegated grandiloquence. Pope, as we have seen, translated it with an industrious reluctance. He turned for guidance to the criticism of the Greek Dionysius of Halicarnassus, an urbane first-century rhetorician who had stood in rather the same relationship to the archaisms of Homer as Pope did himself. According to Dionysius, 'being compelled to take words not naturally beautiful, [Homer] places them in a setting of beautiful ones, and neutralises their offensiveness by the shapeliness of the others'. What Dionysius assumed Homer to have done in the first place, Pope converted into a method of damage control for his translation. He gave Homer's negligently repetitive connecting phrases the reassuring polish and striking neatness of his own phrasings, thereby inadvertently reversing the priorities of the original. Interestingly, modernists and post-modernists have focused not on the glorious arrays of epic, nor on the saving flexibility of the underlying language, but on the characteristic *mixture* of the ordinary and the notable in epic lists: John Ashbery's poem 'Into the Dusk-Charged Air' names a good hundred of the world's rivers in a teasing diction that never quite escapes from his self-made conventional phrasings. 'The Nelson is in Canada,/Flowing'. It's semi-banal the way that good chocolate is semi-sweet.

Another tradition of listing begins with François Rabelais in the early sixteenth century. 'Rabelais plays with words as children do with pebbles; he piles them up into heaps,' wrote Anatole France. His enormous entertainment *Gargantua and Pantagruel* piled joke on joke, mock-scholarship on mock-scholarship, neologism on neologism; his comedy is a comedy of elaboration, intentionally neglectful of proportion in narrative. It is also always a *low* comedy, subverting the idioms of learning and formal romance by juxtaposing them with literal illustrations and gutter details. A parade of classical notables clean out the latrines in Hades and sew buttons on the shirts of the dead; a parody anatomy of 'Mr Shrovetide' – who stands for the horrible scarcity of Lent – compares his sluggish imagination to snails crawling out of strawberry leaves. He has a delight in deliberate, incongruous mixture that looks anarchic from the point of view of the conventions he disrupts, but that signals an individual wilfulness all the more clearly for being scarcely disguised or mediated by convention.

[9]

Rabelais was first translated into English by the brilliantly vainglorious seventeenth-century Cavalier Sir Thomas Urquhart, in one of those extraordinarily apt meetings of author and translator that result in versions of the original text which are wild and faithful at the same time. Urquhart, who wrote a cornucopia of bizarre works of his own while imprisoned by Parliament, set the pattern for those choosing self-consciously to be in Rabelais's 'line of descent' as makers of lists. He consumed and produced words greedily; he had a monumental personal pride that he knew was in bitterly funny contrast to the squalor and confusion of his life; and he was a Scot, always conscious of the need to outdo metropolitan English for variety and richness. Joyce, Beckett and Flann O'Brien, the three great twentieth century exponents of the Rabelaisian list in English, fit the Urquhart pattern biographically, critically, and nationally. All sustained themselves on bitter self-regard when there was little other nourishment available; all have been logomaniacs; and all have given their Irishness utterance in an ambivalently competitive attitude towards the English they worked in. That they were also modernists – different kinds of modernist, of different generations – has meant that they challenged linguistic decorum with their pebble-heaps of words in ways that have only the most tenuous link with Rabelais's original disruptions, of course. Continuity is perceptible, however, in their lists' characteristic juxtapositions of 'high' and 'low'.

But Rabelais's influence as a list-maker extended far beyond this genealogically 'Rabelaisian' tradition. He had revealed that if you bring a *corpus* of learning into imaginative writing playfully, the structures of that knowledge – so different from those of imaginative writing, so dryly sequential – become delightfully arbitrary. You can make the rules of a discipline your playground, in rather the same way nonsense poetry does. Medicine, or linguistics, or jurisprudence can be used for games of permutation and combination. Elizabethan pamphleteers engaged in competitively scholarly abuse of each other, with victory often determined by volume. Sterne had Mr Shandy demonstrate to Corporal Trim and Uncle Toby that grammar always gives you something to say about a subject, even if you know absolutely nothing about it: he creates a whole discourse on polar bears from a mock-systematic run-through of pronouns, tenses and auxiliary verbs. In the twentieth century, T. H. White and James Thurber, both writing for children, have used structures of learning turned ridiculous for pure diversion. In *Mistress Masham's Repose* White sets his extravagantly absent-minded professor to search the rooms of a multiply enlarged version of Blenheim Palace, in each of which there is a comic piece of English literary or military or architectural history. Thurber's *The Wonderful O*, a fable written in a prose with some of the rhythms of blank verse, involves a hectic rifling of dictionaries as pirates outlaw everyday objects containing the letter O.

Nor is even this distant debt to Rabelais's methods necessary to some comic elaborations. Well-judged excess is always funny: all that is needed is a willingness to halt a march across the horizontal plains of narrative to build a sudden tower of words of no obvious usefulness.

Lists of metaphors had a brief, specialised vogue in Renaissance lyric poetry. Where a body of conventional reflections had built up around an established poetic topic, such as Sleep or Desire, it was possible to condense a treatment of the topic into a series of glancing summaries, to produce a poem that was – in whatever pattern or lack of one – a series of metaphorical epithets. Philip Sidney's sonnet 'Desire' opens,

> Thou blind man's mark, thou fool's self-chosen snare,
> Fond fancy's scum, and dregs of scattered thought;
> Band of all evils, cradle of causeless care;
> Thou web of wills, whose end is never wrought . . .

Many sonnets began with this introductory medley of four lines. Other poems took a number of images for the chosen topic and cycled through them several times, laying them out differently each time as a way of giving a movement from first reflection to final clinching. This is the first of the two parts of Bolton's 'Palinode':

> As withereth the primrose by the river,
> As fadeth summer's sun from gliding fountains,
> As vanisheth the light-blown bubble ever,
> As melteth snow upon the mossy mountains:
> So melts, so vanisheth, so fades, so withers
> The rose, the shine, the bubble, and the snow
> Of praise, pomp, glory, joy – which short life gathers –
> Fair praise, vain pomp, sweet glory, brittle joy.
> The withered primrose by the mourning river,
> The faded summer's sun from weeping fountains,
> The light-blown bubble vanishèd for ever,
> The molten snow upon the naked mountains,
>   Are emblems that the treasures we up-lay
>   Soon wither, vanish, fade and melt away.

Yet the ultimate refinement of the practice was a list of epithets without any such overt arrangement, any such immediate instructions as to how they should be understood. Those poets, in particular, who formed part of the 'anti-Senecan' reaction against overflowing copiousness, found list poems an attractive demonstration of the self-sufficiency of epigrammatic pithiness. The same fastidiousness of meaning as is manifested in Bacon's

[11]

Essays, the same deliberate control of association and suggestion, shows itself, for example, in Walter Raleigh's 'False Love':

> A fortress foiled, which reason did defend,
> A Syren song, a fever of the mind,
> A maze wherein affection finds no end,
> A ranging cloud that runs before the wind,
> A substance like the shadow of the sun,
> A goal of grief for which the wisest run . . .

It's worth thinking about the type of metaphors being used here. Evidently the usual question of whether metaphors agree with each other – whether they are congruous – has become irrelevant. Why? Partly because of the tone, of course, which invites admiration for the separate sparks of wit, not any attempt to reconcile them. But there is a more fundamental reason. Although metaphors are not reversible (my love may be like a red, red rose, but a red, red rose is not immediately like my love), they usually link things that are, so to speak, of equivalent scale. As my love and the rose are superimposed on one another, the rose-ness of my love is all, for a moment, that she is supposed to be. The metaphors of the list-poems above are different: Donald Davie nicely called them 'the particulars of an abstraction'. False love and a maze are not of equivalent scale at all. The maze may be an entirely truthful representation of false love, yet not even for a moment is it supposed to be the whole truth of false love. It cannot be: the second is too much 'larger' than the first. Consequently, as a matter of the structure of meaning in the poem, no one image for false love ever attains the authority to conflict with another. Instead they replace each other as they are read. It is a thoroughly *intransitive* procedure, and one that has its syntactical origin in a construction of scholastic logic called a 'copula' that is used to place things in categories. For example: *Socrates is an Athenian, Socrates is an old man, Socrates is fat*. A copula can only contain the verb *to be*, and that need not be stated. You could imagine, as an underlying model for Renaissance list-poems, a poem called 'Socrates' that ran: 'An Athenian; old; fat . . .'

Most such poems are unremarkable. Often the elements of the list have been chosen lazily or amateurishly from the most obvious of those available, accidentally giving the lie to the supposed inexhaustibility of the topic in question. Poems on time or mortality were particularly likely to offer permutations of the same familiar images, reconditioned for service in whichever stanza form the poet had chosen. Sometimes, though, skilful advantage was taken of a list-poem's apparent ability to throw a net over a topic that could not otherwise be pinned down. It helped when the peculiar relationship of particular and abstract specifically corresponded to an aspect of the subject-matter, as could be the case when the ineffability of religious

subjects was substituted for the inexhaustibility of profane ones. George
Herbert's famous list-poem, 'Prayer' (and Vaughan's near-imitation of it,
'Sondayes') was made with just such a specific exploitation in mind. The
shuffled metaphors for praying each acknowledge the partiality of their
reflection of a divine mystery, yet insist on the legitimacy of offering earthly
representations of it. At the back of the poem is the example of Christ's
incarnation: if you like, a sacred analogy for the way metaphors are used in
a list-poem, for the concrete, suffering man Jesus was the most purely
truthful representation of the godhead possible, yet did not express all of it.
Herbert's last line ('The land of spices; something understood') signals, in
the witty humbleness of the final formulation, the perpetual mingling of
abstract and particular that was specific to the incarnation.

Herbert's listing response to the mystery of divine ordering was itself
highly orderly. Outside Anglican pietism, though, among the antinomians
and religious radicals of the seventeenth century, lists could be used to
express an exhilaratingly disorderly perception of a reformed incarnational
theology that seemed to promise an immediate suffusion of earthly life by
divine light. The prose of Abiezer Coppe, the most linguistically inventive
of the 'Ranters' who flourished briefly in the early 1650s, deliberately
tangles the totally mundane and the completely sacred. His occasional lists
sweep together clergy and the socially negligible as equal repositories of
prophetic fire; and careful consultation of biblical verses with magical
readings of them that find the blank outside of the holy book as legible as
the printed inside.

A rather more durable line in lists was inaugurated at some point not too
long before the year 1547, when the courtier-poet Surrey produced a
translation, or version, of an epigram by the Roman poet Martial. It listed
the elements of the good life, the fully achieved life; at least as the good life
was seen from the point of view of a conventional veneration for rural
withdrawal, moderation, and quietitude. Surrey, who was Duke of Norfolk
and commanded Henry VIII's armies in France until his recall and execution, included among the wished-for blessings

> The equal friend; no grudge, no strife;
>   No charge of rule, nor governance;
> Without disease the healthy life;
>   The household of continuance . . .

Mingled though the sentiments may (or may not) be with the real fears and
desires of a life of precarious power, it is hard not to wonder whether
Surrey's list had any individuality at all. The contrast between real life and
rosy withdrawal seems entirely formulaic. Yet the apparently inexpressive

contrast proved to be remarkably resilient as a literary exercise. The good life, as a static and temperate model, had sufficient distance and difference from actual lives to contrast neatly with a wide variety of them. Over the next hundred years the Martial epigram was translated by (among others) the prototypical Grub Street operator Greene, the consciously classicising man of letters Jonson, and the absurdly prolific pietist Francis Quarles. All of them wished for modest riches, pleasantly subordinate wives, and plain digestible food. They did so in a range of line- and stanza-forms, which is not surprising, considering the several revolutions of literary fashion and practice over the century. More significantly, however, they also did so with differences of emphasis, and the occasional insertion of a completely new item. Greene's 'mind content', though twice 'quiet', is sweet, unfrowning, mirthful and blissful; the 'careless slumber' he prescribes may have an absence of care about it as well as an absence of cares in the plural. Jonson, typically, makes the attribution to Martial explicit, addressing him in the second line of his version, called, with less temerity and more consciousness of the difficulty of labour, 'The Things that Make the Happ*ier* Life' (my italics); he then asks for such particular things as 'a continewall fire' and specifically *inherited* property, free from litigation. Quarles's 'Perfections', set firmly in the frame of 'our transitory dayes', and multiplied by his facile fluency, have the upbeat Protestant flavour of salvation by works. '*Pastimes*' should be 'ingenious, lawfull, manly, sparing'. In retrospect, then, Surrey's requirements for happiness do seem to have a degree of personal inclination behind them: no one else asks for 'No charge of rule, nor governance'. I am not claiming that the translations of the Martial epigram are particularly revealing. The effect is more of seeing the faint outline of a succession of faces reflected on the still, bland surface of the same pool. The most that can be claimed is that the epigram can be taken as the incidental vehicle for a limited, stiff kind of self-projection.

It is important because it is the forerunner of a whole group of associated ways of using lists for deliberate self-observation. After Quarles's version in 1632, the fashion for translating the epigram seems to have faded away. There had been changes in the perception of selves, coupled with an increasing sophistication, across many genres of writing, in techniques of articulated self-description; lists were beginning to correspond to particular, purposefully fragmented views of the self. One change of obvious relevance is Montaigne's declaration of 'homme ondoyant et divers' against unitary conceptions of humanity's inner nature: in a famous passage of the essay Florio translated in 1603 as 'Of the Inconstancie of our Actions' he listed his own insurmountably contradictory traits. But in addition to a newly fluid selfhood that could sometimes best be expressed in lists, there had arrived habits of consistent religious self-scrutiny which mixed extreme pious rigour with a humble refusal to usurp God's prerogative by assigning a definite ordering to the confused failures and successes of the pilgrim soul. 'When night comes, list thy deeds', advised Henry Vaughan in *Silex Scintillans* (1650). Those of this kind of list that were set down in permanent poetic or prose form could range from highly subtle self-probings to blanket self-excoriations. As a secular parallel to the lists that recorded individual spiritual experience, there could also be lists that celebrated a modest pluralism of worldly preferences. Katherine Philips' poem 'The Virgin' lies ostensibly somewhere between the Martial epigram and conventional praise for chastity. It starts:

> The Things that make a Virgin please,
> She that seeks, will find them these . . .

Yet it becomes clear as the poem continues that it is a personal recommendation, in catalogue form, of the satisfactions of the virgin state *for the virgin*, addressed to the pleasure of the virgin as much as to anyone else that might be 'pleased'. The already specific 'she' of 'She that seeks' suggests an even more specific 'I'. The good life was diversifying.

Because the seventeenth century was the first great age of *things*, when the expansion of national and international trade brought a large proportion of the European population into possession of manufactured goods for the first time, it became possible, too, for individual preferences to be registered in the individual choice of actual possessions, rather than in a selection of ideal future benefits. A character could be recorded, in literature, by itemising the contents of a house or a room or a cabinet or a bag as the projection of a self. The technique had been used for some time in painting, changing its terms of reference over the course of the sixteenth century from the aristocratic and emblematic to the *Bürgerlich* and material. Neither in painting nor in literature, though, were the results of the technique necessarily very comfortable. The depiction of the self in possessions opened up a spectrum of emotion ranging from smooth intimacy to edgy alienation. The investing of things with substantial human value never translated into a complete anthropomorphism: it might be said, with an appropriate mechanistic emphasis, that the resistance of objects to human familiarity grew in exact proportion to the force of familiar interpretation applied to them. The aggressive assurance of possession is countered by a permanent strangeness. Things can never quite be perfectly passive signs of human preference. Lists of them that are supposed to reflect selves can never quite be perfect reflections.

The consequent unease runs, in various ways, through most of the later uses of this kind of list. By the nineteenth century – the proverbial great age of things, of confident, prolific materialism – listing as a method of characterisation had become institutionalised in fictional and non-fictional prose, and so had curiosity about the failures and limits and provisionality of the method. Hence, as well as Dickens's almost reflexive attention to his characters' selections of jugs, furniture and wall-paint, his abiding interest in rubbish, in objects that have outlived their possessor, or been discarded as their possessor changed, or that present a palimpsest of different ownerships, or whose pathetic brokenness challenges confident novelty and implies a wider pathos. Hence Henry Mayhew's speculation about the histories of the garments in the Old Clothes Exchange, and about the future of the rags that were recycled into the tough material called *shoddy*: '. . . the rags which the beggar could no longer hang about him to cover his nakedness, may be a component of the soldier's or sailor's uniform, the carpet of a palace, or the library table-cover of a prime minister'. In the twentieth century literary radicals have sometimes called for a complete break with a practice felt to be fundamentally false – indeed, almost imperial in its wishful disregard for the foreign-ness of objects. Alain Robbe-Grillet suggested, in *Towards a New Novel*, that objects fell into a uniformly distinct category from human experience. To treat them otherwise blurred the actual contours and boundaries of experience. And though the *nouveaux romans* that have been written have by no means followed any single prescription, including Robbe-Grillet's, they do exclude portraits-by-possessions with some rigour. (They contain lists, instead, whose purpose is to defy the ordinary recreation of a fictional world by the reader's imagination, such as minute descriptions that don't allow the reader to visualise what is described. The lists that result are often exceptionally boring to read, precisely because they refuse the rich collation of categories that is such a fundamental tool of the literary list-maker.)

One kind of list of the self that does not raise this kind of issue is the list of memories: memories, unlike objects, are owned with a clear title. They are packages of personal meaning, tidied and finished by repeated recall, organised, often, in mysterious or purely chronological sequences un-touched by the 'syntax' of the conscious mind. The issue they *do* raise, of course, is the issue of verity. It is never possible to tell what artifices, what suppressions, selections and forgettings have formed them. But that ambiguity only improves their potential for deliberate literary use. A list of dying memories in particular works well as a summary of character, as a sort of compressed *envoi* to the variety of life. The anonymous medieval author of the epic *Chanson de Roland* gives the fatally wounded Roland a final look back at a suitably noble selection of moments and men, sufficiently generalised to allow the medieval reader or hearer to supply the particular loyalties from which it would be most painful to be parted. Lytton Strachey, in a diminuendo of carefully purple prose, shows the dying

Queen Victoria's final thoughts unwinding through age and adulthood back to a first, nursery comfort.

All these different ways of listing the self may have eschewed the ordering of syntax, but they could very easily be made to conform to the orderly decorum of the different forms – essays, poems, novels – that they appeared in. Unlike Rabelais's proportionless heaps, they offered no intrinsic challenge to rules of taste: all were organisations of the self for the reader that resisted chaotic language even when they were voicing chaotic self-perceptions, as in Montaigne, or exploiting the disorder of memory. So long as, in the seventeenth and eighteenth centuries, disorder carried an adverse moral implication, truly disordered lists remained at the fringes of literature. Thus, for example, to turn to the variety of lists of the self that probably presents itself first to the modern imagination, though the psychological mechanisms of the train of thought had been explored as early as 1651 in Thomas Hobbes's *Leviathan*, and were discussed with increasing sophistication and interest by the philosophers Locke, Hume and Berkeley over the next hundred years, there were few attempts at the imaginative transcription of a phenomenon so unpatterned during that time except as a joke or a private experiment. Tolerance increased slowly, in parallel with the slowly increasing appreciation of eccentricity in general as a sort of harmless licensed subversion of the rigours of civil society. In *An Essay Concerning Human Understanding* (1689) Locke distinguished carefully between the reasonable association of ideas which have 'a natural Correspondence and Connexion one with another', and the unreasonable 'Connexion of *Ideas* wholly owning to Chance or Custom'. The latter, he suggested, should be weeded out of children's minds as part of the process of education, so as not to deform their adult intellectual habits; though he then notes the 'pleasant oddness' of some of the examples of irrational association he cites. By the time of Hume's *Treatise of Human Nature* (1739), purposely conceived as a a development of Locke's *Essay*, the separate valuation of the two kinds of association has disappeared: the same 'principles of union or cohesion among our simple ideas' govern the whole range of possible associations. But even in *Tristram Shandy* (1759–66), the most formally bold of eighteenth-century novels and one dedicated by Sterne exactly to a Lockean 'pleasant oddness', trains of thought are playfully discussed, but never reproduced in the raw form of a list. It took the Romantic loosening of the tasteful Augustan sentence (symbolised by a preference for dashes over full stops), and the Romantic openness towards *whatever* was found within the self, to make it acceptable to display in serious writing, unmediated and unpolished, the bizarre sequences of consciousness. Coleridge's listing notebook entry of 1810 – in which, paradoxically, he engages in free association in order to elucidate a *disagreement* with 'an

Idolater of Hume' – makes it clear he thinks of his private web of associations ('strong as Steel yet subtle as the Ether') as being multiply interconnected with his whole poetic enterprise. Thomas de Quincey, a little later still, argues that an associative principle is at the root of most remembered emotions, with an obvious implication for the way emotion should be constructed in writing: 'far more of our deepest thoughts and feelings pass to us through perplexed combinations of *concrete* objects . . . than ever reach us *directly* and in their own abstract shapes'. As always in literary history, once there was a willingness to engage with apparent disorder, new orderings were discovered. After the constraints of the previous century, observations like de Quincey's enabled naturalistic responses to consciousness. Of course, they allowed for the development of far more than *lists* of consciousness; but it did inaugurate at last a confident, if sporadic, tradition of using lists for that purpose. The modernist cliché of the 'stream of consciousness' represents, in fact, an extreme reworking of a tradition rather than an invention.

The eighteenth century's decorous prescriptions for serious writing had had other effects on the use of lists. Really strict neo-classicism avoided them altogether, except when pointing specifically to the kind of mistake of perception they were supposed to represent. There is only one list in Racine's entire dramatic output. It appears in *Bérénice* (1670), to suggest how the unfortunate Jewish queen is able to miss the clear likelihood that Roman custom will prevent the Emperor Titus, her lover, from marrying a foreign monarch. Bérénice sees Rome in glorious pieces – 'Ces aigles, ces faisceaux, ce peuple, cette armée' – and therefore cannot grasp the essential truth of its, or her, situation. A century later, Gibbon used the same perceived contrast between the distracting fragmentariness of a list and the centrality of moral judgement to make a neat, ironic turn in the first chapter of the *Decline and Fall*: 'This long enumeration of provinces, whose broken fragments have formed so many powerful kingdoms, might almost induce us to forgive the vanity or ignorance of the ancients.' Almost, but evidently not quite.

It was more usual, while the Augustan remit ran, to consign listing to styles and genres that made no direct claim to high literary authority. Lists could be whimsical, as in Shenstone's essays. Lists could be deployed as part of the bubbling, exaggerated biliousness of satire. Lists could lightly approach the age's preoccupation with the vexed relationship of words and things. Lists could represent nature's raw contrasted to art's cooked, as in Addison's sketch of the way a coffeehouse audience misunderstood matters when he dropped his notes for the next issue of *The Spectator*. Lists could be the jokes that preceded full, articulated treatments of themes: Pope's *Rape of the Lock*, a work whose satire on vanity contains a single list one line long, draws on a mock-inventory of a dead beau's possessions in *The Tatler* and on Mary Evelyn's lengthy but unassuming list-poem 'A Voyage to Marryland'. Lists could sometimes reliably indicate not only the author's distance from the more important orthodox goals of literature, but his parallel distance from sanity: Christopher Smart's praises of God from Bedlam have the category-mangling infinite extensibility of obsession.

Lists have a traditional role in writing by men about women and romance; and an occasional role in writing by women about men and romance. Love, for one thing, is an abstraction like Sleep or Death, of which there are so many particular aspects that it is possible to make a contradictory portrait of it from a list of them alone. These portraits are, naturally, prescriptive in their selection of 'obvious' details; in general they are most interesting when the social or critical intention is openly avowed, as in the entry on 'Love' in *The Ladies' Dictionary* of 1694, where the female reader in search of advice is told, and perhaps by a female writer, mainly that love is *not* to be understood in terms of the (listed) crises and dramas of romance. Against such lists must be set the comparatively shallow turns and oppositions of poems like the medieval 'Love is wele, love is wo', which offer few surprises in their catalogue of received (male) experience.

But if the list's fundamental paradox of authority faintly haunts general characterisations of Love, it fairly shrieks down the corridors of the romantic lists that itemise the characteristics of the beloved. Most prominent in the lyric poetry of the Renaissance but a part of the vocabulary of stylised courtship in every age, these approach their object, whether she be real or ideal or a variably perverse combination of the two, with an institutionalised apparent humility. The topos of the writer-as-supplicant common to all love literature finds a particular expression in the romantic list's insistence that the pieces of the beloved are being examined so as not to be dazzled by the unendurable beauty of the whole. Yet the severing, in a romantic list of this kind, of the love-object's self as it might be articulated were she a subject rather than an object, is complete. The beloved is at the disposal, within the power, of the observer who treats her as a sequence of kneecaps, breasts, and deep, deep eyes. Reverence and metaphorical dismemberment run extremely close together. Is the writer assembling, or deconstructing, the body he describes? Does the writer read from the body of the beloved, or write onto it, the separate segments of the list he makes? It may be naïve, in the context of the kinds of writing likely to contain such lists, to look for the clear signs of an individual presence as the guarantor of reverence; but it is relatively easy to trace out the degrees of abstraction from a real presence with which a writer approaches real reverence's opposite. At the limit of the kind of abstraction that still (just) wishes to claim a single object are found romantic poems like Richard Crashaw's laughable and worrying 'Wishes. To his (supposed) Mistresse', published in a miscellany of 1646, which sets out a check-list for an imagined perfect bride, chaste and carnal in just the right proportion for a shy evangelical poet. It leaves in the mind of the reader an impression of a sort of incomplete tailor's dummy. And then there are lists of the characteristics of Woman, with no pretence at all of particular observation, like the vehemently misogynistic Burton list Keats so enjoyed for its alphabetic comprehensiveness.

I am not being perverse, I think, in seeing assaults on 'Woman' as closely related to the techniques of listing used by men in dealing with romance. Just as the authority of lists finds one of its most shocking illustrations in the treatment of love-objects, so wider questions of gender in list-writing most clearly congregate around the issue of authority. Over most of the centuries of writing on which this anthology draws, the structures of power in society gave women who wrote a restricted sense of the authority they could claim as authors. This restricted authority inevitably shaped the ways they could and could not make use of lists in writing. There are very few counterparts by women to men's lists of the characteristics of the beloved, or to men's lists of conquests, or to men's slap-happy way with the characterisation of 'Woman'. In addition to the social arrangements that excluded women from collecting enough lovers to fill a list of philanderings, for example, a set of presumptions about the use of language ruled out, for most women writers at most times, the casually powerful enumeration of them. There are a great many different versions of the Don Juan story, but very few with a (fictional or non-fictional) female protagonist. When the reduction of lovers to the elements of a series is such an unequal prerogative, it is almost a relief to be able to turn from Byron's letter of 1819, listing by surname the women he has slept with in Venice, to the moment in Aphra Behn's farce *The Emperor of the Moon* (1687) when the character Bellamante is allowed to salivate at the *quantity* of delectable men she sights at church. Pleasure for the reader, indeed, begins to creep back into sexual arithmetic when we can imagine lovers made into one-word annotations against the grain of power, rather than with it. Likewise, though three and a half centuries separate them, it is nice to compare Burton's list with the venomous collection of types of evil men drawn up by Valerie Solanas in her scum *Manifesto* of 1967. Her wilful disregard for ordinary categorisations – she includes 'owners of greasy spoons' as well as rapists – denudes his, in retrospect, of the seriousness that uncontested power allowed him to claim. His misogyny remains unlovely, but it shrinks a little into comedy.

The gendered difference of access to the authoritativeness of lists has

[20]

given their use by women a different texture, at times, from their use by their male contemporaries, even in the same school of writing. Generalisation is dangerous, but female Modernists, for example, seem to have approached the newly-perceived fragmentation of phenomena with a separate understanding of the possibilities it offered to writing. Virginia Woolf's Mrs Dalloway feels the coloured, shimmering *everything* of London as a constant flux. Multiple impressions touch, in sequence, an equally fluid self. It is not a passive form of observation, yet it figures the 'I' at the centre of the novel as the receiver of a divided world rather than as the divider of it. Perhaps this different balance of power explains the distance between Woolf's consistently rich impressionistic lists and the paucity of 'Rocks, moss, stonecrop, iron, merds' in Eliot's 'Gerontion'.

There are, finally, those lists in which authors aim at a deliberate aesthetic of mixture. As distinct from all the lists in which the author may well have taken a pleasure in mixture, but only in passing, they are almost entirely the product of the last two centuries. Maybe they begin with the Romantics' pantheistic reverence for the immanent meanings of nature: one of the moments of spiritual revelation in *The Prelude* turns on a sudden, heightened reading of the legible mixture of a road, a forest and a rainstorm. Maybe, on the other hand, their genesis lies in the Victorian preference for what Peter Conrad calls 'irregularity and the pursuit of detail at the expense of the whole'. In 1846, according to his autobiography *Praeterita* (1885–9), John Ruskin saddened his father by 'my now constant habit of making little patches and scratches of the sections and fractions of things . . . instead of the former Proutesque or Robertsian outline of the grand buildings and sublime scenes'. Later he was to praise the disordered architecture of the English suburban villa for its 'particular points, and miniature details'. At any rate, by the middle of the nineteenth century, new subject-matter – the incoherence of city life, the bewildering proliferation of commodities, the anarchy of individual taste, the geological lamination of the past in the earth – was finding a ready reflection for itself in telling arrangements of details, 'patches' and 'scratches'. For English Victorians, at least, there was nothing hermetic or obscure about a literary practice that ran so parallel to the larger movement of ideas. Public culture divested itself steadily of general explanations, replacing them with general syntheses that could reach further into a demonstrably un-unified world. Baroque statistics flourished: Mayhew cheerfully calculated that London street-merchants sold, per year, among many other things, 36,750,000 bloaters, about 30,500 'pottles' of mulberries, seventy-two dozen roots of lilies of the valley, 4,798,000 bottles of ginger beer, and £93 worth of 'mock-indecent' literature. The long series of international Exhibitions rejoiced in profusion, juxtaposing objects from opposite ends of the globe. And both light verse and the most solemn of writing celebrated mixed forms – Thackeray sent his comic Irish persona 'Molony' off to the Crystal Palace to hymn the fans and shandrydans assembled there, while Tennyson composed a chorale for the opening of the Exhibition of 1862 that compared the blend of warlike and pacific objects to the inevitable alternation of love and hate in life.

But more could be done with mixtures that did lead away from accessibility into difficulty, into Rimbaud's *'alchimie du verbe'* or into unexplained *montage* and *bricolage*, into the defiant orderings and anti-orderings of experiment. With the change in the status of the word associated with modernity came an interest in the self-sufficiency of the elements of a list, as the sufficient containers and concealers of a writer's intention. In the first two decades of the twentieth century Imagism (in Britain and America) and Acmeism (in Russia), to name only two of a number of related movements, attempted to create a poetics that needed no articulation other than the play of images against each other. The Acmeist Osip Mandelstam compared the 'movement' of a poem from image to image to someone running across a river by jumping from moving boat to moving boat, mapping a zig-zag course determined by the energy and direction of each landing-place. Mandelstam himself also gave his poems rigorous metrical structures, which, for example, those Imagists who drew on Chinese ideograms had no place for; but the mysteriousness of such work depends less on the particular diction than on the reader's inability to be sure of rightly identifying what is inherent in each element. As with the Renaissance poetry of accumulated images, only the 'purest' examples of Imagism were completely without articulated syntax and directions as to the way to understand the variety of images on offer. Lists, again, represented the most problematic edge of a fashion. But the problem and the promise were inextricably intertwined. Though a 'pure' list might require a reading that was largely a decoding, the poets who used them felt they had restored a connection with the organic nature of language which had been mythically disrupted by the huge, indifferent volume of nineteenth-century writing. The 'inherent' meaning they claimed to find, and use, in a word, included the shapes and shades of its history, as if the past were delivered to them in each contact with language, and they could choose, magus-like, between senses and interpretations of it. Putting words next to each other in the simple yet baffling juxtapositions of a list could be a graphic demonstration of the writer's freedom in time, a game with past and present, with the worlds of association that had grown within words.

It would be absurd to claim a unity for twentieth-century literature, or even for twentieth-century lists in literature, around this set of Imagist, or early Modernist, perceptions. But the writer's newly-perceived freedom to manipulate all that inheres in language when making a list – a strong new attachment to the permanent authoritative possibilities of lists – underlies, with surprising consistency, many of the century's later literary movements. I need not, I hope, run through all the inflections of lists as they have been employed deliberately by Surrealists, second generation Modernists, and post-modern meta-writers; or try to explain the careful presence in a Marianne Moore poem of items from Iran, the Virgin Islands and the San Antonio public health department; or go into the fascination with mathematical axioms that makes 'list' much too loose a word for most of the work of Oulipo (the *Ouvroir de la Littérature Potentielle*) in the fifties, sixties and seventies. Each violently divergent line of experiment with language retains the claim that, in a list, the purposeful mixture of elements conjures a purposeful mixture of worlds. *The* world may be unattainable as far as representation is concerned, but the texture of its confusion and resistance to easy transcription can be captured in little. Such lists are necessarily beyond genre. They invent their rules as they go along: they all declare a seriousness shaped only by their present purpose. Whatever the form of their experiment with language, they mimic in miniature the absence of generic constraints. They have some of the intensity of a manifesto. Here, in a way, mixedness *is* seriousness. It testifies to a hunger of the word for the world that will no longer be sated straightforwardly.

A Note on the Contents

My enthusiasm for lists led me to assemble this book; but my enthusiasm grew slowly and piecemeal, taking in a list here and a list there, usually from such technically deliberate and inventively extravagant modern writers as Calvino and Borges. It wasn't until I was actually engaged in gathering material that I began to think about the range of less self-conscious kinds of listing, and consequently about a definition of 'a list' that I could use to set limits on the book. In the end, for the reasons of uncontrollable variety discussed in the first part of the introduction, all I could settle on was a simple rule-of-thumb: for my purposes, a list was any sequence in which there were more than three items; and in which, as far as syntax was concerned, nothing other than sequence linked the items, whether they were single words or larger units of prose or poetry. So bare and basic a definition did have some uses. The more-than-three part of the rule helped me to put aside temptation and exclude Milton's synthetic description of religious conformity ('a stark and dead congealment of wood and hay and stubble'), with its irrelevant but interesting implications for seventeenth-century tolerance of chaos. Sticking faithfully to the syntactical part of the rule neatly dealt with the tricky question of whether to include any of Dickens's great, orchestratedly repetitive descriptions – like the famous passage about the London fog at the beginning of *Bleak House*, which may proceed from place to place where the fog has settled, but does so with an 'unlistlike' momentum and connectedness. But the rule-of-thumb obviously gave little guidance in more complicated matters of editorial policy. How international should the anthology be? Should I try, with my choice of lists, to offer a constant and coherent coverage of the literatures from which they came? The answers to both these questions turned out, I am afraid, to be mostly dictated by accident, advice, my own tastes, and my own particular areas of knowledge. As it stands, the book is weighted towards Englishness, and if readers should find particular omissions infuriating I will have to take refuge in Dr Johnson's excuse for mistaking the meaning of 'pastern' in his *Dictionary* – 'Ignorance, Madam, pure ignorance.'

Some explanation is also required for the organisation of what follows. Unlike most anthologies, this one is not arranged chronologically, but thematically, in the hope that the pleasurable juxtapositions of lists can be reproduced to some extent on the scale of a book. Some of the placings against each other of lists widely separated by date and purpose of composition are intended to be ironic, others to trace out one or other of the possibilities of lists that I have described, others still to hint at connections between writers that may not be visible except in the peculiar perspective of list-making. Original titles, given to lists by their authors, are placed in inverted commas to distinguish them from those I have supplied myself. I have included a number of non- or semi-literary catalogues and inventories, for rather the same reason that biological experiments have 'control groups' of animals to which no drugs are given. They are supposed to give an idea of the underlying sensibilities with which different times regarded sequences and assemblages of things, and to provide references to the kinds of list-reading from which purposeful list-writing could be approached. All of them, I hope, are diverting in themselves.

The world's a Floore, whose swelling heaps retein
    The mingled wages of the Ploughman's toyl;
The world's a heap, whose yet unwinnowed grain
    Is lodg'd with chaff and buried in her soyl;
All things are mixt, the usefull with the vain;
    The good with bad, the noble with the vile;
The world's an Ark, wherein things pure and grosse
    Present their lossefull gain, and gainfull losse;
Where ev'ry dram of gold conteins a pound of drosse.

FRANCIS QUARLES

. . . then straight arose a wicked race of deceivers, who . . . took
the virgin Truth, hewed her lovely form into a thousand pieces,
and scattered them to the four winds. From that time ever since,
the sad friends of Truth, such as durst appear, imitating the
careful search that Isis made for the mangled body of Osiris,
went up and down gathering up limb by limb still as they could
find them.

JOHN MILTON

'The time has come,' the Walrus said
'To talk of many things:
Of shoes – and ships – and
sealing-wax –
Of cabbages – and kings –
Of why the sea is boiling hot –
And whether pigs have wings.'

LEWIS CARROLL

I sing of *Brooks*, of *Blossomes*, *Birds*, and
    Bowers;
Of *April*, *May*, of *June*, and *July*-Flowers.
I sing of *May-poles*, *Hock-carts*, *Wassails*,
    Wakes, .
Of *Bride-grooms*, *Brides*, and of their
    Bridall-cakes.

[27]

I write of *Youth*, of *Love*, and have Accesse
By these, to sing of cleanly-*Wantonnesse*.
I sing of *Dewes*, of *Raines*, and piece by piece
Of *Balme*, of *Oyle*, of *Spice*, and *Amber-Greece*.
I sing of *Times trans-shifting*; and I write
How *Roses* first came *Red*, and *Lilies White*.
I write of *Groves*, of *Twilights*, and I sing
The Court of *Mab*, and of the *Fairie-King*.
I write of *Hell*; I sing (and ever shall)
Of *Heaven*, and hope to have it after all.

ROBERT HERRICK

Puffs, powders, patches, Bibles, billet-doux.

ALEXANDER POPE

One

EPIC CATALOGUES

I expected him to make the songs of the nation but he seems content to make the inventories.

RALPH WALDO EMERSON, *of Walt Whitman*

The Catalogue of the Ships

Say, Virgins, seated round the Throne Divine,
All-knowing *Goddesses!* immortal Nine!
Since Earth's wide Regions, Heav'n's unmeasur'd Height,
And Hell's Abyss hide nothing from your sight,
(We, wretched Mortals! lost in Doubts below,
But guess by Rumour, and but boast we know)
Oh say what Heroes, fir'd by Thirst of Fame,
Or urg'd by Wrongs, to *Troy*'s Destruction came?
To count them all, demands a thousand Tongues,
A Throat of Brass, and Adamantine Lungs.
Daughters of *Jove* assist! inspir'd by You
The mighty Labour dauntless I pursue:
What crowded Armies, from what Climes they bring,
Their Names, their Numbers, and their Chiefs I sing.

The hardy Warriors whom *Boeotia* bred,
Peneleus, Leitus, Prothoënor led;
With these *Arcesilaus* and *Clonius* stand,
Equal in Arms, and equal in Command.
These head the Troops that Rocky *Aulis* yields,
And *Eteon*'s Hills, and *Hyrie*'s watry Fields,
And *Schoenos, Scolos, Græa* near the Main,
And *Mycalessia*'s ample Piny Plain.
Those who in *Peteon* or *Ilesion* dwell,
Or *Harma* where Apollo's Prophet fell;
Heleon and *Hylè*, which the Springs o'erflow;
And *Medeon* lofty, and *Ocalea* low;
Or in the Meads of *Haliartus* stray,
Or *Thespia* sacred to the God of Day.
Onchestus, Neptune's celebrated Groves;
Copæ, and *Thisbè*, fam'd for silver Doves,
For Flocks *Erythræ, Glissa* for the Vine;
Platæa green, and *Nisa* the divine.
And they whom *Thebè*'s well-built Walls inclose,
Where *Mydè, Eutresis, Coronè* rose;
And *Arnè* rich, with purple Harvests crown'd;
And *Anthedon, Boeotia*'s utmost Bound.
Full fifty Ships they send, and each conveys
Twice sixty Warriors thro' the foaming Seas.

To these succeed *Aspledon*'s martial Train,
Who plow the spacious *Orchomenian* Plain.
Two valiant Brothers rule th'undaunted Throng,
Iälmen and *Ascalaphus* the strong:
Sons of *Astyochè* the Heav'nly Fair,
Whose Virgin-Charms subdu'd the God of War:
(In *Actor*'s Court as she retir'd to Rest,
The Strength of *Mars* the blushing Maid comprest)
Their Troops in thirty sable Vessels sweep
With equal Oars, the hoarse-resounding Deep.

The *Phocians* next in forty Barks repair,
Epistrophus and *Schedius* head the War.
From those rich Regions where *Cephisus* leads
His silver Current thro' the flow'ry Meads;
From *Panopëa*, *Chrysa* the Divine,
Where *Anemoria*'s stately Turrets shine,
Where *Pytho*, *Daulis*, *Cyparissus* stood,
And fair *Lilæa* views the rising Flood.
These rang'd in Order on the floating Tide,
Close, on the left, the bold *Boeotians* side.

Fierce *Ajax* led the *Locrian* Squadrons on,
Ajax the less, *Oïleus*' valiant Son;
Skill'd to direct the flying Dart aright;
Swift in Pursuit, and active in the Fight.
Him, as their Chief, the chosen Troops attend,
Which *Bessa*, *Thronus* and rich *Cynos* send:
Opus, *Calliarus*, and *Scarphe*'s Bands;
And those who dwell where pleasing *Augia* stands,
And where *Boägrius* floats the lowly Lands,
Or in fair *Tarphe*'s Sylvan Seats reside;
In forty Vessels cut the yielding Tide.

Euboea next her martial Sons prepares,
And sends the brave *Abantes* to the Wars:
Breathing Revenge, in Arms they take their Way
From *Chalcis*' Walls, and strong *Eretria*;
Th' *Isteian* Fields for gen'rous Vines renown'd,
The fair *Carystos*, and the *Styrian* Ground;
Where *Dios* from her Tow'rs o'erlooks the Plain,
And high *Cerinthus* views the neigh'bring Main.
Down their broad Shoulders falls a length of Hair;
Their Hands dismiss not the long Lance in Air;
But with protended Spears in fighting Fields,

Pierce the tough Cors'lets and the brazen Shields.
Twice twenty Ships transport the warlike Bands,
Which bold *Elphenor*, fierce in Arms, commands.
   Full fifty more from *Athens* stem the Main,
Led by *Menestheus* thro' the liquid Plain,
(*Athens* the fair, where great *Erectheus* sway'd,
That ow'd his Nurture to the blue-ey'd Maid,
But from the teeming Furrow took his Birth,
The mighty Offspring of the foodful Earth.
Him *Pallas* plac'd amidst her wealthy Fane,
Ador'd with Sacrifice and Oxen slain;
Where as the Years revolve, her Altars blaze,
And all the Tribes resound the Goddess' Praise.)
No Chief like thee, *Menestheus!* *Greece* could yield,
To marshal Armies in the dusty Field,
Th'extended Wings of Battel to display
Or close th'embody'd Host in firm Array.
Nestor alone, improv'd by Length of Days,
For martial Conduct bore an equal Praise.
   With these appear the *Salaminian* Bands,
Whom the Gigantic *Telamon* commands;
In twelve black Ships to *Troy* they steer their Course,
And with the great *Athenians* join their Force.
   Next move to War the gen'rous *Argive* Train,
From high *Troezenè*, and *Maseta*'s Plain,
And fair *Ægina* circled by the Main:
Whom strong *Tyrinthè*'s lofty Walls surround,
And *Epidaure* with Viny Harvests crown'd:
And where fair *Asinen* and *Hermion* show
Their Cliffs above, and ample Bay below.
These by the brave *Euryalus* were led,
Great *Sthenelus*, and greater *Diomed*,
But chief *Tydides* bore the Sov'reign Sway;
In fourscore Barks they plow the watry Way.
   The proud *Mýcoenè* arms her martial Pow'rs,
Cleonè, *Corinth*, with Imperial Tow'rs,
Fair *Arethyrea*, *Ornia*'s fruitful Plain,
And *Ægion*, and *Adrastus*' ancient Reign;
And those who dwell along the sandy Shore,
And where *Pellenè* yields her fleecy Store,
Where *Helicè* and *Hyperesia* lie,
And *Gonoëssa*'s Spires salute the Sky.

Great *Agamemnon* rules the num'rous Band,
A hundred Vessels in long Order stand,
And crowded Nations wait his dread Command.
High on the Deck the King of Men appears,
And his refulgent Arms in Triumph wears;
Proud of his Host, unrival'd in his Reign,
In silent Pomp he moves along the Main.
  His Brother follows, and to Vengeance warms
The hardy *Spartans*, exercis'd in Arms:
Phares and *Brysia*'s valiant Troops, and those
Whom *Lacedæmon*'s lofty Hills inclose:
Or *Messë*'s Tow'rs for silver Doves renown'd,
Amyclæ, Laäs, Augia's happy Ground,
And those whom *Oetylos*' low Walls contain,
And *Helos*, on the Margin of the Main.
Those, o'er the bending Ocean, *Helen*'s Cause
In sixty Ships with *Menelaus* draws:
Eager and loud, from Man to Man he flies,
Revenge and Fury flaming in his eyes;
While vainly fond, in Fancy oft he hears
The Fair one's Grief, and sees her falling Tears.

From Alexander Pope's translation of Homer's *The Iliad*, 1715

  Who dwelt in *Pylos* sandie soyle, and *Arene* the faire;
In *Thyron*, near *Alphæus* flood, and *Aepy* full of aire;
In *Cyparisseus, Amphygen*, and little *Pteleon*;
The towne where all the Iliots dwelt, and famous *Doreon*;
Where all the Muses (opposite, in strife of Poesie,
To ancient *Thamyris* of *Thrace*) did use him cruelly;
He coming from *Eurytus* court, the wise *Oechalian* king:
Because he proudly durst affirme, he could more sweetly sing,
Then that Pyerean race of *Iove*; who (angrie with his vant)
Bereft his eye-sight, and his song, that did the eare enchant;
And of his skill to touch his Harpe, disfurnished his hand:
All these in ninetie hollow keeles, grave *Nestor* did command.
  The richly blest inhabitants of the Arcadian land
Below *Cyllenes* mount, that by, *Epyrus* tombe did stand;
Where dwell the bold neare-fighting men; who did in *Phæneus* live:
And *Orchomen*, where flockes of sheepe, the shepheards clustering
    drive:

[33]

In *Rypé* and in *Stratié*, the faire Mantinean towne;
And strong *Enispe*, that for height, is ever weather-blowne;
Tegea, and in *Stimphalus*; *Parrhasia* strongly wall'd;
All these *Alcæus* sonne, to field (king *Agapenor*) call'd;
In sixtie barks he brought them on, and everie barke well mand,
With fierce *Arcadians*, skild to use, the utmost of a band.
King *Agamemnon* on these men, did well-built ships bestow,
To pass the gulfie purple sea, that did no sea rites know.
    They who in *Hermin*, *Buphrasis*, and *Elis* did remaine,
What *Olens* Cliffes, *Alisius*, and *Myrsin* did containe;
Were led to warre by twise two Dukes, and each ten ships did bring,
Which many venterous *Epyans*, did serve for burthening.
    Beneath *Alphimacus* his charge, and valiant *Talphius*,
Sonne of *Euritus Actor*, one; the other *Cteatus*;
Diores Amarincides, the other did imploy;
The fourth divine *Polixenus*, *Agasthenis* his ioy:
The king of faire *Angeiades*, who from *Dulichius* came,
And from *Euchinaus* sweet Iles, which hold their holy frame
By ample *Elis* region, *Meges Phelides* led:
Whom Duke *Phyleux*, *Ioves* belov'd, begat, and whilome fled
To large *Dulychius* for the wrath, that fir'd his fathers breast.
Twise twentie ships with Ebon sailes, were in his charge addrest.
    The war-like men of *Cephale*, and those of *Ithaca*,
Wooddy *Nerytus*, and the men, of wet *Crocilia*:
Sharpe *Ægilipha*, *Samos* Ile, *Zacynthus*, sea-enclos'd;
Epyrus, and the men that hold, the Continent oppos'd;
All these did wise *Ulysses* leade, in counsell Peere to *Iove*:
Twelve ships he brought, which in their course, vermilion sternes did
        move.
    Thoas, *Andremons* wel-spoke sonne, did guide th'Etolians well;
Those that in *Pleuron*, *Olenon*, and strong *Pylene* dwell:
Great *Calcis* that by sea-side stands, and stony *Calydon*;
For now no more of *Oeneus* sonnes, surviv'd; they all were gone:
No more his royall selfe did live, no more his noble sonne,
The golden Meleager; now, their glasses all were run.
All things were left to him in charge, the Ætolians Chiefe he was,
And fortie ships to Troian warres, the seas with him did pass.
    The royall souldier *Idomen*, did leade the Cretans stout:
The men of *Gnossus*, and the towne, *Cortima*, wall'd about.
Of *Lictus and Myletus* towres, of white *Lycastus* state,
Of *Phestus* and of *Rhistias*, the cities fortunate:
And all, the rest inhabiting, the hundred townes of *Crete*;

Whom warre-like *Idomen* did leade, copartner in the fleete,
With kil-man *Merion*; eightie ships, with them did Troy invade.
  Tlepolemus Heraclides, right strong and bigly made,
Brought nine tall ships of warre from *Rhodes*, which hautie *Rhodians*
    mand,
Who dwelt in three dissever'd parts, of that most pleasant land;
Which *Lyndus* and *Ialissus* were, and bright *Camyrus*, cald:
Tlepolemus commanded these, in battell unappald:
Whom faire *Atioche* brought forth, by force of *Hercules*;
Led out of *Ephyr* with his hand, from river *Sellees*;
When many townes of princely youths, he leveld with the ground.
Tlepolem (in his fathers house, for building much renownd,
Brought up to head-strong state of youth) his mothers brother slue,
The flowre of armes, *Lycymnius*, that somewhat aged grew:
Then straight he gathred him a fleete, assembling bands of men,
And fled by sea, to shun the threats, that were denounced then,
By other sonnes and nephews of, th'Alciden fortitude.
He in his exile came to *Rhodes*, driven in with tempests rude:
The Rhodians were distinct in tribes, and great with *Iove* did stand,
The king of men and Gods, who gave, much treasure to their land.
  Nireus, out of *Symas* haven, three wel-built barkes did bring;
Nireus faire *Aglaias* sonne, and *Charopes* the king:
Nireus was the fairest man, that to faire *Ilion* came,
Of all the Greekes, save *Peleus* sonne; who past for generall frame.
But weake this was, not fit for warre, and therefore few did guide.
  Who did in *Cassus, Nisyrus*, and *Crapathus* abide,
In *Co, Euripilus* his towne, and in *Calydnas* soyles,
Phydippus and bold *Antiphus*, did guide to Troian toyles;
The sonnes of crowned *Thessalus*, deriv'd from *Hercules*,
Who went with thirtie hollow ships, well ordred to the seas.
  Now will I sing the sackfull troopes, Pelasgian *Argos* held,
That in deepe *Alus, Alopé*, and soft *Trechina* dweld;
In *Pytha* and in *Hellade*, where live the lovely dames,
The *Myrmidons, Helenians* and *Achives*, robd of Fames:
All of which the great *Æacides*, in fiftie ships did leade.
For, these forgat warres horride voice, because they lackt their head,
That would have brought them bravely foorth; but now at fleete did
    lie,
That wind-like user of his feet, faire *Thetis* progenie;
Wroth for bright-cheekt *Bryseis* losse; whom from *Lyrnessus* spoiles,
(His owne exploit) he brought away, as trophee of his toiles,
When that towne was depopulate; he sunke the Theban towres;

[35]

Myneta, and *Epistrophus*, he sent to *Plutoes* bowres,
Who came of king *Euenus* race, great *Helepiades*:
Yet now he idely lives enrag'd, but soone must leave his ease.

From George Chapman's translation of *The Iliad*, 1598

From Phylace, and from the flow'ry fields
Of Pyrrhasus, a land to Ceres giv'n
By consecration, and from Iton green,
Mother of flocks; from Antron by the sea,
And from the grassy meads of Pteleus, came
A people, whom while yet he lived, the brave
Protesilaüs led; but him the earth
Now cover'd dark and drear. A wife he left,
To rend in Phylace her bleeding cheeks,
And an unfinished mansion. First he died
Of all the Greeks; for as he leap'd to land
Foremost by far, a Dardan struck him dead.
Nor had his troops, though filled with deep regret,
No leader; them Podarces led, a Chief
Like Mars in battle, brother of the slain,
But younger born, and from Iphiclus sprung
Who sprang from Phylacus the rich in flocks.
But him Protesilaüs, as in years,
So also in desert of arms excelled
Heroic, whom his host, although they saw
Podarces at their head, still justly mourn'd;
For he was fierce in battle, and at Troy
With forty sable-sided ships arrived.
   Eleven galleys, Pherae on the lake,
And Boebe, and Jölchus, and the vale
Of Glaphyræ supplied with crews robust
Under Eumelus; him, Alcestis, praised
For beauty above all her sisters fair,
To Thessaly to King Admetus bore.
   Methone, and Olizon's craggy coast,
With Meliboea and Thaumasia sent
Sev'n ships; their rowers were good archers all,
And ev'ry vessel dipp'd into the wave
Her fifty oars. Them Philoctetes, skilled
To draw with sinewy arm the stubborn bow,

Commanded; but he suffering anguish keen
Inflicted by a serpent's venom'd tooth,
Lay sick in Lemnos; him the Grecians there
Had left sore-wounded, but were destined soon
To call to dear remembrance whom they left.
Meantime, though sorrowing for his sake, his troops
Yet wanted not a Chief; them Medon ruled,
Whom Rhena to the far-famed conqueror bore
Oïleus, fruit of their unsanction'd loves.

   From Tricca, from Ithome rough and rude
With rocks and glens, and from Oechalia, town
Of Eurytus Oechalian-born, came forth
Their warlike youth by Podalirius led
And by Machaon, healers both expert
Of all disease, and thirty ships were theirs.

   The men of Ormenus, and from beside
The fountain Hypereia, from the tops
Of chalky Titan, and Asteria's band;
Them ruled Eurypylus, Evæmon's son
Illustrious, whom twice twenty ships obeyed.

   Orthe, Gyrtone, Oloösson white,
Argissa and Helone; they their youth
Gave to controul of Polypoetes, son
Undaunted of Pirithoüs, son of Jove.
Him, to Pirithoüs, (on the self-same day,
When he the Centaurs punish'd, and pursued
Sheer to Æthicæ driv'n from Pelion's heights
The shaggy race) Hippodamia bore.
Nor he alone them led. With him was join'd
Leonteus, dauntless warrior, from the bold
Coronus sprung, who Cæneus call'd his sire.
Twice twenty ships awaited their command.

   Guneus from Cyphus twenty and two ships
Led forth; the Enienes him obey'd,
And the robust Peroebi, warriors bold,
And dwellers on Dodona's wintry brow.
To these were join'd, who till the pleasant fields
Where Titaresius winds; the gentle flood
Pours into Peneus all his limpid stores,
But with the silver-eddied Peneus flows
Unmixt as oil; for Stygian is his stream,
And Styx is the inviolable oath.

Last with his forty ships, Tenthreden's son,
The active Prothoüs came. From the green banks
Of Peneus his Magnesians far and near
He gather'd, and from Pelion forest-crowned.
  These were the Princes and Chiefs of Greece.
Say, Muse, who most in personal desert
Excelled, and whose were the most warlike steeds
And of the noblest strain. Their hue, their age,
Their height the same, swift as the winds of heaven
And passing far all others, were the mares
Which drew Eumelus: on Pierian hills
The heavenly archer of the silver bow,
Apollo, bred them. But of men, the chief
Was Telamonian Ajax, while wrath-bound
Achilles lay; for He was worthier far,
And more illustrious were the steeds which bore
The noble son of Peleus; but revenge
On Agamemnon leader of the host
Was all his thought, while in his gallant ships
Sharp-keel'd to cut the foaming flood, he lay.
Meantime, along the margin of the deep
His soldiers hurled the disk, or bent the bow,
Or to its mark dispatch'd the quivering lance.
Beside the chariots stood th'unharness'd steeds
Cropping the lotus, or at leisure browzed
On celery wild, from wat'ry freshes gleaned.
Beneath the shadow of the shelt'ring tent
The chariot stood, while they, the charioteers
Roam'd here and there the camp, their warlike lord
Regretting sad, and idle for his sake.

From William Cowper's translation of *The Iliad*, 1791

A Catalogue of Later Greeks

... the Greek world, with all its absorptions and dispersals and its Odyssean ramifications, is an inexhaustible Pandora's box of eccentricities and exceptions to all conceivable rule. I thought of the abundance of strange communities: the scattered Bektashi and the Rufayan, the Mevlevi dervishes of the Tower of the Winds, the Liaps of Souli, the Pomaks of the Rhodope, the Kizilbashi near Kechro, the Fire-Walkers of Mavrolevki, the

Lazi from the Pontic shores, the Linovamvaki – crypto-Christian Moslems of Cyprus – the Dönmehs – crypto-Jewish Moslems of Salonika and Smyrna – the Slavophones of Northern Macedonia, the Koutzo-Vlachs of Samarina and Metzovo, the Chams of Thesprotia, the scattered Souliots of Roumeli and the Heptanese, the Albanians of Argolis and Attica, the Kravarite mendicants of Aetolia, the wandering quacks of Eurytania, the phallus-wielding Bounariots of Tyrnavos, the Karamanlides of Cappadocia, the Tzakones of the Argolic gulf, the Ayassians of Lesbos, the Francolevantine Catholics of the Cyclades, the Turkophone Christians of Karamania, the dyers of Mt Ossa, the Mangas of Piraeus, the Venetian nobles of the Ionian, the Old Calendrists of Keratea, the Jehovah's Witnesses of Thasos, the Nomad Sarakatzáns of the north, the Turks of Thrace, the Thessalonican Sephardim, the sponge-fishers of Calymnos and the Caribbean reefs, the Maniots of Corsica, Tuscany, Algeria and Florida, the dying Grecophones of Calabria and Otranto, the Greek-speaking Turks near Trebizond on the banks of the Of, the omnipresent Gypsies, the Chimarriots of Acroceraunia, the few Gagauzi of eastern Thrace, the Mardaïtes of the Lebanon, the half-Frankish Gazmouli of the Morea, the small diasporas of Armenians, the Bavarians of Attic Herakleion, the Cypriots of Islington and Soho, the Sahibs and Boxwallahs of Nicosia, the English remittance men of Kyrenia, the Basilian Monks, both Idiorrhythmic and Cenobitic, the anchorites of Mt Athos, the Chiots of Bayswater and the Guards' Club, the merchants of Marseilles, the cotton-brokers of Alexandria, the shipowners of Panama, the greengrocers of Brooklyn, the Amariots of Lourenço Marques, the Shqip-speaking Atticans of Sfax, the Cretan fellaheen of Luxor, the Elasites beyond the Iron Curtain, the brokers of Trieste, the Krim-Tartar-speaking Lazi of Marioupol, the Pontics of the Sea of Azov, the Caucasus and the Don, the Turcophone and Armenophone Lazi of southern Russia, the Greeks of the Danube Delta, Odessa and Taganrog, the *rentiers* in eternal *villaggiatura* by the lakes of Switzerland, the potters of Syphnos and Messenia, the exaggerators and the ghosts of Mykonos, the Karagounides of the Thessalian plain, the Nyklians and the Achamnómeri of the Mani, the little bootblacks of Megalopolis, the Franks of the Morea, the Byzantines of Mistra, the Venetians and Genoese and Pisans of the archipelago, the boys kidnapped for janissaries and the girls for harems, the Catalan bands, the Kondaritika-speaking lathmakers of the Zagarochoria, the Loubinistika-speakers of the brothels, the Anglo-Saxons of the Varangian Guard, ye olde Englisshe of the Levant company, the Klephts and the Armatoles, the Kroumides of Colchis, the Koniarides of Loxada, the smugglers of Aï-Vali, the lunatics of Cephalonia, the admirals of Hydra, the Phanariots of the Sublime Porte, the princes and boyars of Moldowallachia, the Ralli Brothers of India, the Whittals of Constantinople, the lepers of Spinalonga, the political prisoners of the Macronisos, the Hello-boys back from the States, the two pig-roasting Japanese ex-convicts of Crete, the solitary negro of Canea and a wandering Arab I saw years ago in Domoko, the Chinese tea-pedlar of Kalonaki, killed in Piraeus during the war by a bomb – if all these, to name a few, why not the crypto-Jews of the Taygetus?

From *Mani* by Patrick Leigh Fermor, 1958

The Begats

1 The sons of Levi; Gershon, Kohath, and Merari.
2 And the sons of Kohath; Amram, Izhar, and Hebron, and Uzziel.
3 And the children of Amram; Aaron, and Moses, and Miriam. The sons also of Aaron; Nadab, and Abihu, Eleazar, and Ithamar.
4 Eleazar begat Phinehas, Phinehas begat Abishua,
5 And Abishua begat Bukki, and Bukki begat Uzzi,
6 And Uzzi begat Zerahiah, and Zerahiah begat Meraioth,
7 Meraioth begat Amariah, and Amariah begat Ahitub,
8 And Ahitub begat Zadok, and Zadok begat Ahimaaz,
9 And Ahimaaz begat Azariah, and Azariah begat Johanan,
10 And Johanan begat Azariah, (he it is that executed the priest's office in the temple that Solomon built in Jerusalem:)
11 And Azariah begat Amariah, and Amariah begat Ahitub,
12 And Ahitub begat Zadok, and Zadok begat Shallum,
13 And Shallum begat Hilkiah, and Hilkiah begat Azariah,
14 And Azariah begat Seraiah, and Seraiah begat Jehozadak,
15 And Jehozadak went into captivity, when the LORD carried away Judah and Jerusalem by the hand of Nebuchadnezzar.

From *Chronicles* 1:6

To Each an Award

Men pass through doors and travel to the sea, stand grouped in attitudes of play or labour, bending to children, raising equal's glass, are many times together, man with woman. To each an award, suitable to his sex, his class and the power.

One charms by thickness of wrist; one by variety of positions; one has a beautiful skin, one a fascinating smell. One has prominent eyes, is bold at accosting. One has water sense; he can dive like a swallow without using his hands. One is obeyed by dogs, one can bring down snipe on the wing. One can do cart wheels before theatre queues; one can slip through a narrow ring. One with a violin can conjure up images of running water; one is skilful at improvising a fugue; the bowel tremors at the pedal-entry. One amuses by pursing his lips; or can imitate the neigh of a randy stallion. One casts metal in black sand; one wipes the eccentrics of a great engine with cotton waste. One jumps out of windows for profit. One makes leather instruments of torture for titled masochists; one makes ink for his son out of oak galls and rusty nails. One makes bedsteads, adorned with carvings, at the request of friends. One in a red-brick villa makes designs for a bridge, creates beauty for a purpose. One is eloquent, persuades committees of the value of spending: one announces weddings in a solemn voice. One is told secrets at night, can stop a young girl biting her nails. One can extirpate a goitre with little risk. One can foretell the migrations of mackerel; one can distinguish the eggs of sea-birds. One is a lightning calculator; he is a young one. One is clumsy but amazes by his knowledge of time-tables. One delivers buns in a van, halting at houses. One can emend a mutilated text; one can estimate the percentage of moisture in a sample of nitre. One decorates a room for a lady in black and silver; one manufactures elephant drums for a circus. One has an extraordinary capacity for organising study circles. One fosters snowdrops in a green bowl. One does nothing at all but is good.

From *The Orators* by W. H. Auden, 1932

The Healing of Sir Urry

Than kynge Arthur lette calle that lady and aske her the cause why she brought that hurte knyght into that londe.

'My moste noble kynge,' seyde that lady, 'wyte you well I brought hym hyddir to be heled of hys woundis, that of all thys seven yere myght never be hole.'

And thus she tolde the kynge, and where he was wounded and with whom, and how hys modir discoverde hit in her pryde how she had worought by enchauntemente that he sholde never be hole untyll the beste knyght of the worlde had serched hys woundis.

'And so I have passed all the landis crystynde thorow to have hym healed excepte thys londe, and gyff I fayle here in thys londe I woll never take more payne uppon me. And that ys grete pité, for he was a good knyght and of grete nobeles.'

[41]

'What ys hys name?' seyde kynge Arthure.

'My good and gracious lorde,' she seyde, 'his name ys sir Urré of the Mounte.'

'In good tyme,' seyde the kynge. 'And sythyn ye ar com into thys londe, ye ar ryght wellcome. And wyte you welle, here shall youre son be healed and ever ony Crystyn man [may] heale hym. And for to gyff all othir men off worshyp a currayge, I myself woll asay to handyll your sonne, and so shall all the kynges, dukis and erlis that ben here presente at thys tyme, nat presumying uppon me that I am so worthy to heale youre son be my dedis, but I woll corrayge othir men of worshyp to do as I woll do.'

And than the kynge commaunded all the kynges, dukes and erlis and all noble knyghtes of the Rounde Table that were there that tyme presente to com into the medow of Carlehyll.

And so at that tyme there were but an hondred an ten of the Rounde Table, for forty knyghtes were that tyme away. And so here we muste begynne at kynge Arthur, as was kyndely to begynne at hym that was that tyme the moste man of worshyp crystynde.

Than kynge Arthur loked uppon sir Urré, and he thought he was a full lykly man whan he was hole. And than the kynge made to take hym downe of the lyttar and leyde hym uppon the erth, and anone there was a layde a cussheon of golde that he shulde knele uppon. And than kynge Arthur sayde,

'Fayre knyght, my rewyth of thy hurte, and for to corrayge all other knyghtes I woll pray the sofftely to suffir me to handyll thy woundis.'

'My moste noble crystynd kynge, do ye as ye lyste,' seyde sir Urré, 'for I am at the mercy of God and at youre commaundemente.'

So than kynge Arthur softely handeled hym. And than som of hys woundis renewed uppon bledynge.

Than kynge Claryaunce of Northumbirlonde serched, and hit wolde nat be. And than sir Barraunte le Apres, that was called the Kynge with the Hundred Knyghtes, he assayed and fayled.

So ded kynge Uryence of the londe of Gore. So ded kynge Angwysh of Irelonde, and so ded kynge Newtrys of Garloth. So ded kynge Carydos of Scotlonde. So ded the duke sir Galahalt the Haute Prynce. So ded sir Constantyne that was kynge Cadors son of Cornwayle. So ded duke Chalaunce of Claraunce. So ded the erle of Ulbawys. So ded the erle Lambayle. So ded the erle Arystanse.

Than cam in sir Gawayne wyth hys three sunnes, sir Gyngalyn, sir Florence, and sir Lovell (thes two were begotyn uppon sir Braundeles syster), and all they fayled. Than cam in sir Aggravayne, sir Gaherys, and sir Mordred, and the good knyght sir Gareth that was of verry knyghthod worth all the brethirn.

So cam in the knyghtes of sir Launcelottis kyn, but sir Launcelot was nat [that] tyme in the courte, for he was that tyme uppon his adventures. Than sir Lyonell, sir Ector de Marys, sir Bors de Ganys, sir Blamour de Ganys, sir Bleoberys de Gaynys, sir Gahalantyne, sir Galyhodyn, sir Menaduke, sir Vyllars the Valyaunte, sir Hebes le Renowné, all thes were of sir Launcelottis kynne, and all they fayled.

Than cam in sir Sagramour le Desyrus, sir Dodynas le Saveage, sir Dynadan, sir Brewne le Noyre that sir Kay named La Cote Male Tayle, and sir Kay le Senesciall, sir Kay d'Estraunges, sir Mellyot de Logris, sir Petipace of Wynchylsé, sir Galleron of Galway, sir Melyon of the Mountayne, sir Cardoke, sir Uwayne les Avoutres, and sir Ozanna le Cure Hardy. Than cam in sir Ascamour, and sir Grummor and Grummorson, sir Crosseleme, sir Severause le Brewse that was called a passynge stronge knyght.

For, as the booke seyth, the chyff lady of the Lady off the Lake fested sir Launcelot and sir Severause le Brewse, and whan she had fested them both at sundry tymes, she prayde hem to gyff her a done, and anone they graunted her. And than she prayde sir Severause that he wolde promyse her never to do batayl ayenste sir Launcelot, and in the same wyse she prayde sir Launcelot never to do bataye ayenste sir Severause, and so aythir promysed her. (For the Freynshe booke sayth that sir Severause had never corayge nor grete luste to do bataye ayenste no man but if hit we[re] ayenste gyauntis and ayenste dragons and wylde bestis.)

So leve we thys mater and speke we of them that at the kynges rekeyste were [there] at the hyghe feste, as knyghtes of the Rounde Table, for to serche Sir Urré. And to thys entente the kynge ded hit, to wyte whych was the moste nobelyste knyght amonge them all.

Than cam in sir Agglovale, sir Durnor and sir Tor that was begotyn uppon the cowardis wyff, but he was begotyn afore Aryes wedded her (and kynge Pellynor begate them all: firste sir Tor, sir Agglovale, sir Durnor, sir Lamorak, the moste nobeleste knyght one of them that ever was in kynge Arthurs dayes as for a wordly knyght, and sir Percivale that was pyerles, excepte sir Galahad, in holy dedis. But they dyed in the queste of the Sangreall).

Than cam in sir Gryfflet le Fyze de Du, sir Lucan the Butlere, sir Bedyvere, hys brothir, sir Braundeles, sir Constantyne, sir Cadors son of Cornwayle that was kynge aftir Arthurs dayes, and sir Clegis, sir Sadok, sir Dynas le Senesciall de Cornwayle, sir Fergus, sir Dryaunte, sir Lambegus, sir Clarrus off Cleremownte, sir Cloddrus, sir Hectymere, sir Edwarde of Carnarvan, sir Pryamus whych was crystynde by the meanys of sir Trystram, the noble knyght, and thes three were brethirn; sir Helayne le Blanke that was son unto sir Bors, for he begate hym uppon kynge

Brandygorys daughter, and sir Bryan de Lystenoyse; sir Gauter, sir Raynolde, sir Gyllymere, were three brethirn whych sir Launcelot wan uppon a brydge in sir Kayes armys; sir Gwyarte le Petite, sir Bellyngere le Bewse that was son to the good knyght sir Alysaundir le Orphelyn that was slayne by the treson of kynge Marke.

Also that traytoure kynge slew the noble knyght sir Trystram as he sate harpynge afore hys lady, La Beall Isode, with a trenchaunte glayve, for whos dethe was the moste waylynge of ony knyght that ever was in kynge Arthurs dayes, for there was never none so bewayled as was sir Tristram and sir Lamerok, for they were with treson slayne: sir Trystram by kynge Marke, and sir Lamorake by sir Gawayne and hys brethirn.

And thys sir Bellynger revenged the deth of hys fadir, sir Alysaundir, and sir Trystram, for he slewe kynge Marke. And La Beall Isode dyed sownyng uppon the crosse of sir Trystram, whereof was grete pité. And all that were with kynge Marke whych were of assente of the dethe of sir Trystram were slayne, as sir Andred and many othir.

Than cam sir Hebes, sir Morganoure, sir Sentrayle, sir Suppynabiles, sir Belyaunce le Orgulus that the good knyght sir Lamorak wan in playne batayle, sir Neroveus and sir Plenoryus, two good knyghtes that sir Launcelot wanne, sir Darras, sir Harry le Fyze Lake, sir Ermynde, brother to kyng Hermaunce, for whom sir Palomydes faught at the Rede Cité with two brethirn; and sir Selyses of the Dolerous Towre, sir Edward of Orkeney, sir Ironsyde that was called the noble knyght of the Rede Laundis, that sir Gareth wan for the love of da[m]e Lyones; sir Arrok, sir Degrevaunt, sir Degrave Saunze Vylony that faught wyth the gyaunte of the Blak Lowe; sir Epynogrys that was the kynges son of Northumbir-londe, sir Pelleas that loved the lady Ettarde (and he had dyed for her sake, had nat bene one of the ladyes of the lake whos name was dame Nynyve; and she wedde sir Pelleas, and she saved hym ever aftir, that he was never slayne by her dayes; and he was a full noble knyght); and sir Lamyell of Cardyff that was a grete lovear, sir Playne de Fors, sir Melyaus de Lyle, sir Boarte le Cure Hardy that was kynge Arthurs son, sir Madore de la Porte, sir Collgrevaunce, sir Hervyse de la Foreyst Saveayge, sir Marrok the good knyght that was betrayed with his wyff, for he made him seven yere a warwolff; sir Persaunt, sir Pertolope, hys brothir, that was called the Grene Knyght, and sir Perymones, brother unto them bothe, whych was called the Rede Knyght, that sir Gareth wanne whan he was called Bewmaynes.

All thes hondred knyghtes and ten serched sir Urryes woundis by the commaundemente of kynge Arthur.

'Mercy Jesu!' seyde kynge Arthur, 'where ys sir Launcelot du Lake, that he ys nat here at thys tyme?'

And thus as they stood and spake of many thyngis, there one aspyed sir Launcelot that com rydynge towarde them, and anone they tolde the kynge.

'Pees,' seyde the kynge, 'lat no man say nothyng untyll he be com to us.'

So whan sir Launcelot had aspyed kynge Arthur he descended downe frome hys horse and cam to the kynge and salewed hym and them all.

And anone as the damesell, sir Urryes syster, saw sir Launcelot, she romed to her brothir thereas he lay in hys lyttar and seyde,

'Brothir, here ys com a knyght that my harte gyveth gretly unto.'

'Fayre sister,' seyde sir Urré, 'so doth my harte lyghte gretly ayenste hym, and my harte gyvith me more unto hym than to all thes that hath serched me.'

Than seyde kynge Arthur unto sir Launcelot, 'Sir, ye muste do as we have done', and tolde hym what they had done and shewed hym all that had serched hym.

'Jesu defende me,' seyde sir Launcelot, 'whyle so many noble kyngis and knyghtes have fayled, that I shulde presume uppon me to enchyve that all ye, my lordis, myght nat enchyve.'

'Ye shall nat chose,' seyde kynge Arthur, 'for I commaunde you to do as we all have done.'

'My moste renowmed lorde,' seyde sir Launcelot, 'I know well I dare nat, nor may nat, disobey you. But and I myght or durst, wyte you well I wolde nat take uppon me to towche that wounded knyght in that entent that I shulde passe all othir knyghtes. Jesus deffende me frome that shame!'

'Sir, ye take hit wronge,' seyde kynge Arthur, 'for ye shall nat do hit for no presumpcion, but for to beare us felyshyp, insomuche as ye be a felow of the Rounde Table. And wyte you well,' seyde kynge Arthur, 'and ye prevayle nat and heale hym, I dare sey there ys no knyght in thys londe that may hele hym. And therefore I pray you do as we have done.'

And than all the kyngis and knyghtes for the moste party prayed sir Launcelot to serche hym. And than the wounded knyght, sir Urré, set hym up waykely and seyde unto sir Launcelot.

'Now, curteyse knyght, I requyre the, for Goddis sake, heale my woundis! For methynkis ever sytthyn ye cam here my woundis grevyth me nat so muche as they ded.'

'A, my fayre lorde,' seyde sir Launcelot, 'Jesu wolde that I myght helpe you! For I shame sore with myselff that I shulde be thus requyred, for never was I able in worthynes to do so hyghe a thynge.'

Than sir Launcelot kneled downe by the wounded knyght, saiyng, 'My lorde Arthure, I muste do youre commaundemente, whych ys sore ayenste my harte.' And than he hylde up hys hondys and loked unto the este, saiynge secretely unto hymselff, 'Now, Blyssed Fadir and Son and Holy Goste, I beseche The of Thy mercy that my symple worshyp and honesté

[45]

be saved, and Thou Blyssed Trynyté, Thou mayste yeff me power to hele thys syke knyght by the grete vertu and grace of The, but, Good Lorde, never of myselff.'

And than sir Launcelot prayde sir Urré to lat hym se hys hede; and than, devoutly knelyng, he ransaked the three woundis, that they bled a lytyll; and forthwithall the woundis fayre heled and semed as they had bene hole a seven yere. And in lyke wyse he serched hys body of othir three woundis, and they healed in lyke wyse. And than the laste of all he serched hys honde, and anone hit fayre healed.

Than kynge Arthur and all the kynges and knyghtes kneled downe and gave thankynges and lovynge unto God and unto Hys Blyssed Modir. And ever sir Launcelote wepte, as he had bene a chylde that had bene beatyn!

From the *Works* of Sir Thomas Malory (d. 1471)

ffines Announces

'Her Grace, the Duchess of Valmouth; the Honourable Mrs Manborough of Castle Malling' – ffines' voice filled the room.

'You shall hold Baby, Lieutenant, while I –' Mrs Hurstpierpoint flapped expressively her loose-winged sleeves.

'Sir William West-Wind, Mr Peter Caroon, Mrs Trotter-Stormer, Sir Wroth and Lady Cleobulina Summer-Leyton, Sir Victor Vatt, Master Xavier Tanoski, Lady Lucy Saunter, Miss à Duarté, Miss Roxall, Lady Jane Congress, Lady Constance Cadence-Stewart, Mrs Q. Comedy, Lady Lauraguay, Lady Lukin de Lukin, Mrs Lumlum, Mr Argrove, Mrs Lositer, General George Obliveon, Lady Parvula de Panzoust.'

From *Valmouth* by Ronald Firbank, 1919

The Mayor Congratulates

On the lawn-sward couples were revolving beneath the festooned trees that twinkled convivially with fairy-lamps, but the centre of attraction, perhaps, at present was the Mayor.

'Congratulations,' his voice pealed out, 'to Peggy Laugher, Ann and Zillah Bottom, Almeria Goatpath, Thisbe Brownjohn, Teresa Twistleton, Rebecca Bramblebrook, Junie Jones, Susannah Sneep, Peter Palafox, Flo Flook, Simon Toole, Molly Ark, Nellie Knight, Fanny Beard, May Thatcher, May Heaven, George Kissington, Tircis Tree, Gerry Bosboom,

Gilbert Soham, Lily Quickstep, Doris Country, Anna Clootz, Mary Teeworthy, Dorothy Tooke, Patrick Flynn, Rosa Sweet, Laurette Venum, Violet Ebbing, Horace Hardly, Mary Wilks –'

'*In saeculum saeculi*, apparently!' Mrs Hurstpierpoint shrugged.

From *Valmouth* by Ronald Firbank, 1919

How Kilhwch Won Olwen

'I will tell thee,' said the youth, 'I am Kilhwch, the son of Kilydd, the son of Prince Kelyddon, by Goleuddydd, my mother, the daughter of Prince Anlwadd.' 'That is true,' said Arthur; 'thou art my cousin. Whatsoever boon thou mayest ask, thou shalt receive, be it what it may that thy tongue shall name.' 'Pledge the truth of Heaven and the faith of thy kingdom thereof.' 'I pledge it thee gladly.' 'I crave of thee then, that thou obtain for me Olwen, the daughter of Yspaddaden Penkawr; and this boon I likewise seek at the hands of thy warriors. I seek it from Kai, and Bedwyr, and Greidawl Galldonyd, and Gwythyr the son of Greidawl, and Greid the son of Eri, and Kynndelig Kyvarwydd, and Tathal Twyll Goleu, and Maelwys the son of Baeddan, and Crychwr the son of Nes, and Cubert the son of Daere, and Percos the son of Poch, and Lluber Beuthach, and Corvil Bervach, and Gwynn the son of Nudd, and Edeyrn the son of Nudd, and Garwy the son of Geraint, and Prince Fflewddur Fflam ... and Morvyran the son of Tegid ['Seagull, son of Beauty'] (no one struck him in the battle of Camlan by reason of his ugliness; all thought he was an auxiliary devil. Hair had he upon him like the hair of a stag). And Sandde Bryd Angel (no one touched him with a spear in the battle of Camlan because of his beauty; all thought he was a ministering angel). And Kynwyl Sant (the third man that escaped from the battle of Camlan, and he was the last who parted from Arthur on Hengroen his horse). And Uchtryd the son of Erim, and Eus the son of Erim, and Henwas Adeinawg the son of Erim, and Henbedestyr ['Ancient-Walker'] the son of Erim, and Sgilti Yscawndroed ['Sgilti Light-Foot'] the son of Erim. (Unto these three men belonged these three qualities, – With Henbedestyr there was not any one who could keep pace, either on horseback or on foot; with Henwas Adeinawg, no four-footed beast could run the distance of an acre, much less could it go beyond it; and as to Sgilti Yscawndroed, when he intended to go upon a message for his Lord, he never sought to find a path, but knowing whither he was to go, if his way lay through a wood he went along the tops of the trees. During his whole life, a blade of reed-grass bent not beneath his feet, much less did one ever break, so lightly did he tread.) Teithi Hên the son of Gwynhan (his

[47]

dominions were swallowed up by the sea, and he himself hardly escaped, and he came to Arthur; and his knife had this peculiarity, that from the time that he came there no haft would ever remain upon it, and owing to this a sickness came over him, and he pined away during the remainder of his life, and of this he died). And Carneddyr the son of Govynyon Hên, and Gwenwynwyn the son of Nav Gyssevin, Arthur's champion, and Llysgadrudd Emys, and Gwrbothu Hên (uncles unto Arthur were they, his mother's brothers). Kulvanawyd the son of Goryon, and Llenlleawg Wyddel from the headland of Ganion, and Dyvynwal Moel, and Dunard king of the North, Teirnon Twryf Bliant, and Tegvan Gloff, and Tegyr Talgellawg, Gwrdinal the son of Ebrei, and Morgant Hael, Gwystyl ['Hostage'] the son of Rhun ['Grand'] the son of Nwython ['Whims'], and Llwyddeu the son of Nwython, and Gwydre the son of Llwyddeu (Gwenabwy the daughter of [Kaw] was his mother, Hueil his uncle stabbed him, and hatred was between Hueil and Arthur because of the wound). Drem the son of Dremidyd ['Sight, son of Seer'] (when the gnat arose in the morning with the sun, he could see it from Gelli Wic in Cornwall, as far off as Pen Blathaon in North Britain). And Eidyol the son of Ner, and Glwyddyn Saer (who constructed Ehangwen ['Broad-White'], Arthur's Hall). Kynyr Keinvarvawc (when he was told he had a son born he said to his wife, 'Damsel, if thy son be mine, his heart will always be cold, and there will be no warmth in his hands; and he will have another peculiarity, if he is my son he will always be stubborn; and he will have another peculiarity, when he carries a burden, whether it be large or small, no one will be able to see it, either before him or at his back; and he will have another peculiarity, no one will be able to resist fire and water as well as he will; and he will have another peculiarity, there will never be a servant or an officer equal to him'). Henwas ['Old-Servant'], and Henwyneb ['Old Face'] (an old companion to Arthur). Gwallgoyc (another; when he came to a town, though there were three hundred houses in it, if he wanted anything, he would not let sleep come to the eyes of anyone while he remained there). Berwyn, the son of Gerenhir, and Paris king of France, and Osla Gyllellvawr ['Big-Knife'] (who bore a short broad dagger. When Arthur and his hosts came before a torrent, they would seek for a narrow place where they might pass the water, and would lay the sheathed dagger across the torrent, and it would form a bridge sufficient for the armies of the three Islands of Britain, and of the three islands adjacent, with their spoil). Gwyddawg the son of Menestyr (who slew Kai, and whom Arthur slew, together with his brothers, to revenge Kai). Garanwyn the son of Kai, and Amren the son of Bedwyr, and Ely Amyr, and Rheu Rhwyd Dyrys, and Rhun Rhudwern, and Eli, and Trachmyr (Arthur's chief huntsmen). And Llwyddeu the son of Kelcoed, and Hunabwy the son of Gwryon, and Gwynn Godywron, and Gweir

Datharwenniddawg, and Gweir the son of Cadell the son of Talaryant, and Gweir Gwrhyd Ennwir, and Gweir Paladyr Hir (the uncles of Arthur, the brothers of his mother). The sons of Llwch Llawwynnyawg (from beyond the raging sea). Llenlleawg Wyddel, and Ardderchawg Prydain. Cas the son of Saidi, Gwrvan Gwallt Avwyn, and Gwyllennhin the king of France, and Gwittart the son of Oedd king of Ireland, Gaselit Wyddel, Panawr Per. Bagad, and Fflendor the son of Nav, Gwynnhyvar mayor of Cornwall and Devon (the ninth man that rallied the battle of Camlan). Keli and Kueli, and Gilla Coes Hydd ['Dear-Legs'] (he would clear three hundred acres at one bound: the chief leaper of Ireland was he). Sol, and Gwadyn ['Sole'] Ossol, and Gwadyn Odyeith ['Rare-Sole']. (Sol could stand all day upon one foot. Gwadyn Ossol, if he stood upon the top of the highest mountain in the world, it would become a level plain under his feet. Gwadyn Odyeith, the soles of his feet emitted sparks of fire when they struck upon things hard, like the heated mass when drawn out of the forge. He cleared the way for Arthur when he came to any stoppage.) Hirerwm and Hiratrwm. (The day they went on a visit three Cantrevs provided for their entertainment, and they feasted until noon and drank until night, when they went to sleep. And then they devoured the heads of the vermin through hunger, as if they had never eaten anything. When they made a visit they left neither the fat nor the lean, neither the hot nor the cold, the sour nor the sweet, the fresh nor the salt, the boiled nor the raw.) Huarwar the son of Aflawn ['Easily Satisfied, son of Never'full'] (who asked Arthur such a boon as would satisfy him. It was the third great plague of Cornwall when he received it. None could get a smile from him but when he was satisfied). Gware Gwallt Euryn. The two cubs of Gast Rhymi, Gwyddrud and Gwyddneu Astrus. Sugyn the son of Sugnedydd ['Sucker, son of Pump'] (who would suck up the sea on which were three hundred ships, so as to leave nothing but a dry strand. He was broad-chested). Rhacymwri, the attendant of Arthur (whatever barn he was shown, were there the produce of thirty ploughs within it, he would strike it with an iron flail until the rafters, the beams, and the boards were no better than the small oats in the mow upon the floor of the barn). Dygyflwng, and Anoeth Veidawg ['Obstacle-Overcomer']. And Hir Eiddyl, and Hir Amreu (they were two attendants of Arthur). And Gwevyl ['Lips'] the son of Gwestad (on the day that he was sad, he would let one of his lips drop below his waist, while he turned up the other like a cap upon his head). Uchtryd Varyf Draws ['Uchtryd Beard Across'] (who spread his red untrimmed beard over the eight-and-forty rafters which were in Arthur's Hall). Elidyr Gyvarwydd. Yskyrdav, and Yscudydd ['Runner'] (two attendants of Gwenhwyvar were they. Their feet were swift as their thoughts when bearing a message). Brys the son of Bryssethach ['Hurry, son of Hurryier'] (from the Hill of the Black Fernbrake in North Britain).

And Grudlwyn Gorr. Bwlch ['Notch'], and Kyfwlch ['Equal-Notch'], and Sefwlch, the sons of Cleddyf Kyfwlch, the grandsons of Cleddyf Difwlch ['Glaive-without-Notch']. (Their three shields were three gleaming glitterers; their three spears were three pointed piercers; their three swords were three griding gashers; Glas, Glessic, and Gleisad ['Blue, Bluish, and Bluesome']. Their three dogs, Call ['Wise'], Cuall ['Foolish'], and Cavall. Their three horses, Hwyrdyddwc, and Drwgdyddwc, and Llwyrdyddwg ['Late-Bringer, Evil-Bringer, and Thorough-Bringer']. Their three wives, Och, and Garym, and Diaspad ['Oh, Cry and Shriek']. Their three grandchildren, Lluched ['Lightning'], and Neved, and Eissiwed ['Want']. Their three daughters, Drwg, and Gwaeth, and Gwaethav Oll ['Bad, Worse, and Worst']. Their three handmaids, Eheubryd the daughter of Kyfwlch, Gorascwrn the daughter of Nerth ['Bone, daughter of Strength'], Gwaedan the daughter of Kynvelyn Keudawd Pwyll the half-man.) Dwnn Diessic Unbenn, Eiladyr the son of Pen Llarcau, Kyeudyr Wyllt the son of Hettwn Talaryant, Sawyl Ben Uchel, Gwalchmai the son of Gwyar, Gwalhaved the son of Gwyar, Gwrhyr Gwastawd Ieithoedd ['Long Man, Translator of Tongues'] (to whom all tongues were known), and Kethtrwm the Priest. Clust the son of Clustveinad ['Ear, son of Hearkening'] (though he were buried seven cubits beneath the earth, he would hear the ant fifty miles off rise from her nest in the morning). Medyr ['Skill'] the son of Methredydd (from Gelli Wic he could, in a twinkling, shoot the wren through the two legs upon Esgeir Oervel in Ireland). Gwiawn Llygad Cath ['Gwiawn Cat's-Eye'] (who could cut a haw from the eye of the gnat without hurting him). Ol the son of Olwydd [Trail, son of Scent'] (seven years before he was born his father's swine were carried off, and when he grew up a man he tracked the swine and brought them back in seven herds). Bedwini the Bishop (who blessed Arthur's meat and drink). For the sake of the golden-chained daughters of this island. For the sake of Gwenhwyvar its chief lady, and Gwennhwyach her sister, and Rathtyeu the only daughter of Clemenhill, and Rhelemon the daughter of Kai, and Tannwen the daughter of Gweir Datharweniddawg. Gwenn Alarch the daughter of Kynwyl Canhwch. Eurneid the daughter of Clydno Eiddin. Eneuawc the daughter of Bedwyr. Enrydreg the daughter of Tudvathar. Gwennwledyr the daughter of Gwaledyr Kyrvach. Erdutvul the daughter of Tryffin. Eurolwen the daughter of Gwdolwyn Gorr. Teleri the daughter of Peul. Indeg the daughter of Garwy Hir. Morvudd the daughter of Urien Rheged. Gwenllian Deg the majestic maiden. Creiddylad the daughter of Lludd Llaw Ereint. (She was the most splendid maiden in the three Islands of the mighty, and in the three Islands adjacent, and for her Gwythyr the son of Greidawl and Gwynn the son of Nudd fight every first of May until the day of doom.) Ellylw the daughter of Neol Kynn-Crog (she lived three ages). Essyllt

Vinwen, and Essyllt Vingul.' And all these did Kilhwch son of Kilydd adjure to obtain his boon.

Then said Arthur, 'O chieftain, I have never heard of the maiden of whom thou speakest, nor of her kindred, but I will gladly send messengers in search of her. Give me time to seek her.' And the youth said, 'I will willingly grant from this night to that at the end of the year to do so.'

From *The Mabinogion*, translated by Lady Charlotte Guest, 1838–49

The Lion Calls All the Beasts to His Parliament

The Lepoardis come with Croun off massie gold;
Beirand thay brocht unto that hillis hicht,
With Jaspis Jonit, and Royall Rubeis rold,
And mony divers Dyamontis dicht,
With towis proud ane Palyeoun doun thay picht;
And in that Throne thair sat ane wild Lyoun,
In Rob Royall, with Sceptour, Swerd, and Croun.

Efter the tennour off the cry befoir,
That gais on all fourfuttit beistis in eird,
As thay commandit we withoutin moir,
Befoir thair Lord the Lyoun that appeird:
And quhat thay wer, to me as Lowrence leird,
I sall reheirs ane part of everilk kynd,
Als fer as now occurris to my mynd.

The Minotaur, ane Monster mervelous,
Bellerphont that beist of Bastardrie,
The Warwolff, and the Pegase perillous,
Transformit be assent of sorcerie.
The Linx, the Tiger full off Tiranie:
The Elephant, and eik the Dromedarie;
The Cameill with his Cran nek furth can carie.

The Leopard, as I haif tauld beforne,
The Anteloip, the Sparth furth couth speid,
The peyntit Pantheir, and the Unicorne;
The Rayndeir Ran throw Reveir; Rone, and Reid,
The Jolie Gillet, and the gentill Steid,

[51]

The Asse, the Mule, the Hors of everilk kynd;
The Da, the Ra, the hornit Hart, the Hynd.

The Bull, the Beir, the Bugill, and the Bair,
The tame Cat, Wildcat, and the Wildwod Swyne,
The Hardbakkit Hurcheoun, and the Hirpland Hair,
Baith Otter and Aip, and Pennit Porcupyne;
The Gukit Gait, the selie Scheip, the Swyne,
The wyld Once, the Buk, the Welterand Brok,
The Fowmart, with the Fibert ffurth can flok.

The gray Grewhound, with Sleuthond furth can slyde,
With Doggis all divers and different;
The Rattoun ran, the Glebard furth can glyde,
The quhrynand Quhitret, with the Quhasill went,
The Feitho that hes furrit mony fent,
The Mertrik, with the Cunning and the Con,
The Bowranbane, and eik the Lerioun.

The marmisset the Mowdewart couth leid,
Because that Nature denity had hir sicht;
Thus dressit thay all ffurth, ffor dreid off deid;
The musk, the lytill Mous with all hir micht
With haist scho haikit unto that hill of hicht;
And mony kynd of beistis I couth not knaw,
Befoir thair Lord the Lyoun thay loutit law.

From 'The Taill of the Sone and Air of the Foxe' in *The Morall Fabillis
of Esope the Phrygian* by Robert Henryson, fifteenth century

The Sea Nymphs

And after these the Sea Nymphs marched all,
  All goodly damzels, deckt with long greene haire,
  Whom of their sire *Nereides* men call,
  All which the Oceans daughter to him bare
  The gray eyde *Doris*: all which fifty are;
  All which she there on her attending had.
  Swift *Proto*, milde *Eucrate*, *Thetis* faire,
  Soft *Spio*, sweet *Eudore*, *Sao* sad,
Light *Doto*, wanton *Glauce*, and *Galene* glad.

White hand *Eunica*, proud *Dynamene*,
   Ioyous *Thalia*, goodly *Amphitrite*,
   Louely *Pasithee*, kinde *Eulimene*,
   Light foote *Cymothoe*, and sweete *Melite*,
   Fairest *Pherusa*, *Phao* lilly white,
   Wondred *Agaue*, *Poris*, and *Nesoea*,
   With *Erato* that doth in loue delite,
   And *Panopoe*, and wise *Protomedoea*.
And snowy neckd *Doris*, and milkewhite *Galathoea*.

Speedy *Hippothoe*, and chaste *Actea*,
   Large *Lisianassa*, and *Pronoea* sage,
   Euagore, and light *Pontoporea*,
   And she, that with her least word can asswage
   The surging seas, when they do sorest rage,
   Cymodoce, and stout *Autonoe*,
   And *Neso*, and *Eione* well in age,
   And seeming still to smile, *Glauconome*,
And she that hight of many heastes *Polynome*.

Fresh *Alimeda*, deckt with girlond greene;
   Hyponeo, with salt bedewed wrests
   Laomedia, like the christall sheene;
   Liagore, much praised for wise behests;
   And *Psamathe*, for her brode snowy brests;
   Cymo, *Eupompe*, and *Themiste* iust;
   And she that vertue loues and vice detests
   Euarna, and *Menippe* true in trust,
And *Nemerlea* learned well to rule her lust.

From *The Faerie Queene* by Edmund Spenser, 1596

The Rivers of Ireland

Ne thence the Irishe Riuers absent were,
   Sith no lesse famous then the rest they bee,
   And ioyne in neighbourhood of kingdom nere,
   Why should they not likewise in loue agree,
   And ioy likewise this solemne day to see?
   They saw it all, and present were in place;

Though I them all according their degree,
  Cannot recount, nor tell their hidden race,
Nor read the salvage cuntreis, thorough which they pace.

There was the Liffy rolling downe the lea,
  The sandy Slane, the stony Aubrian,
  The spacious Shenan spreading like a sea,
  The pleasant Boyne, the fishy fruitfull Ban,
  Swift Awniduff, which of the English man
  Is cal'de Blacke water, and the Liftar deep,
  Sad Trowis, that once his people ouerran,
  Strong Allo tombling from Slowlogher steep,
And Mulla mine, whose waues I whilom taught to weep.

From *The Faerie Queene* by Edmund Spenser, 1596

The Element Fire Boasts of the Constellations

... Yet men and beasts, astronomers will tell
Fixed in heavenly constellations dwell,
My planets of both sexes whose degree
Poor heathen judged worthy a deity:
There's Orion armed attended by his dog;
The Theban stout Alcides with his club;
The valiant Perseus, who Medusa slew,
The horse that killed Belerophon, then flew.
My crab, my scorpion, fishes you may see
The maid with balance, wain with horses three,
The ram, the bull, the lion, and the beagle,
The bear, the goat, the raven, and the eagle
The crown, the whale, the archer, Bernice's hair,
The hydra, dolphin, boys that water bear,
Nay more than these, rivers 'mongst stars are found,
Eridanus, where Phaeton was drowned.
Their magnitude, and height, should I recount
My story to a volume would amount;
Out of a multitude these few I touch,
Your wisdom out of little gathers much ...

From 'The Four Elements' in *The Tenth Muse, Lately Sprung
Up In America* by Anne Bradstreet, 1650

[54]

'The Shires'

Hervordshir, shild and spere;
Wosetershir, wringe pere.
Glousetershir, shoo and naile;
Bristowshir, ship and saile.
Oxonfordshir, gird mare;
Warwikshir, bind beare.
London, globber;
Sothery, great bragger.
Shropshir, my shines been sharpe,
Lay wood to the fire, and yef me my harpe.
Lankashir, a fair archer;
Cheshir, thacher.
Northumberland, hasty and hot;
Westmorland, tot for sote.
Yorkeshir, full of knightes;
Lincolnshir, men full of mightes.
Cambridgeshir, full of pikes;
Holland, full of dikes.
Suffolk, full of wiles;
Norfolk, full of giles.
Essex, good houswives;
Middlesex, full of strives.
Kent, as hot as fire;
Sussex, full of mire.
Southhampton, drie and wete;
Somersetshir, good for whete.
Devinshir, wight and strong;
Dorcetshir will have no wrong.
Wiltshir, fair and plaine;
Barkshir, fill vaine.
Harvodshir, full of wood;
Huntingdonshir, corne full good.
Bedfordshir is not to lack;
Buckinghamshir is his mak.
Northampton, full of love
Beneath the girdel and not above.
Nottinghamshir, full of hogges;
Darbyshir, full of dogges.
Leicestershir, full of benes;

Staffordshir, full of shrewd quenes.
Cornewall, full of tinne;
Wales, full of gentlemen.

Anon., c.1500

The Names of Norman Towns

If my health had grown stronger and my parents allowed me, if not actually
to go down to stay at Balbec, at least to take, just once, in order to become
acquainted with the architecture and landscapes of Normandy or of
Brittany, that 1.22 train into which I had so often clambered in imagination,
I should have wished to stop, for preference, at the most beautiful of its
towns; but in vain did I compare and contrast them – how to choose, any
more than between individual persons who are not interchangeable,
between Bayeux, so lofty in its noble coronet of russet lacework, whose
pinnacle was illumined by the old gold of its second syllable; Vitré, whose
acute accent barred its ancient glass with wooden lozenges; gentle Lam-
balle, whose whiteness ranged from egg-shell yellow to pearl grey;
Coutances, a Norman cathedral which its final consonants, rich and
yellowing, crowned with a tower of butter; Lannion with the rumbling
noise, in the silence of its village street, of a coach with a fly buzzing after it;
Questambert, Pontorson, ridiculous and naïve, white feathers and yellow
beaks strewn along the road to those well-watered and poetic spots;
Benodet, a name scarcely moored that the river seemed to be striving to
drag down into the tangle of its algae; Pont-Aven, pink-white flash of the
wing of a lightly poised coif, tremulously reflected in the greenish waters of
a canal; Quimperlé, more firmly anchored, ever since the Middle Ages,
among its babbling rivulets threading their pearls in a grey iridescence like
the patterns made, through the cobwebs on a church window, by rays of
sunlight changed into blunted points of tarnished silver?

From *Du Côté du chez Swann* by Marcel Proust, 1913, translated from
the French by C. K. Scott Moncrieff and Terence Kilmartin

'American Feuillage'

America always!

Always our own feuillage!

Always Florida's green peninsula! Always the priceless delta of
Louisiana! Always the cotton-fields of Alabama and Texas!

Always California's golden hills and hollows – and the silver
mountains of New Mexico! Always soft-breathed Cuba!

Always the vast slope drained by the Southern Sea – inseparable with
the slopes drained by the Eastern and Western Seas!

The area the eighty-third year of these States – the three and a half
millions of square miles;

The eighteen thousand miles of sea-coast and bay-coast on the main
– the thirty thousand miles of river navigation,

The seven millions of distinct families, and the same number of
dwellings – Always these, and more, branching forth into
numberless branches;

Always the free range and diversity! Always the continent of
Democracy!

Always the prairies, pastures, forests, vast cities, travellers, Canada,
the snows;

Always these compact lands – lands tied at the hips with the belt
stringing the huge oval lakes;

Always the West, with strong native persons – the increasing density
there – the habitants, friendly, threatening, ironical, scorning
invaders;

All sights, South, North, East – all deeds, promiscuously done at all
times,

All characters, movements, growths – a few noticed, myriads
unnoticed.

Through Mannahatta's streets I walking, these things gathering.

On interior rivers, by night, in the glare of pine knots, steamboats
wooding up:

Sunlight by day on the valley of the Susquehanna, and on the valleys
of the Potomac and Rappahannock, and the valleys of the Roanoke
and Delaware;

In their northerly wilds beasts of prey haunting the Adirondacks, the
hills – or lapping the Saginaw waters to drink;

In a lonesome inlet, a sheldrake, lost from the flock, sitting on the
water, rocking silently;

In farmers' barns, oxen in the stable, their harvest labour done – they
   rest standing – they are too tired;
Afar on arctic ice, the she-walrus lying drowsily, while her cubs play
   around;
The hawk sailing where men have not yet sailed – the farthest polar
   sea, ripply, crystalline, open, beyond the floes;
White drift spooning ahead, where the ship in the tempest dashes.
On solid land, what is done in cities, as the bells all strike midnight
   together;
In primitive woods, the sounds there also sounding – the howl of the
   wolf, the scream of the panther, and the hoarse bellow of the elk;
In winter beneath the hard blue ice of Moosehead Lake, in summer
   visible through the clear waters, the great trout swimming;
In lower latitudes, in warmer air, in the Carolinas, the large black
   buzzard floating slowly, high beyond the tree-tops,
Below, the red cedar, festooned with tylandria – the pines and
   cypresses, growing out of the white sand that spreads far and flat;
Rude boats descending the big Pedee – climbing plants, parasites,
   with coloured flowers and berries, enveloping huge trees,
The waving drapery on the live oak, trailing long and low,
   noiselessly waved by the wind;
The camp of Georgia waggoners, just after dark – the supper-fires,
   and the cooking and eating by whites and negroes,
Thirty or forty great waggons – the mules, cattle, horses, feeding
   from troughs,
The shadows, gleams, up under the leaves of the old sycamore-trees
   – the flames – also the black smoke from the pitch-pine, curling
   and rising;
Southern fishermen fishing – the sounds and inlets of North
   Carolina's coast – the shad-fishery and the herring-fishery – the
   large sweep-seines – the windlasses on shore worked by horses –
   the clearing, curing, and packing houses;
Deep in the forest, in piney woods, turpentine dropping from the
   incisions in the trees – There are the turpentine works,
There are the negroes at work, in good health – the ground in all
   directions is covered with pine straw.
– In Tennessee and Kentucky, slaves busy in the coalings, at the
   forge, by the furnace-blaze, or at the corn-shucking;
In Virginia, the planter's son returning after a long absence, joyfully
   welcomed and kissed by the aged mulatto nurse.
On rivers, boatmen safely moored at nightfall, in their boats, under
   shelter of high banks,

Some of the younger men dance to the sound of the banjo or fiddle –
others sit on the gunwale, smoking and talking;

Late in the afternoon the mocking-bird, the American mimic, singing
in the Great Dismal Swamp – there are the greenish waters, the
resinous odour, the plenteous moss, the cypress-tree, and the
juniper-tree.

– Northward, young men of Mannahatta – the target company from
an excursion returning home at evening – the musket-muzzles all
bear branches of flowers presented by women;

Children at play – or on the father's lap a young boy fallen asleep,
(how his lips move! how he smiles in his sleep!)

The scout riding on horseback over the plains west of the Mississippi
– he ascends a knoll and sweeps his eye around.

California life – the miner, bearded, dressed in his rude costume – the
staunch California friendship – the sweet air – the graves one, in
passing, meets, solitary, just aside the horse-path;

Down in Texas, the cotton-field, the negro-cabins – drivers driving
mules or oxen before rude carts – cotton-bales piled on banks and
wharves.

Encircling all, vast-darting, up and wide, the American Soul, with
equal hemispheres – one Love, one Dilation or Pride.

– In arriere, the peace-talk with the Iroquois, the aborigines – the
calumet, the pipe of good-will, arbitration, and endorsement,

The sachem blowing the smoke first toward the sun and then toward
the earth,

The drama of the scalp-dance, enacted with painted faces and guttural
exclamations,

The setting-out of the war-party – the long and stealthy march,

The single-file – the swinging hatchets – the surprise and slaughter of
enemies.

– All the acts, scenes, ways, persons, attitudes of these States –
reminiscences, all institutions.

All these States, compact – Every square mile of these States, without
excepting a particle – you also – me also.

Me pleased, rambling in lanes and country fields, Paumanok's
fields,

Me, observing the spiral flight of two little yellow butterflies,
shuffling between each other, ascending high in the air;

The darting swallow, the destroyer of insects – the fall-traveller
southwards, but returning northward early in the spring;

The country boy at the close of the day, driving the herd of cows,
and shouting to them as they loiter to browse by the roadside;

The city wharf – Boston, Philadelphia, Baltimore, Charleston, New
  Orleans, San Francisco,
The departing ships, when the sailors heave at the capstan;
Evening – me in my room – the setting sun,
The setting summer sun shining in my open window, showing the
  swarm of flies, suspended, balancing in the air in the centre of the
  room, darting athwart, up and down, casting swift shadows in
  specks on the opposite wall, where the shine is.
The athletic American matron speaking in public to crowds of
  listeners;
Males, females, combinations – the copiousness – the individuality of
  the States, each for itself – the money-makers;
Factories, machinery, the mechanical forces – the windlass, lever,
  pulley – All certainties,
The certainty of space, increase, freedom, futurity;
In space, the sporades, the scattered islands, the stars – on the firm
  earth, the lands, my lands!
O lands! O all so dear to me – what you are (whatever it is), I
  become part of that, whatever it is.
Southward there, I screaming, with wings slow-flapping, with the
  myriads of gulls wintering along the coasts of Florida – or in
  Louisiana, with pelicans breeding,
Otherways, there, atwixt the banks of the Arkansaw, the Rio Grande,
  the Nueces, the Brazos, the Tombigbee, the Red River, the
  Saskatchewan, or the Osage, I with the spring waters laughing and
  skipping and running;
Northward, on the sands, on some shallow bay of Paumanok, I, with
  parties of snowy herons wading in wet to seek worms and aquatic
  plants;
Retreating, triumphantly twittering, the king-bird, from piercing the
  crow with its bill, for amusement – And I triumphantly twittering;
The migrating flock of wild geese alighting in autumn to refresh
  themselves – the body of the flock feed – the sentinels outside
  move around with erect heads watching, and are from time to time
  relieved by other sentinels – And I feeding and taking turns with
  the rest;
In Canadian forests, the moose, large as an ox, cornered by hunters,
  rising desperately on his hind-feet, and plunging with his fore-feet,
  the hoofs as sharp as knives – And I plunging at the hunters,
  cornered and desperate;
In the Mannahatta, streets, piers, shipping, store-houses, and the
  countless workmen working in the shops,

And I too of the Mannahatta, singing thereof – and no less in myself
   than the whole of the Mannahatta in itself,
Singing the song of These, my ever-united lands – my body no more
   inevitably united part to part, and made one identity, any more
   than my lands are inevitably united, and made ONE IDENTITY;
Nativities, climates, the grass of the great pastoral plains,
Cities, labours, death, animals, products, good and evil – these me, –
These affording, in all their particulars, endless feuillage to me and to
   America, how can I do less than pass the clue of the union of them,
   to afford the like to you?
Whoever you are! how can I but offer you divine leaves, that you
   also be eligible as I am?
How can I but, as here, chanting, invite you for yourself to collect
   bouquets of the incomparable feuillage of these States?

Walt Whitman, 1858–9

Sights of Middle America

We inspected the world's largest stalagmite in a cave where three south-
eastern states have a family reunion; admission by age; adults one dollar;
pubescents sixty cents. A granite obelisk commemorating the Battle of Blue
Licks, with old bones and Indian pottery in the museum nearby, Lo a dime,
very reasonable. The present log cabin boldly simulating the past log cabin
where Lincoln was born. A boulder, with a plaque, in memory of the author
of *Trees* (by now we are in Poplar Cove, NC, reached by what my kind,
tolerant, usually so restrained tour book angrily calls 'a very narrow road,
poorly maintained', to which, though no Kilmerite, I subscribe). From a
hired motor-boat operated by an elderly, but still repulsively handsome
White Russian, a baron they said (Lo's palms were damp, the little fool),
who had known in California good old Maximovitch and Valeria, we could
distinguish the inaccessible 'millionaire's colony' on an island, somewhere
off the Georgia coast. We inspected further: a collection of European hotel
picture post cards in a museum devoted to hobbies at a Mississippi resort,
where with a hot wave of pride I discovered a coloured photo of my father's
Mirana, its striped awnings, its flag flying above the retouched palm trees.
'So what?' said Lo, squinting at the bronzed owner of an expensive car who
had followed us into the Hobby House. Relics of the cotton era. A forest in
Arkansas and, on her brown shoulder, a raised purple-pink swelling (the
work of some gnat) which I eased of its beautiful transparent poison
between my long thumbnails and then sucked till I was gorged on her spicy

blood. Bourbon Street (in a town named New Orleans) whose sidewalks, said the tour book, 'may [I like the 'may'] feature entertainment by pickaninnies who will [liked the 'will' even better] tap-dance for pennies' (what fun), while 'its numerous small and intimate night clubs are thronged with visitors' (naughty). Collections of frontier lore. Ante-bellum homes with iron-trellis balconies and hand-worked stairs, the kind down which move ladies with sun-kissed shoulders run in rich Technicolor, holding up the fronts of their flounced skirts with both little hands in that special way, and the devoted Negress shaking her head on the upper landing. The Menninger Foundation, a psychiatric clinic, just for the heck of it. A patch of beautifully eroded clay; and yucca blossoms, so pure, so waxy, but lousy with creeping white flies. Independence, Missouri, the starting point of the Old Oregon Trail; and Abilene, Kansas, the home of the Wild Bill Something Rodeo. Distant mountains. Near mountains. More mountains; bluish beauties never attainable, or ever turning into inhabited hill after hill; south-eastern ranges, altitudinal features as alps go; heart- and sky-piercing snow-veined grey colossi of stone, relentless peaks appearing from nowhere at a turn of the highway; timbered enormities, with a system of neatly overlapping dark firs, interrupted in places by pale puffs of aspen; pink and lilac formations. Pharaonic, phallic, 'too prehistoric for words' (blasé Lo); buttes of black lava; early spring mountains with young-elephant lanugo along their spines; end-of-the-summer mountains, all hunched up, their heavy Egyptian limbs folded under folds of tawny moth-eaten plush; oatmeal hills, flecked with green round oaks; a last rufous mountain with a rich rug of lucerne at its foot.

Moreover, we inspected: Little Iceberg Lake, somewhere in Colorado, and the snow banks, and the cushionets of tiny alpine flowers, and more snow; down which Lo in red-peaked cap tried to slide, and squealed, and was snowballed by some youngsters, and retaliated in kind *comme on dit*. Skeletons of burned aspens, patches of spired blue flowers. The various items of a scenic drive. Hundreds of scenic drives, thousands of Bear Creeks, Soda Springs, Painted Canyons. Texas, in a drought-struck plain. Crystal Chamber in the longest cave in the world, children under twelve free, Lo, a young captive. A collection of a local lady's home-made sculptures, closed on a miserable Monday morning, dust, wind, witherland. Conception Park, in a town on the Mexican border which I dared not cross. There and elsewhere, hundreds of grey hummingbirds in the dusk, probing the throats of dim flowers. Shakespeare, a ghost town in New Mexico, where bad man Russian Bill was colourfully hanged seventy years ago. Fish hatcheries. Cliff dwellings. The mummy of a child (Florentine Bea's Indian contemporary). Our twentieth Hell's Canyon. Our fiftieth Gateway to something or other *vide* that tour book, the cover of which had been lost by that time. A tick in my groin. Always the same three old men, in hats and suspenders, idling away the summer afternoon under the trees near the public fountain. A hazy blue view beyond railings on a mountain pass, and the backs of a family enjoying it (with Lo, in a hot, happy, wild, intense, hopeful, hopeless whisper – 'Look, the McCrystals, please, let's talk to them, please' – let's talk to them, reader! – 'please! I'll do anything you want, oh, please . . .'). Indian ceremonial dances, strictly commercial. ART: American Refrigerator Transit Company. Obvious Arizona, pueblo dwellings, aboriginal pictographs, a dinosaur track in a desert canyon, printed there thirty million years ago, when I was a child. A lanky, six-foot, pale boy with an active Adam's apple, ogling Lo and her orange-brown bare midriff, which I kissed five minutes later, Jack. Winter in the desert, spring in the foothills, almonds in bloom. Reno a dreary town in Nevada, with a nightlife said to be 'cosmopolitan and mature'. A winery in California, with a church built in the shape of a wine barrel. Death Valley. Scotty's Castle. Works of Art collected by one Rogers over a period of years. The ugly villas of handsome actresses. R. L. Stevenson's footprint on an extinct volcano. Mission Dolores: good title for book. Surf-carved sandstone festoons. A man having a lavish epileptic fit on the ground in Russian Gulch State Park. Blue, blue Crater Lake. A fish hatchery in Idaho and the State Penitentiary. Sombre Yellowstone Park and its coloured hot springs, baby geysers, rainbows of bubbling mud – symbols of my passion. A herd of antelopes in a wildlife refuge. One hundredth cavern, adults one dollar, Lolita fifty cents. A château built by a French marquess in ND. The Corn Palace in SD; and the huge heads of presidents carved in towering granite. The Bearded Woman read our jingle and now she is no longer single. A zoo in Indiana where a large troop of monkeys lived on a concrete replica of Christopher Columbus' flagship. Billions of dead, or half-dead, fish-smelling May flies in every window of every eating place all along a dreary sand shore. Fat gulls on big stones as seen from the ferry *City of Cheboygan*, whose brown woolly smoke arched and dipped over the green shadow it cast on the aquamarine lake. A motel whose ventilator pipe passed under the city sewer. Lincoln's home, largely spurious, with parlour books and period furniture that most visitors reverently accepted as personal belongings.

From *Lolita* by Vladimir Nabokov, 1955

Items Absent in America

The negative side of the spectacle on which Hawthorne looked out, in his contemplative saunterings and reveries, might, indeed, with a little ingenuity, be made almost ludicrous; one might enumerate the items of high civilization, as it exists in other countries, which are absent from the texture of American life, until it should become a wonder to know what was left. No State, in the European sense of the word, and indeed barely a specific national name. No sovereign, no court, no personal loyalty, no aristocracy, no church, no clergy, no army, no diplomatic service, no country gentlemen, no palaces, no castles, nor manors, nor old country-houses, nor parsonages, nor thatched cottages nor ivied ruins; no cathedrals, nor abbeys, nor little Norman churches; no great Universities nor public schools – no Oxford, nor Eton, nor Harrow; no literature, no novels, no museums, no pictures, no political society, no sporting class – no Epsom nor Ascot. Some such list as that might be drawn up of the absent things in American life – especially in the American life of forty years ago, the effect of which, upon an English or a French imagination, would probably as a general thing be appalling. The natural remark, in the almost lurid light of such an indictment, would be that if these things are left out, everything is left out. The American knows that a good deal remains; what it is that remains – that is his secret, his joke, as one may say.

From *Hawthorne* by Henry James, 1879

Items Present in Americans

Other states indicate themselves in their deputies: but the genius of the United States is not best or most in its executives or legislatures, nor in its ambassadors or authors or colleges, or churches, or parlours, nor even in its newspapers or inventors, but always most in the common people. Their manners, speech, dress, friendships, – the freshness and candour of their physiognomy – the picturesque looseness of their carriage – their deathless attachment to freedom – their aversion to anything indecorous or soft or mean – the practical acknowledgment of the citizens of one state by the citizens of all other states – the fierceness of their roused resentment – their curiosity and welcome of novelty – their self-esteem and wonderful sympathy – their susceptibility to a slight – the air they have of persons who never knew how it felt to stand in the presence of superiors – the fluency of their speech – their delight in music, the sure symptom of manly tenderness and native elegance of soul – their good temper and open-handedness – the terrible significance of their elections, the President's taking off his hat to them, not they to him – these too are unrhymed poetry. It awaits the gigantic and generous treatment worthy of it.

From the Preface to Leaves of Grass by Walt Whitman, 1855

The Gay Freedom Day Parade 1978

By the time our truck turned onto Market Street, I was in fact too late to see the head of the parade: the Gay American Indian contingent followed by Disabled Gay People and Friends, followed by a ninety-piece marching band and the gay political leaders of the city. But leaving my truck to walk along the sidelines where a crowd was now gathering, I was able to make my way up to number forty-one: the Gay Latino Alliance, or GALA, a group of young men dancing down the street to mariachi music. Just behind them was a group representing the gay Jewish synagogue, a rather serious group of people, the men with yarmulkes on carrying a banner with the Star of David. This contingent was closely followed by a Marilyn Monroe look-alike on stilts batting six-inch-long eyelashes and swaying to the music of the disco float just behind her. Further back there were people in country work clothes with a sign for the Order of Displaced Okies. The Local Lesbian Association Kazoo Marching Band led a number of women's groups, including the San Francisco Women's Centre, UC Berkeley Women's Studies, and Dykes on Bikes. This latter group could be easily located, as every time they came to an intersection, the six or seven petite women in tight jeans, men's undershirts, and boots would rev up their motorcycles, bringing loud applause from the crowd. Farther back, behind the Gay Pagans, the Free Beach Activists, the Zimbabwe Medical Drive, and the Alice B. Toklas Democratic Club, came the float that many had been waiting for: the sequined, spangled, and tulle-wrapped chariot of the Council of Grand Dukes and Duchesses of San Francisco. Somewhere in this neighbourhood there was a truly unfortunate juxtaposition. The Women Against Violence in Pornography and the Media had taken their proper places in line, but then somehow, perhaps as a result of some confusion in the Society of Janus, elements of the sadomasochistic liberation front had moved in just behind them. The pallid-looking men in uniforms were not dragging chains – the parade organisers had counselled against it – but they were carrying a sign of questionable grammar that read BLACK AND BLUE IS BEAUTIFUL.

From Cities on a Hill by Frances Fitzgerald, 1987

A Part of the Spain that Had to be Omitted

If you could make the yellow flames of candles in the sun; that shines on steel of bayonets freshly oiled and yellow patent-leather belts of those who guard the Host; or hunt in pairs through scrub-oak in the mountains for the ones who fell into the trap at Deva (it was a bad long way to come from the Café Rotonde to be garotted in a draughty room with consolation of the church at order of the state, acquitted once and held until the captain general of Burgos reversed the finding of the court) and in the same town where Loyola got his wound that made him think, the bravest of those who were betrayed that year dived from the balcony on to the paving of the court, head first, because he had sworn they would not kill him (his mother tried to make him promise not to take his life because she worried most about his soul but he dived well and cleanly with his hands tied while they walked with him praying); if I could make him; make a bishop; make Candido Tiebas and Toron; make clouds come fast in shadows moving over wheat and the small, careful stepping horses; the smell of olive oil; the feel of leather; rope-soled shoes; the loops of twisted garlics; earthen pots; saddle bags carried across the shoulder; wine skins; the pitchforks made of natural wood (the tines were branches); the early morning smells; the cold mountain nights and long, hot days of summer, with always trees and shade under the trees, then you would have a little of Navarra. But it's not in this book.

From *Death in the Afternoon* by Ernest Hemingway, 1932

A Lament for Afghanistan

But that will not bring back the things we loved: the high, clear days and the blue icecaps on the mountains; the lines of white poplars fluttering in the wind, and the long white prayer-flags; the fields of asphodels that followed the tulips; or the fat-tailed sheep brindling the hills above Chakcharan, and the ram with a tail so big they had to strap it to a cart. We shall not lie on our backs at the Red Castle and watch the vultures wheeling over the valley where they killed the grandson of Genghiz. We will not read Babur's Memoirs in his garden at Istalif and see the blind man smelling his way around the rose bushes. Or sit in the Peace of Islam with the beggars of Gazar Gagh. We will not stand on the Buddha's head at Bamiyan, upright in his niche like a whale in a dry-dock. We will not sleep in the nomad tent, or scale the Minaret of Jam. And we shall lose the tastes – the hot, coarse, bitter bread; the green tea flavoured with cardamoms; the grapes we cooled in the snow-melt; and the nuts and dried mulberries we munched for altitude sickness. Nor shall we get back the smell of the beanfields; the sweet, resinous smell of deodar wood burning, or the whiff of a snow leopard at 14,000 feet. Never. Never. Never.

From the Introduction to Robert Byron's
The Road to Oxiana by Bruce Chatwin, 1981

Kublai's Atlases

The Great Khan owns an atlas where all the cities of the empire and the neighbouring realms are drawn, building by building and street by street, with walls, rivers, bridges, harbours, cliffs. He realises that from Marco Polo's tales it is pointless to expect news of these places, which for that matter he knows well: how at Kambalu, capital of China, three square cities stand one within the other, each with four temples and four gates that are opened according to the seasons; how on the island of Java the rhinoceros rages, charging, with his murderous horn; how pearls are gathered on the ocean bed off the coasts of Malabar.

Kublai asks Marco, 'When you return to the West, will you repeat to your people the same tales you tell me?'

'I speak and speak,' Marco says, 'but the listener retains only the words he is expecting. The description of the world to which you lend a benevolent ear is one thing; the description that will go the rounds of the groups of stevedores and gondoliers on the street outside my house the day of my return is another; and yet another, that which I might dictate late in life, if I were taken prisoner by Genoese pirates and put in irons in the same cell with a writer of adventure stories. It is not the voice that commands the story: it is the ear.

'At times I feel your voice is reaching me from far away, while I am prisoner of a gaudy and unlivable present, where all forms of human society have reached an extreme of their cycle and there is no imagining what new forms they may assume. And I hear, from your voice, the invisible reasons which make cities live, through which perhaps, once dead, they will come to life again.'

The Great Khan owns an atlas whose drawings depict the terrestrial globe all at once and continent by continent, the borders of the most distant realms, the ships' routes, the coastlines, the maps of the most illustrious metropolises and of the most opulent ports. He leafs through the maps before Marco Polo's eyes to put his knowledge to the test. The traveller recognises Constantinople in the city which from three shores dominates a long strait, a narrow gulf, and an enclosed sea; he remembers that Jerusalem is set on two hills, of unequal height, facing each other; he has no hesitation in pointing to Samarkand and its gardens.

For other cities he falls back on descriptions handed down by word of mouth, or he guesses on the basis of scant indications: and so Granada, the streaked pearl of the caliphs; Lübeck, the neat, boreal port; Timbuktu, black with ebony and white with ivory; Paris, where millions of men come home every day grasping a wand of bread. In coloured miniatures the atlas depicts inhabited places of unusual form: an oasis hidden in a fold of the desert from which only palm crests peer out is surely Nefta; a castle amid quicksands and cows grazing in meadows salted by the tides can only suggest Mont-Saint-Michel; and a palace that instead of rising within a city's walls contains within its own walls a city can only be Urbino.

The atlas depicts cities which neither Marco nor the geographers know exist or where they are, though they cannot be missing among the forms of possible cities: a Cuzco on a radial and multipartite plan which reflects the perfect order of its trade, a verdant Mexico on the lake dominated by Montezuma's palace, a Novgorod with bulb-shaped domes, a Lhasa whose white roofs rise over the cloudy roof of the world. For these, too, Marco says a name, no matter which, and suggests a route to reach them. It is known that names of places change as many times as there are foreign languages; and that every place can be reached from other places, by the most various roads and routes, by those who ride, or drive, or row, or fly.

'I think you recognise cities better in the atlas than when you visit them in person,' the emperor says to Marco snapping the volume shut.

And Polo answers, 'Travelling, you realise that differences are lost: each city takes to resembling all cities, places exchange their form, order, distances, a shapeless cloud invades the continents. Your atlas preserves the differences intact: that assortment of qualities which are like the letters in a name.'

The Great Khan owns an atlas in which are gathered the maps of all the cities: those whose walls rest on solid foundations, those which fell in ruins and were swallowed up by the sand, those that will exist one day and in whose place now only hares' holes gape.

Marco Polo leafs through the pages; he recognises Jericho, Ur, Carthage, he points to the landing at the mouth of the Scamander where the Achaean ships waited for ten years to take the besiegers back on board, until the horse nailed together by Ulysses was dragged by windlasses through the Scaean gates. But speaking of Troy, he happened to give the city the form of

Constantinople and foresee the siege which Mohammed would lay for long months until, as astute as Ulysses, he had his ships drawn at night up the streams from the Bosphorus to the Golden Horn, skirting Pera and Galata. And from the mixture of those two cities a third emerged, which might be called San Francisco and which spans the Golden Gate and the bay with long, light bridges and sends open trams climbing its steep streets, and which might blossom as capital of the Pacific a millennium hence, after the long siege of three hundred years that would lead the races of the yellow and the black and the red to fuse with the surviving descendants of the whites in an empire more vast than the Great Khan's.

The atlas has these qualities: it reveals the form of cities that do not yet have a form or a name. There is the city in the shape of Amsterdam, a semicircle facing north, with concentric canals – the princes', the emperor's, the nobles'; there is the city in the shape of York, set among the high moors, walled, bristling with towers; there is the city in the shape of New Amsterdam known also as New York, crammed with towers of glass and steel on an oblong island between two rivers, with streets like deep canals, all of them straight, except Broadway.

The catalogue of forms is endless: until every shape has found its city, new cities will continue to be born. When the forms exhaust their variety and come apart, the end of cities begins. In the last pages of the atlas there is an outpouring of networks without beginning or end, cities in the shape of Los Angeles, in the shape of Kyoto-Osaka, without shape.

From *Invisible Cities* by Italo Calvino, translated from the Italian by William Weaver, 1974

'Into the Dusk-Charged Air'

Far from the Rapahannock, the silent
Danube moves along towards the sea.
The brown and green Nile rolls slowly
Like the Niagara's welling descent.
Tractors stood on the green banks of the Loire
Near where it joined the Cher.
The St Lawrence prods among black stones
And mud. But the Arno is all stones.
Wind ruffles the Hudson's
Surface. The Irawaddy is overflowing.
But the yellowish, gray Tiber
Is contained within steep banks. The Isar

[69]

Flows too fast to swim in, the Jordan's water
Courses over the flat land. The Allegheny and its boats
Were dark blue. The Moskowa is
Gray boats. The Amstel flows slowly.
Leaves fall into the Connecticut as it passes
Underneath. The Liffey is full of sewage,
Like the Seine, but unlike
The brownish-yellow Dordogne.
Mountains hem in the Colorado
And the Oder is very deep, almost
As deep as the Congo is wide.
The plain banks of the Neva are
Gray. The dark Saône flows silently.
And the Volga is long and wide
As it flows across the brownish land. The Ebro
Is blue, and slow. The Shannon flows
Swiftly between its banks. The Mississippi
Is one of the world's longest rivers, like the Amazon.
It has the Missouri for a tributary.
The Harlem flows amid factories
And buildings. The Nelson is in Canada,
Flowing. Through hard banks the Dubawnt
Forces its way. People walk near the Trent.
The landscape around the Mohawk stretches away;
The Rubicon is merely a brook.
In winter the Main
Surges; the Rhine sings its eternal song.
The Rhône slogs along through whitish banks
And the Rio Grande spins tales of the past.
The Loir bursts its frozen shackles
But the Moldau's wet mud ensnares it.
The East catches the light.
Near the Escaut the noise of factories echoes
And the sinuous Humboldt gurgles wildly.
The Po too flows, and the many-colored
Thames. Into the Atlantic Ocean
Pours the Garonne. Few ships navigate
On the Housatonic, but quite a few can be seen
On the Elbe. For centuries
The Afton has flowed.
                    If the Rio Negro
Could abandon its song, and the Magdalena

The jungle flowers, the Tagus
Would still flow serenely, and the Ohio
Abrade its steep banks. The tan Euphrates would
Sidle silently across the world. The Yukon
Was choked with ice, but the Susquehanna still pushed
Bravely along. The Dee caught the day's last flares
Like the Pilcomayo's carrion rose.
The Peace offered eternal fragrance
Perhaps, but the Mackenzie churned livid mud
Like tan chalk-marks. Near where
The Brahmaputra slapped swollen dikes
Was an opening through which the Limmat
Could have trickled. A young man strode the Churchill's
Banks, thinking of night. The Vistula seized
The shadows. The Theiss, stark mad, bubbled
In the windy evening. And the Ob shuffled
Crazily along. Fat billows encrusted the Dniester's
Pallid flood, and the Fraser's porous surface.
Fish gasped amid the Spree's reeds. A boat
Descended the bobbing Orinoco. When the
Marne flowed by the plants nodded
And above the glistering Gila
A sunset as beautiful as the Athabasca
Stammered. The Zambezi chimed. The Oxus
Flowed somewhere. The Paranaiba
Is flowing, like the wind-washed Cumberland.
The Araguaia flows in the rain.
And, through overlying rocks the Isère
Cascades gently. The Guadalquivir sputtered.
Someday time will confound the Indre,
Making a rill of the Huang Ho. And
The Potomac rumbles softly. Crested birds
Watch the Ucayali go
Through dreaming night. You cannot stop
The Yenisei. And afterwards
The White flows strongly to its . . .
Goal. If the Tyne's shores
Hold you, and the Albany's
Arrest your development, can you resist the Red's
Musk, the Meuse's situation?
A particle of mud in the Neckar
Does not turn it black. You cannot

[71]

Like the Saskatchewan, nor refuse
The meandering Yangtze, unleash
The Genesee. Does the Scamander
Still irrigate crimson plains? And the Durance
And the Pechora? The São Francisco
Skulks amid gray, rubbery nettles. The Liard's
Reflexes are slow, and the Arkansas erodes
Anthracite hummocks. The Paraná stinks.
The Ottawa is light emerald green
Among grays. Better that the Indus fade
In steaming sands! Let the Brazos
Freeze solid! And the Wabash turn to a leaden
Cinder of ice! The Marañón is too tepid, we must
Find a way to freeze it hard. The Ural
Is freezing slowly in the blasts. The black Yonne
Congeals nicely. And the Petit-Morin
Curls up on the solid earth. The Inn
Does not remember better times, and the Merrimack's
Galvanized. The Ganges is liquid snow by now;
The Vyatka's ice-gray. The once-molten Tennessee's
Curdled. The Japurá is a pack of ice. Gelid
The Columbia's gray loam banks. The Don's merely
A giant icicle. The Niger freezes, slowly.
The interminable Lena plods on
But the Purus' mercurial waters are icy, grim
With cold. The Loing is choked with fragments of ice.
The Weser is frozen, like liquid air.
And so is the Kama. And the beige, thickly flowing
Tocantins. The rivers bask in the cold.
The stern Uruguay chafes its banks,
A mass of ice. The Hooghly is solid
Ice. The Adour is silent, motionless.
The lovely Tigris is nothing but scratchy ice
Like the Yellowstone, with its osier-clustered banks.
The Mekong is beginning to thaw out a little
And the Donets gurgles beneath the
Huge blocks of ice. The Manzanares gushes free.
The Illinois darts through the sunny air again.
But the Dnieper is still ice-bound. Somewhere
The Salado propels its floes, but the Roosevelt's
Frozen. The Oka is frozen solider
Than the Somme. The Minho slumbers

In winter, nor does the Snake
Remember August. Hilarious, the Canadian
Is solid ice. The Madeira slavers
Across the thawing fields, and the Plata laughs.
The Dvina soaks up the snow. The Sava's
Temperature is above freezing. The Avon
Carols noiselessly. The Drôme presses
Grass banks; the Adige's frozen
Surface is like gray pebbles.

Birds circle the Ticino. In winter
The Var was dark blue, unfrozen. The
Thwaite, cold, is choked with sandy ice;
The Ardèche glistens feebly through the freezing rain.

From *Rivers and Mountains* by John Ashbery, 1966

Two

COMIC
ELABORATIONS

Compleatly Foolish

...but as we have hitherto made choice of the purest and most refined Cream of Wisdom and Sapience for our Counsel, so would I now have to preside and bear the prime Sway in our Consultation as were a *Fool* in the supreme degree. *Triboulet* (quoth *Pantagruel*) is compleatly *foolish*, as I conceive. Yes, truly, (answered *Panurge*) he is properly and totally a *Fool*, a

Pantagruel.	*Panurge.*
Fatal f.	Jovial f.
Natural f.	Mercurial f.
Celestial f.	Lunatick f.
Erratick f.	Ducal f.
Excentrick f.	Common f.
Ætherial and Junonian f.	Lordly f.
Arctick f.	Palatin f.
Heroick f.	Principal f.
Genial f.	Pretorian f.
Inconstant f.	Elected f.
Earthly f.	Courtly f.
Solacious and sporting f.	Primipilary f.
Jocund and wanton f.	Triumphant f.
Pimpled f.	Vulgar f.
Freckled f.	Domestick f.
Bell-tinging f.	Exemplary f.
Laughing and lecherous f.	Rare outlandish f.
Nimming and filching f.	Satrapal f.
Unpressed f.	Civil f.
First broached f.	Popular f.
Augustal f.	Familiar f.
Cesarine f.	Notable f.
Imperial f.	Favourized f.
Royal f.	Latinized f.
Patriarchal f.	Ordinary f.
Original f.	Transcendent f.
Loyal f.	Rising f.
Episcopal f.	Papal f.
Doctoral f.	Consistorian f.
Monachal f.	Conclavist f.

Fiscal f.
Extravagant f.
Writhed f.
Canonical f.
Such another f.
Graduated f.
Commensal f.
Primolicentiated f.
Trainbairing f.
Supererrogating f.
Collateral f.
Haunch and side f.
Nestling, ninny, and youngling f.
Flitting, giddy, and unsteddy f.
Brancher, novice, and cockney f.
Hagard, cross, and froward f.
Gentle, mild, and tractable f.
Mail-coated f.
Pilfring and purloining f.
Tail-gown f.
Gray-peckled f.
Pleonasmical f.
Capital f.
Hairbrained f.
Cordial f.
Intimate f.
Hepatick f.
Cushotten and swilling f.
Splenetick f.
Windy f.
Legitimate f.
Azymathal f.
Almicautarized f.
Proportioned f.
Chinnified f.
Swollen and puffed up f.
Overcockrifedid and lified f.
Corallery f.
Eastern f.
Sublime f.
Crimson f.
Ingrained f.

Bullist f.
Synodal f.
Doating and raving f.
Singular and surpassing f.
Special and excelling f.
Metaphysical f.
Scatical f.
Predicamental and catagorick f.
Predicable and enunciatory f.
Decumane and superlative f.
Dutiful and officious f.
Optical and perspective f.
Algoristick f.
Algebraical f.
Cabalistical and massoretical f.
Talmudical f.
Algamalized f.
Compendious f.
Abbreviated f.
Hyperbolical f.
Anatomastical f.
Allegorical f.
Tropological f.
Micher pincrust f.
Heteroclit f.
Summist f.
Abbridging f.
Morrish f.
Leaden-sealed f.
Mandatory f.
Compassionate f.
Titulary f.
Crooching, showking, ducking f.
Grim, stern, harsh, and wayward f.
Well-hung and timbred f.
Ill-clawed, pounced and pawed f.
Well-stoned f.
Crabbed and unpleasing f.
Winded and tainted f.
Kitchen-haunting f.
Lofty and stately f.
Spitrack f.

[77]

City f.

Basely accoutred f.

Mast-headed f.

Modal f.

Second notial f.

Chearful and buxom f.

Solemn f.

Annual f.

Festival f.

Recreative f.

Boorish and counterfeit f.

Pleasant f.

Privileged f.

Rustical f.

Proper and peculiar f.

Ever ready f.

Diapasonal f.

Resolute f.

Hieroglyphical f.

Authentick f.

Worthy f.

Precious f.

Fanatick f.

Fantastical f.

Lymphatick f.

Panick f.

Limbicked and distilled f.

Comportable f.

Wretched and heartless f.

Fooded f.

Thick and threefold f.

Damasked f.

Fearny f.

Unleavened f.

Barytonant f.

Pink and spot-poudered f.

Musket-proof f.

Pedantick f.

Strouting f.

Wood f.

Greedy f.

Senseless f.

Architrave f.

Pedestal f.

Tetragonal f.

Renowned f.

Reumatick f.

Flaunting and braggadochio f.

Egregious f.

Humorous and capricious f.

Rude, gross, and absurd f.

Large-measured f.

Bable f.

Down-right f.

Broad-lifted f.

Downsical-bearing f.

Stale and overworn f.

Sawcy and swaggering f.

Full bulked f.

Gallant and vainglorious f.

Gorgeous and gawdy f.

Continual and intermitting f.

Rebasing and roundling f.

Prototypal and precedenting f.

Prating f.

Catechetick f.

Cacodoxical f.

Meridional f.

Nocturnal f.

Occidental f.

Trifling f.

Astrological and figure-flinging f.

Genethliack and horoscopal f.

Knavish f.

Idiot f.

Blockish f.

Beetle-headed f.

Grotesk f.

Impertinent f.

Quarrelsom f.

Unmannerly f.

Captious and Sophistical f.

Soritick f.

Catholoproton f.

Godderlich f.

Obstinate f.

Contradictory f.

Pedagogical f.

Daft f.

Drunken f.

Peevish f.

Prodigal f.

Rash f.

Plodding f.

Hoti and Dioti f.

Aaplos and Catati f.

From *Gargantua and Pantagruel* by François Rabelais, 1532–4, translated from the French by Sir Thomas Urquhart, 1653

Rusling Clutterments

He gave us also the Example of the Philosopher, who, when he thought most seriously to have withdrawn himself unto a solitary Privacy; far from the rusling clutterments of the tumultuous and confused World, the better to improve his *Theory*, to contrive, comment and ratiocinate, was, notwithstanding his uttermost endeavours to free himself from all untoward noises, surrounded and environ'd about so with the barking of Currs, bawling of Mastiffs, bleating of Sheep, prating of Parrets, tatling of Jackdaws, grunting of Swine, girning of Boars, yelping of Foxes, mewing of Cats, cheeping of Mice, squeaking of Weasils, croaking of Frogs, crowing of Cocks, kekling of Hens, calling of Partridges, chanting of Swans, chattering of Jays, peeping of Chickens, singing of Larks, creaking of Geese, chirping of Swallows, clucking of Moorfowls, cucking of Cuckows, bumbling of Bees, rammage of Hawks, chirming of Linots, croaking of Ravens, screeching of Owls, whicking of Pigs, gushing of Hogs, curring of Pigeons, grumbling of Cushet-doves, howling of Panthers, curkling of Quails, chirping of Sparrows, crackling of Crows, nuzzing of Camels, wheening of Whelps, buzzing of Dromedaries, mumbling of Rabets, cricking of Ferrets, humming of Wasps, mioling of Tygers, bruzzing of Bears, sussing of Kitnings, clamring of Scarfes, whimpring of Fullmarts, boing of Buffalos, warbling of Nightingales, quavering of Meavises, drintling of Turkies, coniating of Storks, frantling of Peacocks, clattering of Mag-pyes, murmuring of Stockdoves, crouting of Cormorants, cigling of Locusts, charming of Beagles, gnarring of Puppies, snarling of Messens, rantling of Rats, guerieting of Apes, snuttering of Monkies, pioling of Pelicanes, quecking of Ducks, yelling of

Wolves, roaring of Lions, neighing of Horses, crying of Elephants, hissing of Serpents, and wailing of Turtles, that he was much more troubled, than if he had been in the middle of the Crowd at the Fair of *Fontenoy* or *Niort*.

From *Gargantua and Pantagruel* by François Rabelais, 1532–4, translated from the French by Sir Thomas Urquhart, 1653

Epistemon's Visit to Elysium

But, in respect of the damned, he said he was very sorry, that Panurge had so soon called him back into this world again; for, said he, I took wonderful delight to see them. How so? said Pantagruel. Because they do not use them there, said Epistemon, as badly as you think they do. Their estate and condition of living is but only changed after a very strange manner; for I saw Alexander the Great there, mending and patching on clouts upon old breeches and stockings, and thus got a very poor living.

Xerxes was a crier of mustard.
Romulus, a salter, and patcher of pattens.
Numas, a nailsmith.
Tarquin, a porter.
Piso, a clownish swain.
Sylla, a ferryman.
Cyrus, a cowherd.
Themistocles, a glass-maker.
Epaminondas, a maker of mirrors or looking-glasses.
Brutus and Cassius, surveyors or measurers of land.
Demosthenes, a vine-dresser.
Cicero, a fire-kindler.
Fabius, a threader of beads.
Artaxerxes, a rope-maker.
Æneas, a miller.
Achilles was a scald-pated maker of hay-bundles.
Agamemnon, a lick-box.
Ulysses, a hay-mower.
Nestor, a deer-keeper or forester.
Darius, a gold-finder, or jakes-farmer.
Ancus Martius, a ship-trimmer.
Camillus, a foot-post.
Marcellus, a sheller of beans.
Drusus, a taker of money at the doors of play-houses.

Scipio Africanus, a crier of lee in a wooden-slipper.

Asdrubal, a lantern-maker.

Hannibal, a kettle-maker and seller of egg shells.

Priamus, a seller of old clouts.

Lancelot of the Lake was a flayer of dead horses.

All the Knights of the Round Table, were poor day-labourers, employed to row over the rivers of Cocytus, Phlegeton, Styx, Acheron, and Lethe, when my lords the devils had a mind to recreate themselves upon the water, as in the like occasion are hired the boatmen at Lyons, the gondeliers of Venice, and oars of London. But with this difference, that these poor knights have only for their fare a bob or flirt on the nose, and, in the evening, a morsel of coarse mouldy bread.

From *Gargantua and Pantagruel* by François Rabelais, 1532–4,
translated from the French by Sir Thomas Urquhart, 1653

The Inward Parts of Mr Shrovetide

As for the inward Parts of *Shrovetide*, said *Xenomanes*, his *Brain*, is (at least it was in my time) in Bigness, Colour, Substance and Strength, much like the left Cod of a He-hand-worm . . .

His *Memory* he had like a Scarf.

His *Common Sence*, like a buzzing of Bees.

His *Imagination*, like the Chime of a Set of Bells.

His *Thoughts*, like a flight of Starlings.

His *Conscience*, like the unnestling of a parcel of young Herns.

His *Deliberations*, like a Set of Organs.

His *Repentance*, like the Carriage of a double Canon.

His *Undertakings*, like the Ballast of a Galleon.

His *Understanding*, like a torn Breviary.

His *Notions*, like Snails crawling out of Strawberries.

His *Will*, like three Filberts in a Porrenger.

His *Desire*, like six Trusses of Hay.

His *Judgment*, like a Shoing-horn.

His *Discretion*, like the truckle of a Pully.

His *Reason*, like a Cricket.

From *Gargantua and Pantagruel* by François Rabelais, 1532–4,
translated from the French by Peter Le Motteux, 1694

A Universal Answer

Countess: Will your answer serve to fit all questions?
Clown: As fit as ten groats is for the hand of an attorney, as your French
crown is for your taffety punk, as Tib's rush for Tom's forefinger, as a
pancake for Shrove Tuesday, a morris for Mayday, as the nail to his hole,
the cuckold to his horn, as a scolding quean to a wrangling knave, as the
nun's lip to the friar's mouth; nay, as the pudding to his skin.

From *All's Well That Ends Well*, Act II, Scene ii,
by William Shakespeare, 1603–4

How Sir Thomas Urquhart Could Have Used All the Resources of Rhetoric in His Plea for His Release from Prison

I could truly, having before my eyes some known treatises of the author
whose muse I honour and the straine of whose pen to imitate is my greatest
ambition, have enlarged this discourse with a choicer variety of phrase and
made it overflow the field of the reader's understanding with an inundation
of greater eloquence; and that one way, tropolegetically, by metonymical,
ironical, metaphorical and synecdochical instruments of elocution in all
these several kinds artificially affected according to the nature of the
subject; with emphatical expressions in things of great concernment, with
catachrestical in matters of meaner moment, attended on each side respec-
tively with an epiplectick and exegetick modification; with hyperbolical,
either epitatically or hypocoristically as the purpose required to be elated or
extenuated, they qualifying metaphors and accompanied with apostrophes;
and lastly, with allegories of all sorts, whether apologal, affabulatory,
parabolary, aenigmatick or paraemial; and on the other part, schemato-
logetically adorning the proposed theam with the most especial and chief
flowers of the garden of rhetorick and omiting no figure either of diction or
sentence that might contribute to the ear's enchantment or persuasion of the
hearer.

I could have introduced in case of obscurity synonymal, exargastic and
palilogetick elucidations; for sweetness of phrase, antimetathetick com-
mutations of epithets; for the vehement excitation of matter, exclamations
in the front and epiphonemas in the reer. I could have used for the
promptlyer stirring up of passion apostrophal and prosopopoeial diver-

[82]

sions; and for the appeasing and setling of them, some epanorthotick revocations and aposiopetick restraints. I could have inserted dialogismes, displaying their interrogatory part with communicatively psymatick and sustentative flourishes; or proleptically with the refutative schemes of anticipation and subjection, and that part which concerns the responsory with the figures of permission and concession.

Speeches extending a matter beyond what it is auxetically, digressively, transitiously, by ratiocination, aetiology, circumlocution and other wayes I could have made use of; as likewise with words diminishing the worth of a thing, tapinotically, periphrastically, by rejection, translation and other meanes, I could have served my self.

There is neither definition, distribution, epitrochism, increment, caracterism, hypotyposis or any schem figurating a speech by reason of what is in the thing to our purpose thereby signified, that I needed to have omitted; nor, had I been so pleased, would I have past by the figurative expressions of what is without any thing of the matter in hand, whether paradigmatical, ironical, symbolical, by comparison or any other kinde of simile; or yet paradoxical, paramologetick, paradiastolary, antipophoretick, cromatick or any other way of figurating a speech by opposition, being formules of oratory whereby we subjoyn what is not expected; confess something that can do us no harme; yeeld to one of the members, that the other may be removed; allow an argument to oppose a stronger; mixe praise with dispraise and so forth through all manner of illustration and decorement of purposes by contrarieties and repugnance.

All those figures and tropes besides what are not here mentioned (these synecdochically standing for all, to shun the tediousness of a too prolixe enumeration) I could have adhibited to the embellishment of this tractate, had not the matter it self been more prevalent with me then the superficial formality of a quaint discourse.

From *The Jewell* by Sir Thomas Urquhart (1611–60)

Some of the Sublime Works of the Philosopher Theophrastus

He left behind to Posterity several monuments of his sublime Wit, of which I think it but requisite to give the Reader a Catalogue, to the end that thereby it might be known how great a Philosopher he was . . .

. . . *Of Nature*. Three Books of the Gods; one of Enthusiasm; an Epitome of Natural Things; A tract against Naturallists; one Book of Nature; three more of Nature; two Abridgments of natural things; eighteen more of Natural things; seventeen of various Opinions concerning Natural things; one of Natural Problems; three of Motion; two more of Motion; three of Water; one of a River in *Sicily*; two of Meteors; two of Fire; one of Heaven; one of Nitre and Alum; two of things that putrifie; one of Stones; one of Metals; one of things that melt and coagulate; one of the Sea; one of Winds; two of things in dry places; two of Sublime things; one of Hot and Cold; one of Generation; ten of the History of Plants; eight of the causes of them; five of Humours; one of Melancholy; one of Honey; eighteen first Propositions concerning Wine; one of Drunkenness; one of Spirits; one of Hair; another of Juices, Flesh and Leather; one of things the sight of which is unexpected; one of things which are subject to wounds and bitings; seven of Animals, and another six of Animals; one of Man; one of Animals that are thought to participate of Reason; One of the Prudence and Manners, or Inclinations of Animals; one of Animals that dig themselves Holes and Dens; one of fortuitous Animals; 1182 Verses comprehending all sorts of Fruits and Animals; A question concerning the Soul; one of Sleeping and Waking; one of Labours; one of old Age; one of Thoughts; four of the Sight; one of things that change their Colour; one of Tears entituled *Callisthenes*; two of hearing; one of the Diversity of the Voices of Animals of the same sort; one of Odours; two of Torment; one of Folly; one of the Palsie; one of the Epilepsie; one of the Vertigo, and dazling of the Sight; one of the fainting of the Heart; one of Suffocation; one of Sweat; one of the Pestilence.

From *The Lives, Opinions & Remarkable Sayings of the Most Famous Ancient Philosophers*, translated 'by diverse hands' from the Greek of Diogenes Laertius, 1688

Accidents and Occasions

Now, it is not well enough consider'd, to what Accidents and Occasions the World is indebted for the greatest Part of those noble Writings, which hourly start up to entertain it. If it were not for a *rainy Day, a drunken Vigil, a Fit of the Spleen, a Course of Physick, a sleepy Sunday, an ill Run at Dice, a long Taylor's Bill, a Beggar's Purse, a factious Head, a hot Sun, costive Dyet, Want of Books, and a just Contempt of Learning*. But for these Events, I say, and some Others too long to recite, (especially *a prudent Neglect of taking Brimstone inwardly*,) I doubt, the Number of *Authors*, and of *Writings* would dwindle away to a Degree most woful to behold.

From *A Tale of a Tub*, by Jonathan Swift, 1696

The Coffee-House Misunderstands Mr Addison's
List of Materials

When I want Materials for this Paper, it is my Custom to go abroad in quest of Game; and when I meet any proper Subject, I take the first Opportunity of setting down an Hint of it upon Paper. At the same time I look into the Letters of my Correspondents, and if I find any thing suggested in them that may afford Matter of Speculation, I likewise enter a Minute of it in my Collection of Materials. By this means I frequently carry about me a whole Sheetful of Hints, that would look like a Rhapsody of Nonsense to any Body but myself: There is nothing in them but Obbscurity and Confusion, Raving and Inconsistency. In short, they are my Speculations in the first Principles, that (like the World in its Chaos) are void of all Light, Distinction, and Order.

About a Week since there happened to me a very odd Accident, by Reason of one of these my Papers of Minutes which I had accidentally dropped at *Lloyd's* Coffee-house, where the Auctions are usually kept. Before I missed it, there were a Cluster of People who had found it, and were diverting themselves with it at one End of the Coffee-house: It had raised so much Laughter among them before I had observed what they were about, that I had not the Courage to own it. The Boy of the Coffee-house, when they had done with it, carried it about in his Hand, asking every Body if they had dropped a written Paper; but no Body challenging it, he was ordered by those merry Gentlemen who had before perused it, to get up into the Auction Pulpit, and read it to the whole Room, that if any one would own it they might. The Boy accordingly mounted the Pulpit, and with a very audible Voice read as follows.

MINUTES

Sir *Roger de Coverly's* Country Seat – Yes, for I hate long Speeches – Query, if a good Christian may be a Conjurer – *Childermas-day*, Saltseller, House-Dog. Screech-Owl, Cricket – Mr *Thomas Inkle* of *London*, in the good Ship called *The Achilles. Yarico – Ægrescitique medendo* – Ghosts – The Lady's Library – Lion by Trade a Taylor – Dromedary called *Bucephalus* – Equipage the Lady's *summum bonum* – *Charles Lillie* to be taken notice of – Short Face a Relief to Envy – Redundancies in the three Professions – King *Latinus* a Recruit – Jew devouring an Ham of Bacon – *Westminster Abbey* – *Grand Cairo* – Procrastination – *April* Fools – Blue Boars, Red Lions, Hogs in Armour – Enter a King and two Fiddlers *solus* – Admission into the Ugly Club – Beauty, how improveable – Families of true and false Humour – The Parrot's School-Mistress – Face half *Pict* half *British* – no Man to be an Hero of Tragedy under Six foot – Club of Sighers – Letters from Flower-Pots, Elbow-Chairs, Tapestry-Figures, Lion, Thunder – The Bell rings to the Puppet Show – Old-Woman with a Beard married to a smock-faced Boy – my next Coat to be turned up with Blue – Fable of Tongs and Gridiron – Flower Dyers – The Soldier's Prayer – Thank ye for nothing, says the Gally-Pot – *Pactolus* in Stockings, with golden Clocks to them – Bamboos, Cudgels, Drumsticks – Slip of my Landlady's eldest Daughter – the black Mare with a Star in her Forehead – The Barber's Pole – WILL HONEY-COMB'S Coat-pocket – *Cæsar's* Behaviour and my own in Parallel Circumstances – Poem in Patch-work – *Nulli gravis est percussus Achilles* – The Female Conventicler – The Ogle Master.

The reading of this Paper made the whole Coffee-house very merry: some of them concluded it was written by a Madman, and others by some Body that had been taking Notes out of the Spectator. One who had the Appearance of a very substantial Citizen, told us, with several politick Winks and Nods, that he wished there was no more in the Paper than was expressed in it: That for his part, he looked upon the Dromedary, the Gridiron, and the Barber's Pole, to signify something more than what is usually meant by those Words; and that he thought the Coffee-man could not do better than to carry the Paper to one of the Secretaries of State. He further added, that he did not like the Name of the outlandish Man with the golden Clock in his Stockings. A young *Oxford* Scholar, who chanced to be with his Uncle at the Coffee-house, discover'd to us who this *Pactolus* was; and by that means turned the whole Scheme of this worthy Citizen into Ridicule. While they were making their several Conjectures upon this innocent Paper, I reach'd out my Arm to the Boy, as he was coming out of the Pulpit, to give it to me; which he did accordingly. This drew the Eyes of the whole Company upon me; but after having cast a cursory Glance over it, and shook my Head twice or thrice at the reading of it, I twisted it into a kind of Match, and litt my Pipe with it.

Joseph Addison, in *The Spectator*, April 1711

Nothing

French Truth, *Dutch* Prowess, *British* Policy,
Hybernian Learning, *Scotch* Civility,
Spaniards' Dispatch, *Danes'* Wit, are mainly seen in thee.

From 'Upon Nothing' by John Wilmot, Earl of Rochester (1647–80)

A Nullity of Pseudonyms

And now the Storm began to thicken; one Day he would publish, *A Vindication of, &c.* Another, *A Letter to, &c.* A Third, *A Defence of, &c.* Sometimes calling himself ——, or ——, or ——, or ——, or ——, or ——, giving a new Name to every Treatise . . .

From the *Memoirs of the Life of Scriblerus* by Jonathan Swift, 1723

Varieties of Nothing

Now some imagine these several kinds differ in name only. But, without endeavouring to confute so absurd an opinion, especially as these different kinds of Nothing occur frequently in the best authors, I shall content myself with setting them down, and leave it to the determination of the distinguished reader, whether it is probable, or indeed possible, that they should all convey one and the same meaning.

These are, Nothing *per se* Nothing; Nothing at all; Nothing in the least; Nothing in nature; Nothing in the world; Nothing in the whole world; Nothing in the whole universal world. And perhaps many other of which we say – Nothing.

From the 'Essay on Nothing' by Henry Fielding (1707–54)

A Magazine of Conceptions and Conclusions

My father took a single turn across the room, then sat down, and finished the chapter.

The verbs auxiliary we are concerned in here, continued my father, are, *am; was; have; had; do; did; make; made; suffer; shall; should; will; would; can; could; owe; ought; used;* or *is wont.* – And these varied with tenses, *present, past, future*, and conjugated with the verb *see*, – or with the questions added to them; – *Is it? Was it? Will it be? Would it be? May it be? Might it be?* And these again put negatively, *Is it not? Was it not? Ought it not?* – Or affirmatively, – *It is; It was; It ought to be.* Or chronologically, – *Has it been always? Lately? How long ago?* – Or hypothetically, – *If it was? If it was not?* What would follow? – If the French should beat the English? If the Sun go out of the Zodiac?

Now, by the right use and application of these, continued my father, in which a child's memory should be exercised, there is no one idea can enter his brain, how barren soever, but a magazine of conceptions and conclusions may be drawn forth from it. – Didst thou ever see a white bear? cried my father, turning his head round to Trim, who stood at the back of his chair: – No, an' please your honour, replied the corporal. – But thou couldst discourse about one, Trim, said my father, in case of need? – How is it possible, brother, quoth my uncle Toby, if the corporal never saw one? – 'Tis the fact I want, replied my father, – and the possibility of it is as follows.

A WHITE BEAR! Very well. Have I ever seen one? Might I ever have seen one? Am I ever to see one? Ought I ever to have seen one? Or can I ever see one?

Would I had seen a white bear! (for how can I imagine it?)

If I should see a white bear, what should I say? If I should never see a white bear, what then?

If I never have, can, must or shall see a white bear alive; have I ever seen the skin of one? Did I ever see one painted? – described? Have I never dreamed of one?

Did my father, mother, uncle, aunt, brothers or sisters, ever see a white bear? What would they give? How would they behave? How would the white bear have behaved? Is he wild? Tame? Terrible? Rough? Smooth?

– Is the white bear worth seeing? –

– Is there no sin in it? –

Is it better than a BLACK ONE?

From *Tristram Shandy* by Laurence Sterne, 1759–67

Half a Score Things to Do

In less than five minutes I shall have thrown my pen into the fire, and the little drop of thick ink which is left remaining at the bottom of my ink-horn, after it – I have but half a score of things to do in the time – I have a thing to name – a thing to lament – a thing to hope – a thing to promise, and a thing to threaten – I have a thing to suppose – a thing to declare – a thing to conceal – a thing to choose, and a thing to pray for. – This chapter, therefore, I *name* the chapter of THINGS – and my next chapter to it, that is, the first chapter of my next volume, if I live, shall be my chapter upon WHISKERS, in order to keep up some sort of connection in my works.

From *Tristram Shandy* by Laurence Sterne, 1759–67

Subjects for Verse

This poor gentleman caught cold one winter's night, as he was contemplating, by the side of a christal stream, by moonshine. This afterwards terminated in a fever that was fatal to him. Since his death, I have been favoured with the inspection of his poetry, of which I have preserved a catalogue for the benefit of my readers.

OCCASIONAL POEMS

On his dog, that growing corpulent refused a crust when it was offered him.

To the memory of a pair of breeches, that had done him excellent service.

Having lost his trusty walking-staff, he complaineth.

To his mistress, on her declaring that she loved parsnips better than potatoes.

On an ear-wig that crept into a nectarine that it might be swallowed by Cloe.

On cutting an artichoke in his garden the day that Queen Anne cut her little finger.

Epigram on a wooden-peg.

Ode to the memory of that great modern – who first invented shoe-buckles.

From the essay 'An Humourist' by William Shenstone, 1714–63

A Mighty Preference for Every Thing English

– I had a long and interesting Letter from George, cross lines by a short one from Tom yesterday dated Paris – They both send their loves to you – Like most Englishmen they feel a mighty preference for every thing English – the french Meadows the trees the People the Towns the Churches the Books the every thing – although they may be in themselves good; yet when put in comparison with our green Island they all vanish like Swallows in October. They have seen Cathedrals Manuscripts. Fountains, Pictures, Tragedy Comedy, – with other things you may by chance meet with in this Country such a[s] Washerwomen, Lamplighters, Turnpikemen Fish kettles, Dancing Masters, kettle drums, Sentry Boxes, Rocking Horses &c . . .

From a letter by John Keats to Fanny Keats, 10 September 1817

'Vile Things'

The House of Mourning written by Mr Scott, –
  A sermon at the Magdalen, – a tear
  Dropt on a greasy novel, – want of cheer
After a walk up hill to a friend's cot, –
Tea with a Maiden Lady – a curs'd lot
  Of worthy poems with the Author near, –
  A patron lord – a drunkenness from beer, –
Haydon's great picture, – a cold coffee pot
At midnight when the Muse is ripe for labour, –
  The voice of Mr Coleridge, – a french Bonnet
Before you in the pit, – a pipe and tabour, –
A damn'd inseparable flute and neighbour, –
  All these are vile, – But viler Wordsworth's Sonnet
  On Dover: – Dover! – who *could* write upon it?

John Keats, c.1817

'No!'

No sun – no moon!
No morn – no noon –
No dawn – no dusk – no proper time of day –
No sky – no earthly view –
No distance looking blue –
No road – no street – no 't'other side the way' –
No end to any Row –
No indications where the Crescents go –
No top to any steeple –
No recognitions of familiar people –
No courtesies for showing 'em! –
No knowing 'em! –
No travelling at all – no locomotion,
No inkling of the way – no notion –
'No go' – by land or ocean –
No mail – no post –
No news from any foreign coast –
No Park – no Ring – no afternoon gentility –
No company – no nobility –

No warmth, no cheerfulness, no healthful ease,
  No comfortable feel in any member –
No shade, no shine, no butterflies, no bees,
  No fruits, no flow'rs, no leaves, no birds –
    November!

Thomas Hood (1799–1845)

Mr Jingle Encapsulates the City of Rochester

'Magnificent ruin!' said Mr Augustus Snodgrass, with all the poetic fervour that distinguished him, when they came in sight of the fine old castle.

'What a study for an antiquarian!' were the very words that fell from Mr Pickwick's mouth, as he applied the telescope to his eye.

'Ah! fine place,' said the stranger, 'glorious pile – frowning walls – tottering arches – dark nooks – crumbling staircases – Old cathedral too – earthy smell – pilgrims' feet worn away the old steps – little Saxon doors – confessionals like money-takers' boxes at theatres – queer customers these monks – Popes, and Lord Treasurers, and all sorts of old fellows, with great red faces, and broken noses, turning up every day – buff jerkins too – matchlocks – Sarcophagus – fine place – old legends too – strange stories: capital;' and the stranger continued to soliloquise until they reached the Bull Inn, in the High Street, where the coach stopped.

From *The Pickwick Papers* by Charles Dickens, 1836–7

The Reputed Catholic Horrors in the Cellars of the Oratory

... a mob might have swarmed about our innocent dwelling, to rescue certain legs of mutton and pats of butter from imprisonment, and to hold an inquest over a dozen packing-cases, some old hampers, a knife-board, and a range of empty blacking-bottles.

From *Lectures on the Present Position of Catholics in England*
by John Henry Newman, 1851

The Diverse Gifts to Pasha Bailey Ben

His Importance.

Pale Pilgrims came from o'er the sea
To wait on PASHA BAILEY B.,
All bearing presents in a crowd,
For B. was poor as well as proud.

His Presents.

They brought him onions strung on ropes,
And cold boiled beef, and telescopes,
And balls of string, and shrimps, and guns,
And chops, and tacks, and hats, and buns.

More of them.

They brought him white kid gloves, and pails,
And candlesticks, and potted quails,
And capstan-bars, and scales and weights,
And ornaments for empty grates.

Why I mention these.

My tale is not of these – oh no!
I only mention them to show
The divers gifts that divers men
Brought o'er the sea to BAILEY BEN.

From 'Pasha Bailey Ben', in *The Bab Ballads* by W. S. Gilbert (1836–1911)

Great-Aunt Adelaide's Soirée

The next morning, when the children came in from their half-hour of
Healthful Fresh Air before breakfast, this is what they had been doing:
Daniel had pinned up a large notice at the Tradesmen's Entrance, saying:
INFECTOUIS DISEESE, NO ADMITTENS.
*Hannah had mixed some of the schoolroom chalk with water and filled up all
yesterday's milk-bottles with it.*
Tora had painted little red spots on the glass pane of the big front door.
*The other children had dug up lots of worms in case they might come in useful, at
Great-Aunt Adelaide's soirée.*

Cook became more and more mystified as the morning wore on and no butcher or baker or fishmonger arrived with their goods for that evening's party. 'Drat them tradesmen!' she said to Nurse Matilda, over their elevenses in the Servants' Hall. 'And the extra help hasn't come either. But I must say, your young ladies and gentlemen are being very helpful. I never did see such children for helpfulness.'

The children were indeed being very busy assisting with preparations for Great-Aunt Adelaide's soirée.

Jaci had made a little hole in the bottom of the kettle and every time Cook put it on the range, in two minutes it was empty and the fire underneath had gone out.

Hetty was standing beside Cook as she made her sausage rolls, and as fast as Cook filled one, she prodded the sausage out and put it quietly back with the rest. ('I must have mistook me quantities,' said Cook, looking with dismay at the undiminished pile of sausages still waiting to be wrapped around with pastry.)

Sophie was curling the worms up lovingly on the little chocolate cakes. Justin had opened the sandwiches and was putting in a teeny thin layer of wet cotton wool; and closing them up again.

Toni had filled up the coffee tin with earth.

Arabella had wrapped a crêpe bandage round the fruit cake and covered the whole thing with icing.

Clarissa had folded a yellow duster in with the sponge roll and Cook was quite happy, thinking it was apricot jam.

Agatha had sewn together the knees of Gumble's best evening trousers, and the hem of Fiddle (the parlourmaid's) dress.

Sebastian filled the toes of their shoes with a stiff greengage jelly.

All the other children were helping with Great-Aunt Adelaide's party too.

From *Nurse Matilda Goes to Town* by Christianna Brand, 1967

The Professor Tries to Rescue Maria from the Mansion of Malplaquet

When he had passed the Grecian Amphitheatre, and the sixty-foot pyramid in honour of General Burgoyne, the Valley of Concord opened before him, as Capability Brown had always intended that it should, and there was the vast bulk of the mansion at the end of it. Wren, Vanbrugh, Hawksmoor, Kent, and the rest of them had erected its dozen colonnades; Adam, Patrioli, and others had plastered its hundred ceilings; Sheraton, Hepplewhite, Chippendale, etc., had stuffed it with furniture, since sold; and there it lay before the Professor in the evening sunlight, with more rooms than anybody could remember.

He let himself in by a ruined door in the west wing, and began to search.

He searched the Gothic Billiard Room – which had once held a table as big as a swimming-bath, and which still had the coat armour of all Maria's ancestors painted on the imitation wooden tracery of the ceiling. The central achievement had been kindly provided by Horry Walpole, and it had 441 quarterings, including the arms of Boadicea and Herod Antipas. All the bends were sinister and all the wives were on the wrong side of their husbands.

He searched the Orangery, where Gibbon had scratched out a semicolon in the famous last paragraph of *The Decline and Fall of the Roman Empire*, before presenting the eighth volume to the Duke of Gloucester – who had observed affably: 'Another damned thick book! Always scribble, scribble, scribble! Eh, Mr Gibbon?'

He searched the Menagerie, where the Earl of Chesterfield had once been locked by mistake for two days as a monkey, and a pity they did not keep him there for good.

He searched the Chinese Parlour, into which Rousseau had suddenly rushed in 1768, when he had indignantly read out an interminable and incomprehensible letter from himself to Diderot, leaving all hearers completely stunned.

He searched the Rent Room, where the Wicked Earl had once run his estate agent through the body – the former claimed during his trial by the Lords that it had been in a duel, but the agent still walked on Tuesday nights, with the hilt of the sword in the small of his back, which was a good argument to the contrary.

He searched the Chart Room, where one of the viscounts, an admiral, had been accustomed to keep his sextant and other instruments, on retiring from the service after having lost Majorca, Minorca, Bermuda, Goa, Simla, Hecla, and Alabama, in a series of naval engagements.

He searched the Gun Room, out of whose window the Duke of Orleans had been accustomed to shoot larks with the corks from champagne bottles.

He searched the Fertilizer Room, where the Master of Malplaquet, who had invented three separate potato grubbers, had been accustomed to store enormous quantities of Hypersuperextrainfraphosphates, for the use of his tenant farmers.

He even searched the State Room, in which Queen Victoria had held the only Drawing Room ever held outside a royal castle, and in it there was the very chair in which she had sat, with a glass lid over the seat, to preserve the royal imprint.

The Professor lifted the lid and sat down himself, for he was beginning to feel tired.

Then he got up with a sigh and went upstairs to the Clock Room in the pediment of the North Front, which had a clock made by Christopher Pinchbeck II, which played 'When the Heart of a Man Is Depressed with Cares', in four parts, one at each quarter – people got over it in time, and stopped listening.

His quarry was not there.

The Professor began to lose his head, and to hurry from one floor to another, as the different ideas occurred to him.

He searched the Butler's Strong Room, which had at various times held the Derby, Grand National, and Ascot gold cups, as well as an épergne in the shape of a banyan tree which had been presented to the Sixth Duke by the grateful inhabitants of Bombay.

He tried the stables for 144 horses, the kennels for 144 hounds, the attics for 144 abigails or footmen, and the Card Room, where Charles James Fox had once lost £144,000 in a single night, wearing scarlet heels to his shoes and blue powder on his wig.

He even tried the Armoury, which had once housed the accoutrements of the Third Duke's Own Northamptonshire Fencibles – and also a party of visitors who had been mislaid while being shown round the Palace, in aid of charity, by a forgetful butler, in 1915.

His hostage was nowhere to be seen.

The poor Professor sat down on the bare floor of the Armoury for a second rest. Then he pulled himself together for a final effort, and searched afresh.

He searched the Pavilion, where an absent-minded Lord Dudley had once invited Sydney Smith to dinner with the remark: 'Dine with me today, and I will get Sydney Smith to meet you' – to which Mr Sydney Smith had courteously replied that he was engaged to meet him elsewhere.

He searched the Colonnade, where the great Pope himself had walked with William Broome, on the night when he was persuading the latter to persuade Tonson to publish a letter from Lintot, signed however by Cleland, and purporting to have been written by Bolingbroke, in which Lady Mary Wortley Montagu was accused of having suspected a Mr Green of persuading Broome to refuse permission to Tonson to publish a letter by Cleland, purporting to have been signed by Lintot, without the knowledge of Bolingbroke, about the personal habits of Dr Arbuthnot, under the pseudonym of Swift. (On the other hand, a person named Worsdale, a mere tool, calling himself R. Smythe, was to tell Curll that a certain 'PT', a secret enemy of Temple, possessed a copy of the correspondence between Lord Hervey and Colly Cibber: with obvious results.)

He went out of doors at last, and searched the fountain which Boswell had once fallen into, to amuse the Great Lexicographer.

He even poked about under the equestrian statue of dapper little George

II, seated on a horse with no girths, and for that reason perhaps the very one which had run away with him at Dettingen.

Maria was nowhere to be seen.

From *Mistress Masham's Repose* by T. H. White, 1947

Black the Pirate Removes the Letter O from the Island of Ooroo

Test cases were constantly brought to court – or curt, as it was called. 'Somebody will have to clarify the law for everybody, or nobody will know where anybody stands,' the people said. So Black appointed Hyde lawyer, judge, and chief clarifier. 'The more chaotic the clarification,' said Black, 'the better. Remember how I hate that letter.'

This was right up Hyde's dark and devious alley. 'Chaotic is now chatic,' he said, 'a cross between chaos and static.' He decided that farmers could keep their cows if they kept them in herds, for cows in herds are kine or cattle. And so the people had milk and cheese and butter. He decided in favour of hens and eggs, if hens were segregated. 'Keep them out of flocks,' he said, 'for flocks are not only flocks, but also poultry.'

'We have no corn or potatoes, or cauliflower, or tomatoes,' a housewife said one day.

'In a vegetable garden,' said Hyde, 'the things that grow are ninety-five per cent without an O. I could name you twenty such,' he added cockily, 'and then you'd scream in unison for broccoli. Almost all the fruits are yours to eat, from the apple to the tangerine, with a good two dozen in between. I'll stick to those that start with P to show you what I mean: the pear, the peach, the plum, the prune, the plantain and pineapple, the pawpaw and papaya. But you will yearn for things you never ate, and cannot tolerate – I know you women – the pomegranate, for one, and the dull persimmon. No grapefruit, by the way. I hate its bitter juice. I have banned it, under its French name, *pamplemousse*.'

Another wife took the stand one day to complain of things she hadn't. 'Cloves and cinnamon,' she said, 'and marjoram and saffron.'

'You still have dill,' said Hyde, 'and thyme and sage and basil, vinegar, vanilla, and sarsaparilla, salt and pepper and paprika, ginger and the spices. You can't have coffee, but there is tea; to sweeten it, there's sugar.'

A seamstress raised her hand to ask about the O's in textiles, fabrics, and in clothes. 'You're denied a few,' admitted Hyde. 'Corduroy and bombazine, organdy and tricotine, calico and crinoline. But you have silk and satin, velvet, lace and linen, tulle and twill and tweed, damask and denim, madras and muslin, felt and chintz and baize and leather, and twenty more for cool and warm and winter weather.'

Now the boatswain of the crew was a man named Stragg, and the cockswain was a man named Strugg, and the former was allergic to roses, and the latter was allergic to phlox. So Black decided that even the flowers with an O in their names were against him, and he ordered his crew to get rid of roses and phlox in the gardens of the island, and oleanders and moonflowers and morning-glories, and cosmos and coxcomb and columbine, and all the rest with O's.

'But my livelihood is violets and hollyhocks and marigolds,' a gardener complained.

'Lilies are nice for livelihood,' said Hyde, 'and more alliterative. There are also lilacs and the like. I crossbreed certain things myself with more success than failure. Forget-me-nots, when crossed with madwort, lose their O's. I get a hybrid which I call regret-me-evers. Love-in-a-mist, when crossed with bleeding hearts, results in sweethearts quarrels.'

'It's blasphemy or heresy,' the women cried, 'or something!'

'You haven't heard the half of it,' said Hyde. 'Black-eyed susans, crossed with ragged sailors, give me ragged susans. Jack-in-the-pulpit, crossed with devil's paintbrush, should give me devil-in-the-pulpit. And think of the fine satanic chimes that will emerge from hellebore crossed with Canterbury bells.' At this the women rose in anger and dismay and left the curt without a curtsy.

'Why not get rid of all the flowers?' demanded Black one day. 'After all, there is an O in flowers.'

'I thought of that,' said Hyde, 'but we must spare collective nouns, like food, goods, and crops, and tools, and, I should think, the lesser schools. I have taken the carpenter's gouge and boards. It still leaves him much too much, but that's the way it goes, with and without O's. He has his saw and axe and hatchet, his hammer and chisel, his brace and bit, and plane and level, also nails and tacks and brads and screws and staples. But all he can build is bric-a-brac and knick-knack, gew-gaw, kickshaw, and gimcrack. No coop or goathouse, no stoop or boathouse.'

'I would that I could banish body; then I'd get rid of everybody.' Black's eyes gleamed like rubies. 'No more anatomy, no more morphology, physiognomy, or physiology, or people, or even persons. I think about it often in the night. Body is blood and bones and other O's, organs, torso, abdomen, and toes.'

Hyde curled his upper lip. 'I'll build you a better man,' he said, 'of firmer flesh and all complete, from hairy head to metatarsal feet, using A's and I's and U's and E's, with muscular arms and flexible knees; eyes and ears and lids and lips, neck and chest and breast and hips; liver, heart, and lungs and chin, nerves and ligaments and skin; kidneys, pancreas, and flanks, ankles, calves, and shins and shanks; legs and lashes, ribs and spleen –' Black had turned a little green, and then Hyde held up both hands. 'Brains and veins and cells and glands –'

'Silence!' thundered Black. 'I wish that more things had an O.'

Hyde sighed. 'There is no O in everything,' he said. 'We can't change that.'

From The Wonderful O by James Thurber, 1958

'The Wonderful Bag'

I was sitting one day in my shop when a Kurd came up and began bargaining with me for certain of my goods; suddenly he took up a little bag and, without attempting to hide it, tried most openly to walk off with it, as if it had belonged to him ever since he was born. I jumped out into the street and, stopping him by the skirts of his robe, told him to give me back my bag. He only shrugged his shoulders, saying: 'That bag, and all that is in it, belongs to me.' In rising anger, I cried out: 'O Mussulmans, save my goods from this wretched unbeliever!' At once all who were in the market crowded round us, and my fellow merchants advised me to lay a complaint before the kadi without further delay. I agreed to this, and immediately willing hands helped me to drag the Kurd who had stolen my bag into the presence of the kadi. As we all stood respectfully before him, he asked: 'Which of you is the plaintiff and which the defendant?' Without giving me time to open my mouth, the Kurd stepped forward, crying: 'Allah increase the power of our master the kadi! This bag is my bag, and all that it contains belongs to me! I lost it and then found it again on this man's counter.' 'When did you lose it?' asked the kadi. 'I lost it yesterday,' answered the impudent fellow, 'and I could not sleep all night for thinking of it.' 'In that case,' said the judge, 'give me a list of its contents.' Without a moment's hesitation, the Kurd answered: 'O kadi, there are in my bag two crystal flasks filled with kohl, two silver sticks for putting on kohl, a handkerchief, two lemonade glasses with gilded rims, two torches, two ladles, a cushion, two carpets for gaming tables, two water-pots, two basins, one dish, one cook-pot, one earthen water-jar, one kitchen dipper, one large knitting-needle, two provision sacks, a pregnant cat, two bitches, a rice-jar, two donkeys, two bedroom sets for women, a linen garment, two pelisses, a cow, two calves, a sheep with two lambs, a camel with two little camels, two racing dromedaries with their females, a buffalo and two oxen, a lioness and two lions, a female bear, two foxes, one couch, two beds, a palace with two reception halls, two green tents, two canopies, a kitchen with two doors, and an assembly of Kurds of my own kind all ready to swear that the bag is my bag.'

Then the kadi turned to me, saying: 'What answer have you to this?'

I was so astonished by what the Kurd had said, that it was a little time before I was able to advance and answer: 'May Allah lift up and honour our master the kadi! I know that, in my sack, there are only a ruined pavilion, a house without a kitchen, a large dog-kennel, a boys' school, some jolly young fellows playing dice, a brigands' lair, an army with captains, the city of Basrah and the city of Baghdad, the ancient palace of the amir Shaddad son of Ad, a smith's furnace, a fishing net, a shepherd's crook, five pretty boys, twelve untouched girls, and a thousand leaders of caravans all ready to bear witness that this bag is my bag.'

When the Kurd had heard my answer, he burst into tears and cried between his sobs: 'O our master the kadi, my bag is known and well known; it is universally acknowledged to be my property. Beside those things which I mentioned before, it contains two fortified cities and ten towers, two alchemical alembics, four chess players, a mare and two foals, a stallion and two geldings, two long lances, two hares, a buggered boy and two pimps, a blind man and two far-seeing men, a lame man and two paralytics, a sea captain, a ship with sailors, a Christian priest and two deacons, a patriarch and two monks, and a kadi and two witnesses ready to swear that this bag is my bag.' Then the kadi turned to me again, and said: 'What answer have you to all that?'

Being filled with hot rage, even to my nose, I advanced and replied as calmly as I could: 'Allah lighten and make strong the judgment of our master the kadi! I ought to add that there are in the bag, beside the things which I have already mentioned, headache cures, filtres and enchantments, coats of mail and armouries filled with arms, a thousand rams trained for fighting, a deer park, men who love women, boy fanciers, gardens filled with trees and flowers, vines loaded with grapes, apples and figs, shades and phantoms, flasks and cups, new married couples with all their marriage fresh about them, cries and jokes, twelve disgraceful farts and as many odourless funks, friends sitting in a meadow, banners and flags, a bride coming out of the bath, twenty singers, five fair Abyssinian slaves, three Indian women, four Greek women, fifty Turkish women, seventy Persian women, forty women from Kashmir, eighty Kurdish women, as many Chinese women, ninety women from Georgia, the land of Irak, the Earthly Paradise, two stables, a mosque, many hammams, a hundred merchants, a plank, a nail, a black man playing on the clarinet, a thousand dinars, twenty chests full of stuffs, twenty dancers, fifty storehouses, the city of Kufah, the city of Gaza, Damietta, al-Sawan, the palace of Khusran Anushirwan, the palace of Sulaiman, all the lands between Balkh and Isfahan, the Indies and

Sudan, Baghdad and Khurasan, and – may Allah preserve the days of our master the kadi – a shroud, a coffin, and a razor for the beard of the kadi if the kadi does not recognise my rights and say that this bag is my bag!'

When he had heard all this, the kadi looked at us and said: 'As Allah lives, either you two are mocking at the law and its representatives, or else this bag is a bottomless abyss or the Valley of the Day of Judgment itself.'

Finally, to see which one of us had spoken the truth, the kadi opened the bag before his witnesses and found in it a little orange peel and some olive stones.

At once I told the flabbergasted kadi that the bag must belong to the Kurd and that mine had disappeared. Then I went my way.

From *The Thousand Nights and One Night,* translated by
J. C. Mardrus and Powys Mathers

Cyrano's Twenty Wittier Nose Jokes

Le Vicomte: Vous . . . vous avez un nez . . . heu . . . un nez . . . très
   grand.
Cyrano, gravement: Très.
Le Vicomte, riant: Ha!
Cyrano, imperturbable: C'est tout? . . .
Le Vicomte: Mais . . .
Cyrano: Ah! non! c'est un peu court, jeune homme!
On pouvait dire . . . Oh! Dieu! . . . bien des choses en somme . . .
En variant le ton, – par exemple, tenez:
Aggressif: 'Moi, monsieur, si j'avez un tel nez,
Il faudrait sur-le-champ que je me l'amputesse!'
Amical: 'Mais il doit tremper dans votre tasse!
Pour boire, faites-vous fabriquer un hanap!'
Descriptif: 'C'est un roc! . . . c'est un pic! . . . c'est un cap!
Que dis-je, c'est un cap? . . . C'est une péninsule!'
Curieux: 'De quoi sert cette oblongue capsule?
D'écritoire, monsieur, ou de boîte à ciseaux?'
Gracieux: 'Aimez-vous à ce point les oiseaux
Que paternellement vous vous préoccupâtes
De tendre ce perchoir à leurs petites pattes?'
Truculent: 'Cà, monsieur, lorsque vous pétunez,
La vapeur du tabac vous sort-elle du nez
Sans qu'un voisin ne crie au feu de cheminée?'
Prévenant: 'Gardez-vous, votre tête entraînée

Par ce poids, de tomber en avant sur le sol!'
Tendre: 'Faites-lui faire un petit parasol
De peur que sa couleur au soleil ne se fane!'
Pédant: 'L'animal seul, monsieur, qu'Aristophane
Appelle Hippocampelephantocamélos
Dut avoir sous le front tant de chair sur tant d'os!'
Cavalier: 'Quoi, l'ami, ce croc est à la mode?
Pour pendre son chapeau, c'est vraiment très commode!'
Emphatique: 'Aucun vent ne peut, nez magistral,
T'enrhumer tout entier, excepté le mistral!'
Dramatique: 'C'est la Mer Rouge quand il saigne!'
Admiratif: 'Pour un parfumeur, quelle enseigne!'
Lyrique: 'Est-ce une conque, êtes-vous un triton?'
Naïf: 'Ce monument, quand le visite-t-on?'
Respectueux: 'Souffrez, monsieur, qu'on vous salue,
C'est là qui s'appelle avoir pignon sur rue!'
Campagnard: 'Hé, ardé! C'est-y un nez? Nanain!
C'est queuqu'navet géant ou ben queuqu'melon nain!'
Militaire: 'Pointez contre cavalerie!'
Pratique: 'Voulez-vous le mettre en loterie?
Assurément, monsieur, ce sera le gros lot!'
Enfin, parodiant Pyrame en un sanglot:
'Le voilà donc ce nez qui des traits de son maître
A détruit l'harmonie! Il en rougit, le traître!'
– Voilà ce qu'à peu prés, mon cher, vous m'auriez dit
Si vous aviez un peu de lettres et d'ésprit:
Mais d'ésprit, ô le plus lamentable des êtres,
Vous n'en eûtes jamais un atome, et de lettres
Vous n'avez que les trois qui forment le mot: sot!

From *Cyrano de Bergerac* by Edmond Rostand, 1897

The House O'Shea, Known as the Haunted Inkbottle

You brag of your brass castle or your tyled house in ballyfermont? Niggs, niggs and niggs again. For this was a stinksome inkenstink, quite puzzonal to the wrottel. Smatterafact, Angles aftanon browsing there thought not Edam reeked more rare. My wud! The warped flooring of the lair and soundconducting walls thereof, to say nothing of the uprights and imposts, were persianly literatured with burst loveletters, telltale stories, stickyback snaps, doubtful eggshells, bouchers, flints, borers, puffers, amygdaloid almonds, rindless raisins, alphybettyformed verbage, vivlical viasses, ompiter dictas, visus umbique, ahems and ahahs, imeffible tries at speech unasyllabled, you owe mes, eyoldhyms, fluefoul smut, fallen lucifers, vestas which had served, showered ornaments, borrowed brogues, reversibles jackets, blackeye lenses, family jars, falsehair shirts, Godforsaken scapulars, neverworn breeches, cutthroat ties, counterfeit franks, best intentions, curried notes, upset latten tintacks, unused mill and stumpling stones, twisted quills, painful digests, magnifying wineglasses, solid objects cast at goblins, once current puns, quashed quotatoes, messes of mottage, unquestionable issue papers, seedy ejaculations, limerick damns, crocodile tears, spilt ink, blasphematory spits, stale shestnuts, schoolgirl's, young ladies', milkmaids', washerwomen's, shopkeepers' wives, merry widows', ex nuns', vice abbess's, pro virgins', super whores', silent sisters', Charleys' aunts', grandmothers', mothers'-in-laws', fostermothers', godmothers' garters, tress clippings from right, lift and cintrum, worms of snot, toothsome pickings, cans of Swiss condensed bilk, highbrow lotions, kisses from the antipodes, presents from pickpockets, borrowed plumes, relaxable handgrips, princess promises, lees of whine, deoxodised carbons, convertible collars, diviliouker doffers, broken wafers, unloosed shoe latchets, crooked strait waistcoasts, fresh horrors from Hades, globules of mercury, undeleted glete, glass eyes for an eye, gloss teeth for a tooth, war moans, special sighs, longsufferings of longstanding, ahs ohs ouis sis jas jos gias neys thaws sos, yeses and yeses and yeses, to which, if one has the stomach to add the breakages, upheavals distortions, inversions of all this chambermade music one stands, given a grain of goodwill, a fair chance of actually seeing the whirling dervish, Tumult, son of Thunder, self exiled in upon his ego, a nightlong a shaking betwixtween white or reddr hawrors, noondayterrorised to skin and bone by an ineluctable phantom (may the Shaper have mercery on him!) writing the mystery of himsel in furniture.

From *Finnegans Wake* by James Joyce, 1939

The Whole Bloody Business

Personally of course I regret everything. Not a word, not a deed, not a thought, not a need, not a grief, not a joy, not a girl, not a boy, not a doubt, nor a trust, not a scorn, not a lust, not a hope, not a fear, not a smile, not a tear, not a name, not a face, no time, no place, that I do not regret, exceedingly. An ordure, from beginning to end. And yet, when I sat for Fellowship, but for the boil on my bottom ... The rest, an ordure. The Tuesday scowls, the Wednesday growls, the Thursday curses, the Friday howls, the Saturday snores, the Sunday yawns, the Monday morns, the Monday morns. The whacks, the moans, the cracks, the groans, the welts, the squeaks, the belts, the shrieks, the pricks, the prayers, the kicks, the tears, the skelps, and the yelps. And the poor old lousy earth, my earth and my father's and my mother's and my father's father's and my mother's mother's and my father's mother's and my mother's father's and my father's mother's father's and my mother's father's mother's and my father's mother's mother's and my mother's father's father's and my father's father's mother's and my mother's mother's father's and my father's father's father's and my mother's mother's mother's and other people's fathers' and mothers' and fathers' fathers' and mothers' mothers' and fathers' mothers' and mothers' fathers' and fathers' mothers' fathers' and mothers' fathers' mothers' and fathers' mothers' mothers' and mothers' fathers' fathers' and fathers' fathers' mothers' and mothers' mothers' fathers' and fathers' fathers' fathers' and mothers' mothers' mothers'. An excrement. The crocuses and the larch turning green every year a week before the others and the pastures red with uneaten sheep's placentas and the long summer days and the newmown hay and the woodpigeon in the morning and the cuckoo in the afternoon and the corncrake in the evening and the wasps in the jam and the smell of the gorse and the look of the gorse and the apples falling and the children walking in the dead leaves and the larch turning brown a week before the others and the chestnuts falling and the howling winds and the sea breaking over the pier and the first fires and the hooves on the road and the consumptive postman whistling *The Roses Are Blooming in Picardy* and the standard oillamp and of course the snow and to be sure the sleet and bless your heart the slush and every fourth year the February débâcle and the endless April showers and the crocuses and then the whole bloody business starting all over again. A turd.

From *Watt* by Samuel Beckett, 1953

An Irish Plethora

There is scarcely a single word in the Irish (barring, possibly, *Sasanach*) that is simple and explicit. Apart from words with endless shades of cognate meaning, there are many with so complete a spectrum of graduated ambiguity that each of them can be made to express two directly contrary meanings, as well as a plethora of intermediate concepts that have no bearing on either. And all this strictly within the linguistic field. Superimpose on all that the miasma of ironic usage, poetic licence, oxymoron, plamás, Celtic evasion, Irish bullery and Paddy Whackery, and it is a safe bet that you will find yourself very far from home. Here is an example copied from Dineen and from more authentic sources known only to my little self:

Cur, g. *curtha* and cuirthe, m. – act of putting, sending, sowing, raining, discussing, burying, vomiting, hammering into the ground, throwing through the air, rejecting, shooting, the setting or clamp in a rick of turf, selling, addressing, the crown of cast-iron buttons which have been made bright by contact with cliff-faces, the stench of congealing badger's suet, the luminance of glue-lice, a noise made in an empty house by an unauthorised person, a heron's boil, a leprechaun's denture, a sheep-biscuit, the act of inflating hare's offal with a bicycle-pump, a leak in a spirit level, the whine of a sewage farm windmill, a corncrake's clapper, the scum on the eye of a senile ram, a dustman's dumpling, a beetle's faggot, the act of loading every rift with ore, a dumb man's curse, a blasket, a 'kur', a fiddler's occupational disease, a fairy godmother's father, a hawk's vertigo, the art of predicting past events, a wooden coat, a custard-mincer, a blue-bottle's 'farm', a gravy flask, a timber-mine, a toy craw, a porridge-mill, a fair-day donnybrook with nothing barred, a stoat's stomach-pump, a broken –

But what is the use? One could go on and on without reaching anywhere in particular.

From the 'Cruiskeen Lawn' column in the *Irish Times* by
Flann O'Brien (Brian O'Nolan, 1911–66)

The Ambassadors' Gifts

The Western ambassadors file in, bearing their tributes:
A blonde, a flying buttress, some Vikings,
A second blonde, Hadrian's Wall, a fake Rembrandt,
A third blonde, a fourth blonde, a fifth blonde.

The Western ambassadors file in, bearing their tributes:
Two blondes, a half-scale model of the Colosseum,
Polyphony, the square root of two, a Greek vase,
A third blonde, a pedometer, a redhead, Individualism.

The Western ambassadors file in, bearing their tributes:
Gunpowder, Fermat's theorem, bamboo,
Printing, Cologne Cathedral (incomplete):
The blond emperor rises to his feet in a rage.

From *A Bad Day for the Sung Dynasty* by Frank Kuppner, 1984

'Sweet Like a Crow'

'The Sinhalese are beyond
a doubt one of the least
musical peoples in the
world. It would be
quite impossible to have
less sense of pitch,
line, or rhythm.'
– Paul Bowles

Your voice sounds like a scorpion being pushed
through a glass tube
like someone has just trod on a peacock
like wind howling in a coconut
like a rusty bible, like someone pulling barbed wire
across a stone courtyard, like a pig drowning,
a vattacka being fried
a bone shaking hands
a frog singing at Carnegie Hall.
Like a crow swimming in milk,
like a nose being hit by a mango
like the crowd at the Royal-Thomian match,
a womb full of twins, a pariah dog
with a magpie in its mouth
like the midnight jet from Casablanca
like Air Pakistan curry,
a typewriter on fire, like a spirit in the gas
which cooks your dinner,
like a hundred pappadams being crunched, like someone
uselessly trying to light 3 *Roses* matches in a dark room,
the clicking sound of a reef when you put your head into the sea,
a dolphin reciting epic poetry to a sleepy audience,
the sound of a fan when someone throws brinjals at it,
like pineapples being sliced in the Pettah market
like betel juice hitting a butterfly in mid-air
like a whole village running naked onto the street
and tearing their sarongs, like an angry family
pushing a jeep out of the mud, like dirt on the needle,
like 8 sharks being carried on the back of a bicycle
like 3 old ladies locked in the lavatory

like the sound I heard when I was having an afternoon sleep
and someone walked through my room in ankle bracelets.

From Running in the Family by Michael Ondaatje, 1982

Achievements of the Fat

It's likely we also invented some of love,
much of fertility (see the Willensdorf Venus)
parts of theology (divine feasting, Unmoved Movers)
likewise complexity, stateliness, the ox-cart
    and self-deprecation.

From 'Quintets for Robert Morley' by Les A. Murray

After the Riotous Party

After the riotous party, they sail down the lake,
Gathering the debris still floating from the evening before:
A few hats, some torn sheets of paper,
Flowers, a major and a minor poet.

From A Bad Day for the Sung Dynasty by Frank Kuppner, 1984

Comprehensive Death

As the poets have mournfully sung,
Death takes the innocent young,
    The rolling in money,
    The screamingly funny,
And those who are very well hung.

W. H. Auden (1907–73)

Retired Lives

I who recount this tale am Sister Theodora, nun of the order of Saint Columba. I am writing in a convent, from old papers unearthed or talk heard in our parlour here or a few rare accounts by people who were actually present. We nuns have few occasions to speak to soldiery, so what I don't know I try to imagine; how else could I set about it? Not all the story is clear to me yet. I must crave indulgence: we country girls, however noble, have always led retired lives in remote castles and convents; apart from religious ceremonies, triduums, novenas, gardening, harvesting, vintaging, whippings, slavery, incest, fires, hangings, invasions, sacking, rape and pestilence, we have had no experience. What can a poor nun know of this world?

From *The Non-Existent Knight* by Italo Calvino, translated from the Italian by Archibald Colquhoun, 1962

Bizarre Containers

In plain language, we have an inborn capability for intoxication, greed, lust, cruelty and murder: a fact which your thinking moralist will always find more significant than our ingenuity in constructing such bizarre containers of ourselves as the Polaris submarine, Sistine Chapel, and suspenderbelt.

From *1982, Janine*, by Alasdair Gray, 1984

The Monstrous Regiment of Books

In the shop window you have promptly identified the cover with the title you were looking for. Following this visual trail, you have forced your way through the shop past the thick barricade of Books You Haven't Read, which were frowning at you from the tables and shelves, trying to cow you. But you know you must never allow yourself to be awed, that among them there extend for acres and acres the Books You Needn't Read, the Books Made For Purposes Other Than Reading, Books Read Even Before You Open Them Since They Belong To The Category Of Books Read Before Being Written. And thus you pass the outer girdle of ramparts, but then you are attacked by the infantry of the Books That If You Had More Than One Life You Would Certainly Also Read But Unfortunately Your Days Are

Numbered. With a rapid manoeuvre you bypass them and move into the phalanxes of the Books You Mean To Read But There Are Others You Must Read First, the Books Too Expensive Now And You'll Wait Till They're Remaindered, the Books ditto When They Come Out in Paperback, Books You Can Borrow From Somebody, Books That Everybody's Read So It's As If You Had Read Them, Too. Eluding these assaults, you come up beneath the towers of the fortress, where other troops are holding out:

the Books You've Been Planning To Read For Ages,

the Books You've Been Hunting For Years Without Success,

the Books Dealing With Something You're Working On At The Moment,

the Books You Want To Own So They'll Be Handy Just In Case,

the Books You Could Put Aside Maybe To Read This Summer,

the Books You Need To Go With Other Books On Your Shelves,

the Books That Fill You With Sudden, Inexplicable Curiosity, Not Easily Justified.

Now you have been able to reduce the countless embattled troops to an array that is, to be sure, very large but still calculable in a finite number; but this relative relief is then undermined by the ambush of the Books Read Long Ago Which It's Now Time To Reread and the Books You've Always Pretended To Have Read And Now It's Time To Sit Down And Really Read Them.

With a zigzag dash you shake them off and leap straight into the citadel of the New Books Whose Author Or Subject Appeals To You. Even inside this stronghold you can make some breaches in the ranks of the defenders, dividing them into New Books By Authors Or On Subjects Not New (for you or in general) and New Books By Authors Or On Subjects Completely Unknown (at least to you), and defining the attraction they have for you on the basis of your desires and needs for the new and the not new (for the new you seek in the not new and for the not new you seek in the new).

All this simply means that, having rapidly glanced over the titles of the volumes displayed in the bookshop, you have turned toward a stack of *If on a Winter's Night a Traveller* fresh off the press, you have grasped a copy, and you have carried it to the cashier so that your right to own it can be established.

From *If on a Winter's Night a Traveller* by Italo Calvino, translated from the Italian by William Weaver, 1981

Three

RICHES

*Collections, Commodities
and Vanities*

12 Tarshish was thy merchant by reason of the multitude of all kind of riches; with silver, iron, tin, and lead, they traded in thy fairs.

13 Javan, Tubal, and Meshech, they were thy merchants: they traded the persons of men and vessels of brass in thy market.

14 They of the house of Togarmah traded in thy fairs with horses and horsemen and mules.

15 The men of Dedan were thy merchants: many isles were the merchandise of thine hand: they brought thee for a present horns of ivory and ebony.

16 Syria was thy merchant by reason of the multitude of the wares of thy making: they occupied in thy fairs with emeralds, purple, and broidered work, and fine linen, and coral, and agate.

17 Judah, and the land of Israel, they were thy merchants: they traded in thy market wheat of Minnith, and Pannag, and honey, and oil, and balm.

18 Damascus was thy merchant in the multitude of the wares of thy making, for the multitude of all riches; in the wine of Helbon, and white wool.

19 Dan also and Javan going to and fro occupied in thy fairs: bright iron, cassia, and calamus, were in thy market.

20 Dedan was thy merchant in precious clothes for chariots.

21 Arabia, and all the princes of Kedar, they occupied with thee in lambs, and rams, and goats: in these were they thy merchants.

22 The merchants of Sheba and Raamah, they were thy merchants: they occupied in thy fairs with chief of all spices, and with all precious stones, and gold.

23 Haran, and Canneh, and Eden, the merchants of Sheba, Asshur, and Chilmad, were thy merchants.

24 These were thy merchants in all sorts of things, in blue clothes, and broidered work, and in chests of rich apparel, bound with cords, and made of cedar, among thy merchandise.

25 The ships of Tarshish did sing of thee in thy market: and thou wast replenished, and made very glorious in the midst of the seas.

26 Thy rowers have brought thee into great waters: the east wind hath broken thee in the midst of the seas.

27 Thy riches, and thy fairs, thy merchandise, thy mariners, and thy pilots, thy calkers, and the occupiers of thy merchandise, and all thy

men of war, that are in thee, and in all thy company which is in the midst of thee, shall fall into the midst of the seas in the day of thy ruin.

From Ezekiel 27

3 Dedicatory Epigrams from the Greek Anthology

(i)

Piso the fisherman, weighed down by long toil and his right hand already shaky, gives to Hermes these his rods with the lines hanging from their tips, his oar that swam through the sea, his curved hooks whose points bite the fishes' throats, his net fringed with lead, the float that announced where his weel lay, his two wicker creels, the flint pregnant with fire that sets the tinder alight, and his anchor, the trap that holds fast wandering ships.

PHILIPPUS OF THESSALONICA

(ii)

The fruit-watcher dedicated to rustic Priapus, carved out of a trunk, this sacrifice from the trees, a newly split pomegranate, this quince covered with fresh dew, a navelled fig with wrinkled skin, a purple cluster of thick-set grapes, fountain of wine, and a walnut just out of its green rind.

ANON.

(iii)

Callimenes, resting from its long labour his sluggish hand that trembles with age, dedicates to Hermes his disc of lead that running correctly close to the straight ruler can deftly mark its track, the hard steel that eats the pens, the ruler itself, too, guide of the undeviating line, the rough stone on which the double-tooth of the pen is sharpened when blunted by long use, the sponge, wandering Triton's couch in the deep, healer of the pen's errors, and the ink-box with many cavities that holds in one all the implements of calligraphy.

PAULUS SILENTIARIUS

Translations by W. R. Paton, 1916

Elizabethan Trade Goods

Things to be carried with you: kerseys of all orient colours, frizadoes, motleys, bristow friezes, Spanish blankets, bays of all colours, felts of divers colours. Taffeta hats. Deep caps for mariners, whereof if ample vent be found, it would turn to an infinite commodity of the common poor people by knitting.

Quilted caps of Levant taffeta of divers colours, for the night.

Knit stocks of silk of orient colours.

Garters, girdles of buff and all other leather, with gilt and ungilt buckles.

Gloves of all sorts knit, and of leather.

Gloves perfumed.

Shoes of Spanish leather.

Shoes of other leather.

Velvet shoes and pantoufles.

Purses knit, and of leather.

Nightcaps knit.

A garnish of pewter for a show of vent of that English commodity, bottles, flagons, spoons etc. of that metal.

Glasses of English making.

Looking glasses for women, great and fair.

Spectacles of the common sort.

Hour glasses.

Combs of horn.

Linen of divers sorts.

Handkerchiefs with silk of several colours wrought.

Glazen eyes to ride with against dust.

Knives in sheaths both single and double, of good edge.

Needles great and small of every kind.

Buttons.

All the several silver coins of our English monies, to be carried with you to be showed to the governors at Cambalu, which is a thing that shall in silence speak to wise men more than you imagine.

Locks and keys, hinges, bolts, hasps, etc. great and small of excellent workmanship, whereof if vent may be, we shall set our subjects in work, which you may have in great regard. For in finding ample vent of any thing that is to be wrought in this realm, is more worth to our people besides the gain of the merchant, than Christchurch, Bridewell, the Savoy, and all the hospitals of England.

Take with you the map of England set out in fair colours, one of the biggest sort I mean, to make show of your country from whence you come.

And also the large map of London to make show of your city. And let the river be drawn full of ships of all sorts, to make the more show of your great trade and traffic in trade of merchandise.

Rolls of parchment, for that we may vent much without hurt to the realm, and it lieth in small room.

Carry glue, for that we have plenty.

Red ochre for painters. We have great mines of it, and have no vent.

Try what vent you may have of saffron, because this realm yields the best of the world, and the tillage may set the poor greatly in work to their relief.

Black coneys' skins. Try the vent at Cambalu, for we abound with the commodity.

Before you offer your commodities to sale, endeavour to learn what commodities the country there hath. For if you bring thither velvet, taffeta, spice, or any such commodity that you yourself desire to lade yourself home with, you must not sell yours dear, lest hereafter you purchase theirs not so cheap as you would.

Antimony. See whether they have any ample use there for it, for that we may load whole navies of it and have no use for it unless it be for some small portion in founding of bells.

A painted bellows. For that perhaps they have not the use of them.

A pot of cast iron. It is a natural commodity of this realm.

Note especially what excellent dyeing they use in these regions: see their dye houses and the materials and simples that they use about the same, and bring musters and shows of the colours and of the materials.

Take with you for your own use. All manner of engines to take fish and fowl.

Take with you those things that be in perfection of goodness. For false and sophisticated commodities shall draw you and all your commodities into contempt and ill opinion.

From 'Notes given 1580: to Mr Arthur Pet, and to Mr Charles Jackman, sent by the merchants of the Moscovy Company for the discovery of the Northeast Strait' in *The Principal Navigations, Voyages, Traffiques and Discoveries of the English Nation* by Richard Hakluyt, 1589–90 and 1598–1600

Come Buy, Come Buy

Autolycus, singing: Lawn as white as driven snow;
Cypress black as e'er was crow;
Gloves as sweet as damask roses;
Masks for faces and for noses;

Bugle bracelet, necklace amber,
Perfume for a lady's chamber;
Golden quoifs and stomachers,
For my lads to give their dears;
Pins and poking-sticks of steel –
What maids lack from head to heel.
    Come buy of me, come; come buy, come buy;
    Buy lads, or else your lasses cry:
    Come buy.

From *The Winter's Tale*, Act IV Scene iv, by William Shakespeare, c. 1610

John Tradescant's Collection

VARIETY OF RARITIES

Indian morris-bells of shells and fruits.
Indian musicall Instruments.
Indian Idol made of Feathers, in shape of a Dog.
Indian fiddle.
Spanish Timbrell.
Instrument which the Indians sound at Sun-rising.
Portugall musicall Instrument like a hoop, with divers brasse plates.
A choice piece of perspective in black Ivory case.
A Canow & Picture of an Indian with his Bow and Dart, taken 10 leagues at
    Sea. *An°.*-76.
A bundle of Tobacco, *Amazonian.*
Birds-nests from *China.*
Indian Conjurors rattle, wherewith he calls up Spirits.
Indian *Pa* God.
The Idol *Osiris. Anubis*, the sheep, the Beetle, the Dog, which the Egyptians
    worshipped. Mr. *Sandys.*
A Gamaha with *Jesus*, Joseph and *Mary*, in Italian capitall letters.
A Gamaha with a Fish in it.
A Gamaha of a Deaths-head.
A Circumcision-Knife of stone, and the instrument to take up the *praeputium*
    of silver.
Jewes Philacteries with the Commandements, writ in Hebrew.
A piece of Stone of Saint *John Baptists* Tombe.
A piece of the Stone of *Sarrigo*-Castle where *Hellen* of *Greece* was born.
A piece of the Stone of the Oracle of *Apollo.*
A piece of the Stone of *Diana*'s Tomb.

An Orange gathered from a Tree that grew over *Zebulon*'s Tombe.

Severall sorts of Magnifying glasses: Triangular, Prismes, Cylinders.

Antient Iron-Money in crosse-plates, like Anchors, preserved in *Pontefract-Castle, Yorke-shire*.

Severall Assayes of Money.

A Brazen-ball to warme the Nunnes hands.

A piece of one of the Logges of *Bagmere* in *Cheshire*, neer *Breereton*.

A Trunion of Capt: *Drake*'s Ship.

Divers sorts of Indian Jakes.

Severall sorts of Cymballs.

Cassava Bread 2 sorts.

The Padre Guardians staffe of *Jerusalem* made of a branch of one of the 70 Palme-Trees of Elam, which he gave to Sir *Tho: Roe*.

A glasse-horne for annointing Kings.

2 Roman Urnes.

A Roman sacrificing-earthen-Cup, with the word CAMPANION printed in the bottome.

Tarriers of Wood made like our Tyring-Irons.

Tarriers of Wood like Rolles to set Table-dishes on.

Indian Tresles to hang a payr of Skales on, of black varnisht wood.

The plyable Mazer wood, being warmed in water will work to any form.

Blood that rained in the *Isle of Wight*, attested by Sir *Jo: Oglander*.

A Hand of Jet usually given to Children, in *Turky*, to preserve them from Witchcraft.

From *Musæum Tradescantianum*, 1656

Two Selections from a Collection of Lost Things

RARITIES IN PICTURES

26. A fair English Lady drawn *Al Negro*, or in the Æthiopian hue excelling the original White and Red Beauty, with this Subscription, *Sed quandam volo nocte Nigriorem.*

27. Pieces and Draughts in *Caricatura*, of Princes, Cardinals and famous men; wherin, among others, the Painter hath singularly hit the signatures of a Lion and a Fox in the face of Pope *Leo* the Tenth.

28. Some Pieces *A la ventura*, or Rare Chance Pieces, either drawn at random and happening to be like some person, or drawn for some, and happening to be more like another; while the Face, mistaken by the Painter, proves a tolerable Picture of one he never saw.

29. A Draught of famous Dwarfs with this Inscription, *Nos facimus Bruti puerum nos Lagona vivum.*

30. An exact and proper delineation of all sorts of Dogs upon occasion of the practice of *Sultan Achmet*: who in a great Plague at *Constantinople* transported all the Dogs therein unto *Pera*, and from thence into a little Island, where they perished at last by Famine: as also the manner of Priests curing of mad Dogs by burning them in the forehead with Saint *Bellin's Key*.

31. A noble Picture of *Thorismund* King of the Goths as he was killed in his Palace at *Tholouse*, who being let bloud by a Surgeon, while he was bleeding, a stander by took the advantage to stab him.

32. A Picture of rare Fruits with this Inscription, *Credere quæ possis surrepta sororibus Afris.*

ANTIQUITIES AND RARITIES OF SEVERAL SORTS

6. *Mummia Thosolana*; or, The complete Head and Body of Father *Crispin*, buried long ago in the Vault of the Cordeliers at *Tholouse*, where the Skins of the dead so drie and parch up without corrupting that their persons may be known very long after, with this Inscription, *Ecce iterum Crispinus.*

7. A noble *Quandros* or Stone taken out of a Vulture's Head.

8. A large *Ostridges* Egg, whereon is neatly and fully wrought that famous Battel of *Alcazar*, in which three Kings lost their lives.

9. An *Etiudros Alberti* or Stone that is apt to be always moist: usefull unto drie tempers, and to be held in the hand in Fevers instead of Crystal, Eggs, Limmons, Cucumbers.

10. A small Viol of Water taken out of the Stones therefore called *Enhydri*, which naturally include a little Water in them, in like manner as the *Ætites* or *Aëgle* Stone doth another Stone.

11. A neat painted and gilded Cup made out of the *Confiti di Tivoli* and formed up with powder'd Egg-shells; as *Nero* is conceived to have made his *Piscina admirabilis*, singular against Fluxes to drink often therein.

12. The Skin of a Snake bred out of the Spinal Marrow of a Man.

13. Vegetable Horns mentioned by *Linschoten*, which set in the ground grow up like Plants about *Goa*.

14. An extract of the Inck of Cuttle Fishes reviving the old Remedy of *Hippocrates* in Hysterical Passions.

From *Musæum Clausum or Bibliotheca Abscondita* by
Sir Thomas Browne (1605–82)

Art, Nature's Ape

Art, natures Ape, hath many brave things done
    As th'Pyramids, the lake of Meris vast
The Pensile Orchards built in Babylon,
    Psammitch's Labyrinth. (arts Cramping task)
    Archimedes his Engins made for war.
    Romes Golden House. Titus his Theater.

The Clock at Strasburgh, Dresdens Table-Sight
    Regiamonts Fly of Steele about that flew.
Turrian's Wooden Sparrows in a flight.
    And th'Artificiall man Aquinas slew.
    Mark Scaliota's Lock, and Key and Chain
    Drawn by a Flea, in our Queen Betties reign.

Might but my pen in natures Inventory
    Its progress make, 't might make such things to jump
All of which are but Inventions Vents or glory
    Wits Wantonings, and Fancies frollicks plump.
    Within whose maws lies buried Times, and Treasures
    Embalmed up in thick dawbd sinfull pleasures.

Nature doth better work than Art: yet thine
    Out vie both works of nature and of Art.
Natures Perfection and the perfect shine
    Of Grace attend thy deed in ev'ry part.
    A Thought, a Word, and Worke of thine, will kill
    Sin, Satan, and the Curse: and Law fulfill.

From *Preparatory Meditations*, second series, no. 56,
by Edward Taylor of Massachusetts, 1703

The Bravery of Their Tinkling Ornaments

16 Moreover the LORD saith, Because the daughters of Zion are haughty,
and walk with stretched forth necks and wanton eyes, walking and
mincing as they go, and making a tinkling with their feet:

17 Therefore the Lord will smite with a scab the crown of the head of the
daughters of Zion, and the LORD will discover their secret parts.

18 In that day the Lord will take away the bravery of their tinkling ornaments about their feet, and their cauls, and their round tires like the moon,

19 The chains, and the bracelets, and the mufflers,

20 The bonnets, and the ornaments of the legs, and the headbands, and the tablets, and the earrings,

21 The rings, and nose jewels,

22 The changeable suits of apparel, and the mantles, and the wimples, and the crisping pins,

23 The glasses, and the fine linen, and the hoods, and the vails.

24 And it shall come to pass, that instead of sweet smell there shall be stink; and instead of a girdle a rent; and instead of well set hair baldness; and instead of a stomacher a girding of sackcloth; and burning instead of beauty.

From Isaiah 3

From 'A Voyage to Marry-Land; Or, The Ladies Dressing Room'

... But to go on where we left off,
Though you may think what's said enough;
This is not half that does belong
To the fantastick Female Throng:
In Pin-up Ruffles now she flaunts,
About her Sleeves are *Engageants*:
Of Ribbon, various *Echelles*,
Gloves trimm'd, and lac'd as fine as *Nell*'s.
Twelve dozen *Martial*, whole, and half,
Of *Jonquil*, *Tuberose*, (don't laugh)
Frangipan, *Orange*, *Violett*,
Narcissus, *Jassemin*, *Ambrett*:
And some of *Chicken* skin for night,
To keep her Hands plump, soft, and white;
Mouches for pushes, to be sure,
From *Paris* the *tré-fine* procure,
And *Spanish* Paper, Lip, and Cheek,
With Spittle sweetly to belick:
Nor therefore spare in the next place,

The Pocket *Sprunking* Looking-Glass;
Calembuc Combs in *Pulvil* case,
To set, and trim the Hair and Face:
And that the Cheeks may both agree,
Plumpers to fill the Cavity.
The *Settée*, *Cupée* place aright,
Frelange, Fontange, Favorite;
Monté la haut, and *Palisade,*
Sorti, Flandan, (great helps to Trade)
Burgoigne, Jardiné, Cornett,
Frilal next upper Pinner set,
Round which it does our Ladies please
To spread the Hood call'd *Rayonnés*:
Behind the Noddle every Baggage
Wears bundle *Choux,* in *English* Cabbage.
Nor *Cruches* she, nor *Confidents,*
Nor *Passagers* nor *Bergers* wants;
And when this Grace Nature denies,
An Artificial *Tour* supplies;
All which with *Meurtriers* unite,
And *Creve-Coeurs* silly Fops to smite,
Or take in Toil at *Park* or *Play,*
Nor Holy *Church* is safe, they say,
Where decent Veil was wont to hide
The modest Sex Religious Pride:
Lest these yet prove too great a Load,
'Tis all comprised in the *Commode*;
Pins tipt with Diamond Point, and head,
By which the Curls are fastened,
In radiant *Firmament* set out,
And over all the Hood *sur-tout*:
Thus Face that *Erst* near head was plac'd
Imagine now about the Wast,
For *Tour* on *Tour,* and *Tire* on *Tire,*
Like Steeple *Bow,* or *Grantham* Spire,
Or *Septizonium* once at *Rome,*
(But does not half so well become
Fair Ladies Head) you here behold
Beauty by Tyrant Mode controll'd.
The graceful *Oval,* and the *Round,*
This *Horse* Tire does quite confound;
And Ears like *Satyr,* Large and Raw,

And bony Face, and hollow Jaw;
This monstrous Dress does now reveal
Which well plac'd Curls did once conceal.
Besides all these, 'tis always meant
You furnish her Apartment,
With *Moreclack* Tapistry, Damask Bed,
Or Velvet richly embroidered:
Branches, *Brasero, Cassolets,*
A *Cofre-fort,* and Cabinets,
Vases of Silver, *Porcelan,* store
To set, and range about the Floor:
The Chimney Furniture out of Plate,
(For Iron's now quite out of date:)
Tea-Table, *Skreens,* Trunks, and Stand,
Large Looking-Glass richly *Japan'd,*
An hanging Shelf, to which belongs
Romances, Plays, and Amorous Songs;
Repeating Clocks, the hour to show
When to the Play 'tis time to go,
In Pompous Coach, or else Sedan'd
With Equipage along the *Strand,*
And with her new *Beau* Foppling mann'd.
A new Scene to us next presents,
The Dressing-Room, and Implements,
Of Toilet Plate Gilt, and Emboss'd,
And several other things of Cost:
The Table *Miroir,* one Glue Pot,
One for *Pomatum,* and what not?
Of *Washes, Unguents,* and *Cosmeticks,*
A pair of Silver Candlesticks;
Snuffers, and Snuff-dish, Boxes more,
For Powders, Patches, Waters store,
In silver Flasks, or Bottles, Cups
Cover'd, or open, to wash Chaps;
Nor may *Hungarian* Queen's be wanting,
Nor store of Spirits against fainting:
Of other waters rich, and sweet,
To sprinkle Handkerchief is meet;
D'Ange, Orange, Mill-Fleur, Myrtle,
Whole Quarts the Chamber to bequirtle:
Of Essence *rare,* and *le meilleure*
From *Rome,* from *Florence, Montpellier,*

In *Filgran Casset* to repel,
When Scent of *Gousset* does rebel,
Though powder'd *Allom* be as good
Well strew'd on and well understood;
For Vapours that offend the Lass,
Of *Sal-armoniack* a Glass:
Nor Brush for Gown, nor Oval Salver,
Nor Pincushion, nor Box of Silver,
Baskets of *Fil'gran*, long and round,
Or if *Japonian* to be found,
And the whole Town so many yield,
Calembuc Combs by dozens fill'd
You must present, and a world more,
She's a poor Miss can count her store.

From *Mundum Muliebris*, 1690; attributed to Mary Evelyn (1665–85). The
poem is followed by a 'Fop's Dictionary' which explains some, but not all,
of the purposely exotic terms.

All is Gone, All is Dust

What is become now of these great *Merchants of the earth*, and where is the
fruit *of all their labours under the Sun?* Why, truly they are *taken out of the way as
all others, and they are cut off as the tops of the eares of corn.* Their dwelling is in
the dust, and as for their place here, it lies waste, and is not known: *Nettles
and Brambles come up in it, and the Owl and the Raven dwell in it.* But if you will
visit them at their *long homes*, and knock at those *desolate doors*, you shall find
some remains of them, a heap of loathesomeness and corruption. O
miserable and sad mutations! Where is now their *pompous* and *shining train?*
Where are their *triumphs, fireworks, and feasts*, with all the *ridiculous tumults* of a
popular, prodigious pride? Where is their *purple and fine linen*, their chains of
massie gold, and sparkling ornaments of *pearls?* Where are their *Cooks* and
Carvers, their *fowlers* and *fishers?* Where are their curious *Utensils*, their *Cups* of
Agate, Crystal, and *China-earth?* Where are their sumptuous *Chambers*, where
they enclosed themselves in *Cedar, Ivory*, and *Ebony?* Where is their *Musick*,
their *soft* and *delicate dressings, pleasing motions*, and *excellency of looks?* Where
are their rich *perfumes*, costly *Conserves*, with their precious and various store
of *foreign and domestick* wines? Where are their *sons* and their *daughters* fair as
the *flowers*, straight as the *Palm-trees*, and *polished as the corners of the Temple?*
O pitiful and astonishing transformations! all is gone, all is dust, deformity,
and desolation. *Their bones are scattered in the pit, and instead of well-set hair,*

there is baldness, and loathsomeness instead of beauty. This is the state of their *bodies*, and (O blessed *Jesus!*) who knows the state of their *souls?*

From *The Mount of Olives* by Henry Vaughan, 1652

The Inventory of a Dead Beau's Possessions

Whereas the gentleman that behaved himself in a very disobedient and obstinate manner at his late trial in Sheer Lane on the 20th instant, and was carried off dead upon the taking away of his snuff-box, remains still unburied; the Company of Upholders not knowing otherwise how they should be paid, have taken his goods in execution to defray the charge of his funeral. His said effects are to be exposed to sale by auction at their office in the Haymarket on the 4th of January next, and are as follow:

A very rich tweezer-case, containing twelve instruments for the use of each hour in the day.

Four pounds of scented snuff, with three gilt snuff-boxes; one of them with an invisible hinge, and a looking-glass in the lid.

Two more of ivory, with the portraitures on their lids of two ladies of the town; the originals to be seen every night in the side-boxes of the play-house.

A sword with a steel diamond hilt, never drawn but once at May Fair.

Six clean packs of cards, a quart of orange-flower water, a pair of French scissors, a toothpick case, and an eyebrow brush.

A large glass case, containing the linen and clothes of the deceased; among which are, two embroidered suits, a pocket perspective, a dozen pair of red-heeled shoes, three pair of red silk stockings, and an amber-headed cane.

The strong-box of the deceased, wherein were found, five billet-doux, a Bath shilling, a crooked sixpence, a silk garter, a lock of hair, and three broken fans.

A press for books; containing on the upper shelf,

Three bottles of diet-drink.

Two boxes of pills.

A syringe, and other mathematical instruments.

On the second shelf are several miscellaneous works; as,

Lampoons.

Plays.

Tailors' bills.

And an almanac for the year 1700.

On the third shelf,
> A bundle of letters unopened, endorsed (in the hand of the deceased),
> 'Letters from the old gentleman.'
> Lessons for the flute.
> Toland's 'Christianity not Mysterious.' And a paper filled with patterns of several fashionable stuffs.

On the lowest shelf,
> One shoe.
> A pair of snuffers.
> A French grammar.
> A mourning hat-band: and half a bottle of usquebaugh.

There will be added to these goods, to make a complete auction, a collection of gold snuff-boxes and clouded canes, which are to continue in fashion for three months after the sale.

The whole are to be set up and prized by Charles Bubbleboy, who is to open the auction with a speech.

From *The Tatler*, December 1709

Some of the Contents of Alexander Pope's Grotto

Several Pieces of Crystal with a brown Incrustation and a Mixture of Mundic, from the *Hartz* Mines in *Germany*; a fine Piece of Gold Ore from the *Peruvian* Mines; Silver Ore from the Mines of *Mexico*; several Pieces of Silver Ore from *Old Spain*; some large Pieces of Gold Clift, from Mr Cambridge, in Gloucestershire; Lead Ore, Copper Ore, white Spar, petrified Wood, *Brazil* Pebbles, *Egyptian* Pebbles and Blood-stones, from Mr *Brinsden*. Some large Clumps of Amethyst, and several Pieces of White Spar, from the Duchess of *Cleveland*. Some fine Pieces of Red Spar, several fine Isicles, and several sorts of Fossils, from George *Littleton*, Esq; Many Pieces of Coral and petrified Moss, and many other curious Stones from the Island of *St Christopher* in the *West Indies*; with several Humming Birds and their Nests, from Anthony Brown, Esq.

From *A Plan of Mr Pope's Garden* by J. Serle, 1745

Mineral Rejoicings

Let Dew, house of Dew rejoice with Xanthenes a precious stone of an amber colour.

Let Round, house of Round rejoice with Myrmeeites a gem having an Emmet in it.

Let New, house of New rejoice with Nasamonites a gem of a sanguine colour with black veins.

Let Hook, house of Hook rejoice with Sarda a Cornelian – blessed be the name of the Lord Jesus by hook.

Let Crook, house of Crook rejoice with Ophites black spotted marble – Blessed be the name of the Lord Jesus by crook. The Lord enable me to shift.

Let Lime, house of Lime rejoice with Sandareses a kind of gem in Pliny's list.

Let Linnet, house of Linnet rejoice with Tanos, which is a mean sort of emerald.

Let Hind, house of Hind rejoice with Pæderos Opal – God be gracious to Mrs Hind, that lived at Canbury.

Let Tyrrel, house of Tyrrel rejoice with Sardius Lapis an Onyx of a black colour. God speed Hawke's Fleet.

Let Moss, house of Moss rejoice with the Pearl-Oyster behold how God has consider'd for him that lacketh.

Let Ross, house of Ross rejoice with the Great Flabber Dabber Flat Clapping Fish with hands. Vide Anson's Voyage & Psalm 98th, ix.

Let Fisher, house of Fisher rejoice with Sandastros kind of burning stone with gold drops in the body of it. God be gracious to Fisher of Cambridge & to all of his name & kindred.

Let Fuller, house of Fuller rejoice with Perileucos a precious stone with a white thread descending from its face to the bottom.

Let Thorpe, house of Thorpe rejoice with Xystios an ordinary stone of the Jasper-kind.

Let Alban, house of Alban rejoice with Scorpites a precious stone in some degree of the creatures.

Let Wand, house of Wand rejoice with Synochitis a gem supposed by Pliny to have certain magical effects.

Let Freeman, house of Freeman rejoice with Carcinias a precious stone the colour of a sea-crab. The Lord raise the landed interest.

Let Quince, house of Quince rejoice with Onychipuncta a gem of the jasper kind.

Let Manly, house of Manly rejoice with the Booby a tropical bird.

Let Fage, house of Fage rejoice with the Fiddlefish. Blessed be the name of the Lord Jesus in the fish's mouth.

Let Benning, house of Benning rejoice with the Sea-Egg. Lord have mercy on the soul of Benning's wife.

Let Singleton, house of Singleton rejoice with the Hog-Plump. Lord have mercy on the soul of Lord Vane.

Let Thickness, house of Thickness rejoice with The Papah a fruit found at Chequetan.

Let Heartly, house of Heartly rejoice with the Drummer-fish. God be gracious to Heartly of Christ, to Marsh, Hingeston & Bill.

Let Sizer, house of Sizer rejoice with Trichros a precious stone black at bottom, white atop and blood-red in the middle.

Let Chetwind, house of Chetwind rejoice with Hammocrysos, a gem with gold sands on it.

Let Branch, house of Branch rejoice with Hæmatites – Blessed be the name of the Lord Jesus THE BRANCH.

Let Dongworth, house of Dongworth rejoice with Rhymay the Bread-fruit. God be gracious to the immortal soul of Richard Dongworth.

Let Randall, house of Randall rejoice with Guavoes. God give Randall success.

Let Osborne, house of Osborne rejoice with Lithizontes a sort of carbuncle. God be gracious to the Duke of Leeds & his family.

Let Oldcastle, house of Oldcastle rejoice with Leucopthalmos. God put it in heart of King to repair & beautify Dover Castle.

Let Beeson, house of Beeson rejoice with Pyropus, carbuncle opal. God be gracious to Masters of Yoke's Place.

From *Jubilate Agno* by Christopher Smart, 1759–63

Bequests

My father died a month ago
And left me all his riches;
A feather bed, and a wooden leg,
And a pair of leather breeches.

He left me a teapot without a spout,
A cup without a handle,
A tobacco pipe without a lid,
And half a farthing candle.

Nursery rhyme, nineteenth century

Mississippi Flotsam

Another night, when we was up at the head of the island, just before daylight, here comes a frame house down, on the west side. She was a two-storey, and tilted over, considerable. We paddled out and got aboard – clumb in at an upstairs window. But it was too dark to see yet, so we made the canoe fast and set in her to wait for daylight.

The light begun to come before we got to the foot of the island. Then we looked in at the window. We could make out a bed, and a table, and two old chairs, and lots of things around about on the floor; and there was clothes hanging against the wall. There was something laying on the floor in the far corner that looked like a man. So Jim says:

'Hello, you!'

But it didn't budge. So I hollered again, and then Jim says:

'De man ain't asleep – he's dead. You hold still – I'll go en see.'

He went and bent down and looked, and says:

'It's a dead man. Yes, indeedy; naked, too. He's ben shot in de back. I reck'n he's ben dead two er three days. Come in, Huck, but doan' look at his face – it's too gashly.'

I didn't look at him at all. Jim throwed some old rags over him, but he needn't done it; I didn't want to see him. There was heaps of old greasy cards scattered around over the floor, and old whisky bottles, and a couple of masks made out of black cloth; and all over the walls was the ignorantest kind of words and pictures, made with charcoal. There was two old dirty calico dresses, and a sun-bonnet, and some women's under-clothes, hanging against the wall, and some men's clothing, too. We put the lot into the canoe; it might come good. There was a boy's old speckled straw hat on the floor; I took that too. And there was a bottle that had had milk in it; and it had a rag stopper for a baby to suck. We would a took the bottle, but it was broke. There was a seedy old chest, and an old hair trunk with the hinges broke. They stood open, but there warn't nothing left in them that was any account. The way things was scattered about, we reckoned the people left in a hurry and warn't fixed so as to carry off most of their stuff.

We got an old tin lantern, and a butcher knife without any handle, and a bran-new Barlow knife worth two bits in any store, and a lot of tallow candles, and a tin candlestick, and a gourd, and a tin cup, and a ratty old bed-quilt off the bed, and a reticule with needles and pins and beeswax and buttons and thread and all such truck in it, and a hatchet and some nails, and a fish-line as thick as my little finger, with some monstrous hooks on it, and a roll of buckskin, and a leather dog-collar, and a horse-shoe, and some vials of medicine that didn't have no label on them; and just as we was

[126]

leaving I found a tolerable good curry-comb, and Jim he found a ratty old fiddle-bow, and a wooden leg. The straps was broke off of it, but barring that, it was a good enough leg, though it was too long for me and not long enough for Jim, and we couldn't find the other one, though we hunted all around.

And so, take it all around, we made a good haul.

From *The Adventures of Huckleberry Finn* by Mark Twain, 1885

'The Street-Sellers of Second-Hand Articles'

Of these traffickers, then, there are five classes, the mere enumeration of the objects of their traffic being curious enough: –

1. *The Street-Sellers of Old Metal Articles*, such as knives, forks, and butchers' steels; saws, hammers, pincers, files, screw-drivers, planes, chisels, and other tools (more frequently those of the workers in wood than of other artisans); old scissors and shears; locks, keys, and hinges; shovels, fire-irons, trivets, chimney-cranes, fenders, and fire-guards; warming-pans (but rarely now); flat and Italian irons, curling-tongs; rings, horse-shoes, and nails; coffee and tea-pots, urns, trays, and canisters; pewter measures; scales and weights; bed-screws and keys; candlesticks and snuffers; niggards, generally called niggers (*i.e.*, false bottoms for grates); tobacco and snuff-boxes and spittoons; door-plates, numbers, knockers, and escutcheons; dog-collars and dog-chains (and other chains); gridirons; razors; coffee-mills; lamps; swords and daggers; gun and pistol-barrels and locks (and occasionally the entire weapon); bronze and cast metal figures; table, chair, and sofa castors; bell-pulls and bells; the larger buckles and other metal (most frequently brass) articles of harness furniture; compositors' sticks (the depositories of the type in the first instance); the multifarious kinds of tin-wares; stamps; cork-screws; barrel-taps; ink-stands; a multiplicity of culinary vessels and of old metal lids; footmen, broken machinery, and parts of machinery, as odd wheels, and screws of all sizes, &c., &c.

2. *The Street-Sellers of Old Linen, Cotton, and Woollen Articles*, such as old sheeting for towels; old curtains of dimity, muslin, cotton, or moreen; carpeting; blanketing for house-scouring cloths; ticking for beds and pillows; sacking for different purposes, according to its substance and quality; fringes; and stocking-legs for the supply of 'jobbing worsted,' and for re-footing . . .

3. *The Street-Sellers of Old Glass and Crockery*, including the variety of bottles, odd, or in sets, or in broken sets; pans, pitchers, wash-hand basins, and other crockery utensils; china ornaments; pier, convex, and toilet

glasses (often without the frames); pocket ink-bottles; wine, beer, and liqueur glasses; decanters; glass fish-bowls (occasionally); salt-cellars; sugar-basins; and lamp and gas glasses.

4. *The Street-Sellers of Miscellaneous Articles.* There are such as cannot properly be classified under any of the three preceding heads, and include a mass of miscellaneous commodities: Accordions and other musical instruments; brushes of all descriptions; shaving-boxes and razor-strops; baskets of many kinds; stuffed birds, with and without frames; pictures, with and without frames; desks, work-boxes, tea-caddies, and many articles of old furniture; boot-jacks and hooks; shoe-horns; cartouche-boxes; pocket and opera glasses; rules, and measures in frames; backgammon, and chess or draught boards and men, and dice; boxes of dominoes; cribbage-boards and boxes, sometimes with old packs of cards; pope-boards (boards used in playing the game of 'Pope,' or 'Pope Joan,' though rarely seen now); 'fish', or card counters of bone, ivory, or mother of pearl (an equal rarity); microscopes (occasionally); an extensive variety of broken or faded things, new or long kept, such as magic lanterns, dissected maps or histories, &c., from the toy warehouses and shops; Dutch clocks; barometers; wooden trays; shells; music and books (the latter being often odd volumes of old novels); tee-totums, and similar playthings; ladies' head-combs; umbrellas and parasols; fishing-rods and nets; reins, and other parts of cart, gig, and 'two-horse' harness; boxes full of 'odds and ends' of old leather, such as water-pipes; and a mass of imperfect metal things, which had 'better be described,' said an old dealer, 'as from a needle to an anchor.'

5. *The Street-Sellers of Old Apparel,* including the body habiliments, constituting alike men's, women's, boys', girls', and infants' attire: as well as hats, caps, gloves, belts, and stockings; shirts and shirt-fronts ('dickeys'); handkerchiefs, stocks, and neck-ties; furs, such as victorines, boas, tippets, and edgings; beavers and bonnets; and the other several, and sometimes not easily describable, articles which constitute female fashionable or ordinary wear.

I may here observe, that of the wares which once formed a portion of the stock of the street-sellers of the fourth and fifth divisions, but which are now no longer objects of street sale, were, till within the last few years, fans; back and shoulder boards (to make girls grow straight!); several things at one time thought indispensable to every well-nurtured child, such as a coral and bells; belts, sashes, scabbards, epaulettes, feathers or plumes, hard leather stocks, and other indications of the volunteer, militia, and general military spirit of the early part of the present century.

From *London Labour and the London Poor* by Henry Mayhew, 1861–2

The Deposit in the Sewers

I may premise that where the deposit is found the greatest, the sewer is in the worst state. This deposit, I find it repeatedly stated, is of a most miscellaneous character. Some of the sewers, indeed, are represented as the dust-bins and dung-hills of the immediate neighbourhood. The deposit has been found to contain all the ingredients from the breweries, the gas-works, and the several chemical and mineral manufactories; dead dogs, cats, kittens, and rats; offal from slaughter-houses, sometimes even including the entrails of the animals; street-pavement dirt of every variety; vegetable refuse; stable-dung; the refuse of pig-styes; night-soil; ashes; tin kettles and pans (pansherds); broken stoneware, as jars, pitchers, flower-pots, &c.; bricks; pieces of wood; rotten mortar and rubbish of different kinds; and even rags.

From *London Labour and the London Poor* by Henry Mayhew, 1861–2

An Endless Procession of White

She had entered the household linen gallery in order to reach the handkerchief department at the end of it. It was an endless procession of white: the white of cotton, of dimity, of piqués, of calicoes; the white of madapollam, nainsook, muslin and tarlatan; then, in enormous piles built of lengths of material alternating like stones hewn in cubes, came the linens, coarse linens and fine linens of every width, white or unbleached, made from pure flax bleached in the meadows; then the whole thing began all over again and departments for every kind of made-up linen succeeded each other; there was household linen, table linen, kitchen linen, an endless avalanche of white, there were sheets and pillow-cases, innumerable different kinds of table-napkins and table-cloths, of aprons and dishcloths. And as Denise passed through, people were lining her way and the salutations were continuing. In the linen department Baugé had dashed forward to give her a smile, as if she were the well-loved queen of the shop. Finally, after having gone through the blankets department, a room decked with white banners, she went into the handkerchiefs, where the ingenious decorations were sending the crowd into ecstasies – it was all white columns, white pyramids, white castles, complicated architecture built up of nothing but handkerchiefs, handkerchiefs made of lawn, of cambric, of Irish linen, of Chinese silk, initialed handkerchiefs, handkerchiefs embroidered with satin-stitch, trimmed with lace, hemstitched, and with woven designs on them, a whole

town of white bricks of infinite variety, standing out like a mirage against an
oriental sky warmed to white heat.

From *Au Bonheur des Dames* by Émile Zola (1840–1902),
translated from the French by April Fitzlyon

Three Decadent Collections

(i) STRANGE MUSICAL INSTRUMENTS

He collected together from all parts of the world the strangest instruments
that could be found, either in the tombs of dead nations or among the few
savage tribes that have survived contact with Western civilisations, and
loved to touch and try them. He had the mysterious *furuparis* of the Rio
Negro Indians, that women are not allowed to look at, and that even youths
may not see till they have been subjected to fasting and scourging, and the
earthen jars of the Peruvians that have the shrill cries of birds, and flutes of
human bones such as Alfonso de Ovalle heard in Chili, and the sonorous
green jaspers that are found near Cuzco and give forth a note of singular
sweetness. He had painted gourds filled with pebbles that rattled when they
were shaken; the long *clarin* of the Mexicans, into which the performer does
not blow, but through which he inhales the air; the harsh *ture* of the Amazon
tribes, that is sounded by the sentinels who sit all day long in high trees, and
can be heard, it is said, at a distance of three leagues; the *teponaƺili*, that has
two vibrating tongues of wood, and is beaten with sticks that are smeared
with an elastic gum obtained from the milky juice of plants; the *yotl*-bells of
the Aztecs, that are hung in clusters like grapes; and a huge cylindrical
drum, covered with the skins of great serpents, like the one that Bernal Diaz
saw when he went with Cortes into the Mexican temple, and of whose
doleful sound he has left us so vivid a description. The fantastic character of
these instruments fascinated him and he felt a curious delight in the thought
that Art, like Nature, has her monsters, things of bestial shape and with
hideous voices.

(ii) FABRICS

And so, for a whole year, he sought to accumulate the most exquisite
specimens that he could find of textile and embroidered work, getting the
dainty Delhi muslins, finely wrought with gold-thread palmates, and
stitched over with iridescent beetles' wings; the Dacca gauzes, that from
their transparency are known in the East as 'woven air,' and 'running
water,' and 'evening dew;' strange figured cloths from Java; elaborate
yellow Chinese hangings; books bound in tawny satins or fair blue silks,
and wrought with *fleurs de lys*, birds, and images; veils of *lacis* worked in

[130]

Hungary point; Sicilian brocades, and stiff Spanish velvets; Georgian work with its gilt coins, and Japanese *Foukousas* with their green-toned golds and their marvellously-plumaged birds.

(iii) RENAISSANCE VILLAINS

Over and over again Dorian used to read this fantastic chapter, and the two chapters immediately following, in which, as in some curious tapestries or cunningly-wrought enamels, were pictured the awful and beautiful forms of those whom Vice and Blood and Weariness had made monstrous or mad; Filippo, Duke of Milan, who slew his wife, and painted her lips with a scarlet poison that her lover might suck death from the dead thing he fondled; Pietro Barbi, the Venetian, known as Paul the Second, who sought in his vanity to assume the title of Formosus, and whose tiara, valued at two hundred thousand florins, was bought at the price of a terrible sin; Gian Maria Visconti, who used hounds to chase living men, and whose murdered body was covered with roses by a harlot who had loved him; the Borgia on his white horse, with Fratricide riding beside him, and his mantle stained with the blood of Perotto; Pietro Riario, the young Cardinal Archbishop of Florence, child and minion of Sixtus IV, whose beauty was equalled only by his debauchery, and who received Leonora of Aragon in a pavilion of white and crimson silk, filled with nymphs and centaurs, and gilded a boy that he might serve at the feast as Ganymede or Hylas; Ezzelin, whose melancholy could be cured only by the spectacle of death, and who had a passion for red blood, as other men have for red wine – the son of the Fiend, as was reported, and one who had cheated his father at dice when gambling with him for his own soul; Giambattista Cibo, who in mockery took the name of Innocent, and into whose torpid veins the blood of three lads was infused by a Jewish doctor; Sigismondo Malatesta, the lover of Isotta, and the lord of Rimini, whose effigy was burned at Rome as the enemy of God and man, who strangled Polyssena with a napkin, and gave poison to Ginevra d'Este in a cup of emerald, and in honour of a shameful passion built a pagan church for Christian worship; Charles VI, who had so wildly adored his brother's wife that a leper had warned him of the insanity that was coming on him, and who, when his brain had sickened and grown strange, could only be soothed by Saracen cards painted with the images of Love and Death and Madness; and, in his trimmed jerkin and jewelled cap and acanthus-like curls, Grifonetto Baglioni, who slew Astorre with his bride, and Simonetto with his page, and whose comeliness was such that, as he lay dying in the yellow piazza of Perugia, those who had hated him could not choose but weep, and Atlanta, who had cursed him, blessed him.

From *The Picture of Dorian Gray* by Oscar Wilde, 1891

Collections

Nowadays it's rather nobby
To regard one's private hobby
As the objects of one's tenderest affections;
Some excel at Alpine climbing,
Others have a taste for rhyming,
While a lot of people go in for collections.

Such as prints by Hiroshigi,
Edelweiss from off the Rigi,
Jacobean soup tureens,
Early types of limousines,
Pipes constructed from a dry cob,
Baseball hits by Mr Ty Cobb,
Locks of Missus Browning's hair,
Photographs of Ina Claire,
First editions still uncut,
Daily pranks of Jeff and Mutt,
Della Robbia singing boys,
Signatures of Alfred Noyes,
Fancy bantams,
Grecian vases,
Tropic beetles,
Irish laces,
But my favourite pastime
Is collecting country places.

I've a shooting box in Scotland,
I've a château in Touraine,
I've a silly little chalet
In the Interlaken Valley,
I've a hacienda in Spain,
I've a private fjord in Norway,
I've a villa close to Rome,
And in traveling
It's really quite a comfort to know
That you're never far from home!

From 'I've a Shooting Box in Scotland' by Cole Porter, 1916

Antiquities in an Airless Cellar in Damascus

The hotel is owned by M. Alouf, whose children inhabit the top floor. One evening he led us into an airless cellar lined with glass cases and a safe. From these he took the following objects:

A pair of big silver bowls, stamped with Christian symbols and a picture of the Annunciation.

A document written on mud-coloured cloth, between three and four feet long and eighteen inches broad, purporting to be the will of Abu Bakr, the first Caliph, and said to have been brought from Medina by the family of King Hussein in 1925.

A Byzantine bottle of dark-blue glass as thin as an egg-shell, unbroken, and about ten inches high.

A gold Hellenistic head, with parted lips, glass eyes, and bright blue eyebrows.

A gold mummy in a trunk.

And a silver statuette nine and a half inches tall, which, for lack of anything to compare it with, M. Alouf called Hittite. This object, if genuine, must be one of the most remarkable discoveries of recent years in the Near East. The figure is that of a man, with broad shoulders and narrow hips. On his head he wears a pointed cap as tall as his own body. His left arm is broken; his right carries a horned bull in its crook and holds a sceptre. Round the waist are bands of wire. This wire, the sceptre, the tail and horns of the bull, and the cap are all of gold. And the gold is so pliable that M. Alouf gaily bent the sceptre at a right-angle and put it straight again. No persuasions could induce him to let me photograph the object. One wonders when and how it will be rescued from that cellar.

From *The Road to Oxiana* by Robert Byron, 1937

'Inventory'

To reach it, a ladder has to be set up. There is no stair.
What can we be looking for in the attic
but the accumulation of disorder?
There is a smell of damp.
The late afternoon enters by way of the laundry.
The ceiling beams loom close, and the floor has rotted.
Nobody dares to put a foot on it.
A folding cot, broken.

A few useless tools,
the dead one's wheelchair.
The base for a lamp.
A Paraguayan hammock with tassels, all frayed away.
Equipment and papers.
An engraving of Aparicio Saravia's general staff.
An old charcoal iron.
A clock stopped in time, with a broken pendulum.
A peeling gilt frame, with no canvas.
A cardboard chessboard, and some broken chessmen.
A stove with only two legs.
A chest made of leather.
A mildewed copy of Foxe's *Book of Martyrs*, in intricate Gothic
    lettering.
A photograph which might be of anybody.
A worn skin, once a tiger's.
A key which has lost its lock.
What can we be looking for in the attic
except the flotsam of disorder?
To forgetting, to all forgotten objects, I have just erected
    this monument
(unquestionably less durable than bronze) which will be lost
    among them.

From *El oro de los tigres* by Jorge Luis Borges, 1972,
translated from the Spanish by Alastair Reid

Four

THE LISTS OF
THE HEART

We see in Beauty certain airs are found,
Which not one Grace can make, but all compound.

KATHERINE PHILIPS ('ORINDA')

O flouds, O fires, O suns, O showers,
Mixt, and made friends by loves sweet powers.

RICHARD CRASHAW

He called her a melon, a pineapple, an olive tree,
an emerald, and a fox in the snow all
in the space of three seconds . . .

VIRGINIA WOOLF

Love is Wele, Love is Wo

Love is soft, love is swete, love is good sware;
Love is much tene, love is muchel care.
Love is blissene mest, love is bot yare;
Love is wondred and wo with for to fare.

Love is hap, who it laveth; love is good hele.
Love is lecher and less, and leef for to tele.
Love is doughty in the world with for to dele.
Love maketh in the land many unlele.

Love is stalwarde and strong to striden on stede.
Love is loveliche a thing to wommane nede.
Love is hardy and hot as glowinde glede.
Love maketh many may with teres to wede.

Love hath his steward by sty and by strete.
Love maketh many may hire wonges to wete.
Love is hap, who it haveth, on for to hete.
Love is wis, love is war, and wilful ansete.

Love is the softeste thing in herte may slepe.
Love is craft, love is good with cares to kepe.
Love is lees, love is leef, love is longinge.
Love is fol, love is fast, love is frovringe.
Love is sellich an thing, whoso shal sooth singe.

Love is wele, love is wo, love is gladhede.
Love is lif, love is deth, love may us fede.

Were love al so londdrey as he is first kene,
It were the wordlokste thing in worlde were, ich wene.

It is y-said in an song, sooth is y-sene,
Love comseth with care and endeth with tene,
Mid lavedy, mid wive, mid maide, mid quene.

Anon., medieval

If Love In These Be Founded

To live in hell, and heaven to behold;
  To welcome life, and die a living death;
To sweat with heat, and yet be freezing cold;
  To grasp at stars, and lie the earth beneath;
To tread a maze that never shall have end;
  To burn in sighs, and starve in daily tears;
To climb a hill, and never to descend;
  Giants to kill, and quake at childish fears;
To pine for food, and watch th'Hesperian tree;
  To thirst for drink, and nectar still to draw;
To live accursed, whom men hold blest to be,
  And weep those wrongs which never creature saw:
    If this be love, if love in these be founded,
    My heart is love, for these in it are grounded.

From 'Sonnets to Diana' by Henry Constable, 1592–4

Love

'Tis very much like Light, a thing that every Body Knows, and yet none
can tell what to make of it: 'Tis not Money, Fortune, Joynture, Raving,
Stabbing, Hanging, Romancing, Flouncing, Swearing, Ramping, Desiring,
Fighting, Dying, though all those have been, are, and still will be mistaken
and miscalled for it.

From the definition of 'Love' in The Ladies' Dictionary, 1694

Romance

– The play was bad even in comparison with *1818* the Augustan age of the
Drama, 'Comme on sait' as Voltaire says. – the whole was made up of a
virtuous young woman, an indignant brother, a suspecting lover, a libertine
prince, a gratuitous villain, a street in Naples, a Cypress grove, lillies &
roses, virtue and vice, a bloody sword, a spangled jacket, One Lady Olivia,
One Miss ONeil alias Evadné, alias Bellamira, alias – Alias – Yea & I say

unto you a greater than Elias – there was Abbot, & talking of Abbot his name puts me in mind of a Spelling book lesson, descriptive of the whole Dramatis personae – Abbot – Abbess – Actor – Actress –

From a letter by John Keats to George and Georgiana Keats, Feb–May 1819

'Out of Sight in the Direction of my Body'

All the trees all their boughs all their leaves
The grass at the base the rocks the massed houses
Afar the sea that thine eye washes
Those images of one day and the next
The vices the virtues that are so imperfect
The transparence of men in a fume from thy dour questing
Thy fixed ideas virgin-lipped leaden-hearted
The vices the virtues that are so imperfect
The eyes consenting resembling the eyes thou didst vanquish
The confusion of the bodies the lassitudes the ardours
The imitation of the words the attitudes the ideas
The vices the virtues that are so imperfect

Love, is man unfinished.

Paul Éluard (1895–1952), translated from the French by Samuel Beckett

'Casabianca'

Love's the boy stood on the burning deck
trying to recite 'The boy stood on
the burning deck.' Love's the son
      stood stammering elocution
      while the poor ship in flames went down.

Love's the obstinate boy, the ship,
even the swimming sailors, who
would like a schoolroom platform, too,
      or an excuse to stay
      on deck. And love's the burning boy.

Elizabeth Bishop (1911–79)

Intellectual Discussion

... No honey, ah suspect you-all
Of bein' intellectual
And so, instead of gushin' on,
Let's have a big discussion on
Timidity, stupidity, solidity, frigidity,
Aridity, turbidity, Manhattan, and viscidity,
Fatality, morality, legality, finality,
Neutrality, reality, or Southern hospitality,
Pomposity, verbosity,
You're losing your velocity,
But let's not talk about love.

> From 'Let's Not Talk About Love', in *Let's Face It*
> by Cole Porter, 1941

The Shepherd's Enticements

Thou shalt eat curds and cream, all the year lasting;
And drink the crystal stream, pleasant in tasting;
Whig and whey whilst thou burst, and bramble-berries,
Pie-lids and pasty-crust, pears, plums, and cherries.
  Thy garments shall be thin,
  Made of a wether's skin –
  Yet all not worth a pin!
   Phyllida flouts me.

I found a stock-dove's nest, and thou shalt have it.
The cheese-cake, in my chest, for thee I save it.
I will give thee rush-rings, key-nobs, and cushnets,
Pence, purse, and other things, bells, beads, and bracelets.
  My sheep-hook, and my dog,
  My bottle, and my bag –
  Yet all not worth a rag!
   Phyllida flouts me.

> From 'Phyllida Flouts Me', anon., pre-1603

Mr Wilde's Presents

Even when I am stripped of all I have, and am ever to have, and am granted a discharge as a hopeless Insolvent, I have still got to pay my debts. The Savoy dinners – the clear turtle soup, the luscious ortolans wrapped in their crinkled Sicilian vine-leaves, the heavy amber-coloured, indeed almost amber-scented champagne – Dagonet 1880, I think, was your favourite wine? – all have still to be paid for. The suppers at Willis's, the special *cuvée* of Perrier-Jouet reserved always for us, the wonderful *pâtés* procured directly from Strasburg, the marvellous *fine champagne* served always at the bottom of great bell-shaped glasses that its bouquet might be the better savoured by the true epicures of what was really exquisite in life – these cannot be left unpaid, as bad debts of a dishonest *client*. Even the dainty sleeve-links – four heart-shaped moonstones of silver mist, girdled by alternate ruby and diamond for their setting – that I designed, and had made at Henry Lewis's as a special little present to you, to celebrate the success of my second comedy – these even – though I believe you sold them for a song a few months afterwards – have to be paid for.

From *De Profundis* by Oscar Wilde, written to Lord Alfred Douglas from Reading Gaol, 1897

Why Do I Love?

... 'Tis not his Face; I've sence enough to see,
That is not good, though doated on by me:
Nor is't his Tongue, that has this Conquest won;
For that at least is equall'd by my own;
His Carriage can to none obliging be,
'Tis Rude, Affected, full of Vanity:
Strangely Ill-natur'd, Peevish, and Unkind,
Unconstant, False, to Jealousie inclin'd;
His Temper cou'd not have so great a Pow'r,
'Tis mutable, and changes every hour:
Those vigorous Years that Women so Adore,
Are past in him: he's twice my Age and more;
And yet I love this false, this worthless Man,
With all the Passion that a Woman can ...

From 'To one that ask'd me why I lov'd *J.G.*' by 'Ephelia', in *Female Poems on Several Occasions*, 1679

Bérénice Enumerates the Triumph of Titus

Bérénice: Le temps n'est plus, Phénice, où je pouvais trembler.
Titus m'aime, il peut tout, il n'a plus qu'à parler.
Il verra le sénat m'apporter ses hommages,
Et le peuple, de fleurs couronner ses images.
De cette nuit, Phénice, as-tu vu la splendeur?
Tes yeux ne sonts-ils pas tout pleins de sa grandeur?
Ces flambeaux, ce bûcher, cette nuit enflamée,
Ces aigles, ces faisceaux, ce peuple, cette armée,
Cette foule de rois, ces consuls, ce sénat,
Qui tous, de mon amant empruntaient leur éclat;
Cette pourpre, cet or, que rehaussait sa gloire,
Et ces lauriers encor témoins de sa victoire;
Tous ces yeux qu'on voyait venir de toutes parts
Confondre sur lui seul leurs avides regards;
Ce port majestueux, cette doux présence.

    Bérénice: The time for trembling's past, I've Titus' love.
He can do anything. He's but to speak.
He'll see the senate bow the knee to me,
The people crown his images with flowers.
The splendour of that night did you behold?
Are not your eyes full of his majesty?
This pyre, these torches, this inflamèd night.
These eagles, fasces, people, army, and
This host of kings, consuls and senators,
Borrowing their radiance from my beloved;
This gold, this purple that his glory gilds,
These laurels, witness of his victory;
And all of these eyes gazing from every side
Focused on him alone their eager looks;
This royal carriage and this gentleness.

      From *Bérénice* by Jean Racine, 1670, translated from the
French by John Cairncross

'To Electra'

More white than whitest Lillies far,
Or Snow, or whitest Swans you are:
More white than are the whitest Creames,
Or Moone-light tinselling the streames:
More white than *Pearls*, or *Juno's* thigh;
Or *Pelops* Arme of *Yvorie*.
True, I confesse; such Whites as these
May me delight, not fully please:
Till, like *Ixion's* Cloud you be
White, warme, and soft to lye with me.

From *Hesperides* by Robert Herrick, 1648

Fedele's Song

I serve a mistress whiter than the snow,
  Straighter than cedar, brighter than the glass,
Finer in trip and swifter than the roe,
  More pleasant than the field of flowering grass;
More gladsome to my withering joys that fade,
Than winter's sun or summer's cooling shade.

Sweeter than swelling grape of ripest wine,
  Softer than feathers of the fairest swan,
Smoother than jet, more stately than the pine,
  Fresher than poplar, smaller than my span,
Clearer than beauty's fiery pointed beam,
Or icy crust of crystal's frozen stream.

Yet is she curster than the bear by kind,
  And harder-hearted than the aged oak,
More glib than oil, more fickle than the wind,
  Stiffer than steel, no sooner bent but broke.
Lo! thus my service is a lasting sore;
Yet will I serve, although I die therefore.

From *Fedele and Fortunio* by Anthony Munday, 1585

Stella's Kiss

Sweet kiss, thy sweets I fain would sweetly indite
Which even of sweetness sweetest sweetener art,
Pleasingst consort, where each sense holds a part,
Which, coupling doves, guides Venus' chariot right;
Best charge and bravest retrait in Cupid's fight,
A double key which opens to the heart,
Most rich when most his riches it impart;
Nest of young joys, schoolmaster of delight,
Teaching the means at once to take and give;
The friendly fray, where blows both wound and heal,
The pretty death, while each in other live.
Poor hope's first wealth, hostage of promist weal,
Breakfast of love. But lo, lo, where she is,
Cease we to praise: now pray we for a kiss.

From *Astrophel and Stella* by Sir Philip Sidney (1554–86)

Lovers' Comparisons

All the gracious elogies, metaphors, hyperbolical comparisons of the best things in the world, the most glorious names; whatsoever, I say, is pleasant, amiable, sweet, grateful, and delicious, are too little for her.

> *Phoebo pulchrior et sorore Phoebi.*
> His Phoebe is so fair, she is so bright,
> She dims the sun's lustre, and the moon's light.

Stars, suns, moons, metals, sweet-smelling flowers, odours, perfumes, colours, gold, silver, ivory, pearls, precious stones, snow, painted birds, doves, honey, sugar, spice, cannot express her, so soft, so tender, so radiant, sweet, so fair is she.

From *The Anatomy of Melancholy* by Robert Burton, 1621

Olivia's Face

Viola: 'Tis beauty truly blent, whose red and white
Nature's own sweet and cunning hand laid on.
Lady, you are the cruell'st she alive,
If you will leave these graces to the grave,
And leave the world no copy.
Olivia: O, sir, I will not be so hard-hearted; I will give out divers schedules
of my beauty. It shall be inventoried, and every particle and utensil labell'd
to my will: as – item, two lips indifferent red; item, two grey eyes with lids
to them; item, one neck, one chin, and so forth. Were you sent hither to
praise me?

From *Twelfth Night*, Act I Scene v, by William Shakespeare, 1600

Sonnet

Il n'est point tant de barques à Venise,
D'huitres à Bourg, de lièvres en Champagne,
D'ours en Savoie et de veaux en Bretagne,
De cygnes blancs le long de la Tamise;

Ni tant d'amours se traitant en l'église,
Ni différends aux peuples d'Allemagne,
Ni tant de gloire à un seigneur d'Espagne,
Ni tant se trouve à la cour de feintise;

Ni tant y a de monstres en Afrique,
D'opinions en une république,
Ni de pardons à Rome aux jours de fête;

Ni d'avarice aux hommes de pratique,
Ni d'arguments en une Sorbonnique,
Que m'amie a de lunes en la tête.

Mellin de Saint-Gelais (1491–1558)

'You're the Top'

You're the top!
You're the Colosseum.
You're the top!
You're the Louvre Museum.
You're a melody from a symphony by Strauss,
You're a Bendel bonnet,
A Shakespeare sonnet,
You're Mickey Mouse.
You're the Nile,
You're the Tow'r of Pisa,
You're the smile
On the Mona Lisa.
I'm a worthless check, a total wreck, a flop,
But if, baby, I'm the bottom
You're the top!

You're the top!
You're Mahatma Gandhi.
You're the top!
You're Napoleon brandy.
You're the purple light of a summer night in Spain,
You're the National Gall'ry,
You're Garbo's sal'ry,
You're cellophane.
You're sublime,
You're a turkey dinner,
You're the time
Of the Derby winner.
I'm a toy balloon that is fated soon to pop,
But if, baby, I'm the bottom
You're the top!

You're the top!
You're a Ritz hot toddy.
You're the top!
You're a Brewster body.
You're the boats that glide on the sleepy Zuider Zee,
You're Nathan panning,
You're Bishop Manning,

You're broccoli.
You're a prize,
You're a night at Coney,
You're the eyes
Of Irene Bordoni.
I'm a broken doll, a fol-de-rol, a blop,
But if, baby, I'm the bottom
You're the top!

You're the top!
You're an Arrow collar.
You're the top!
You're a Coolidge dollar.
You're the nimble tread of the feet of Fred Astaire,
You're an O'Neill drama,
You're Whistler's mama,
You're Camembert.
You're a rose,
You're Inferno's Dante,
You're the nose
Of the great Durante.
I'm just in the way, as the French would say
'De trop,'
But if, baby, I'm the bottom
You're the top!

You're the top!
You're a Waldorf salad.
You're the top!
You're a Berlin ballad.
You're a baby grand of a lady and a gent,
You're an old Dutch master,
You're Mrs Astor,
You're Pepsodent.
You're romance,
You're the steppes of Russia,
You're the pants on a Roxy usher.
I'm a lazy lout that's just about to stop,
But if, baby, I'm the bottom
You're the top!

You're the top!
You're a dance in Bali.
You're the top!
You're a hot tamale.
You're an angel, you, simply too, too, too diveen,
You're a Botticelli,
You're Keats,
You're Shelley,
You're Ovaltine.
You're a boon,
You're the dam at Boulder,
You're the moon over Mae West's shoulder.
I'm the nominee of the G.O.P. or GOP,
But if, baby, I'm the bottom
You're the top!

You're the top!
You're the Tower of Babel.
You're the top!
You're the Whitney Stable.
By the river Rhine,
You're a sturdy stein of beer,
You're a dress from Saks's,
You're next year's taxes,
You're stratosphere.
You're my thoist,
You're a Drumstick Lipstick,
You're da foist
In da Irish Svipstick.
I'm a frightened frog
That can find no log
To hop,
But if, baby, I'm the bottom
You're the top!

From *Anything Goes* by Cole Porter, 1934

Specifications for a Perfect Lover

A well-tam'd Heart,
For whose more noble smart,
Love may bee long chusing a Dart.

Eyes, that bestow
Full quivers on loves Bow;
Yet pay lesse Arrowes than they owe.

Smiles, that can warme
The blood, yet teach a charme,
That Chastity shall take no harme.

Blushes, that bin
The burnish of no sin,
Nor flames of ought too hot within.

Joyes, that confesse,
Vertue their Mistresse,
And have no other head to dress.

Fears, fond and flight,
As the coy Brides, when Night
First does the longing lover right.

Teares, quickly fled,
And vaine, as those are shed
For a dying Maidenhead.

Dayes, that need borrow
No part of their good Morrow
From a fore spent night of sorrow.

Dayes, that in spight
Of Darkenesse, by the Light
Of a cleere mind are Day all Night.

Nights, sweet as they,
Made short by lovers play,
Yet long for th'absence of the Day.

Life, that dares send
A challenge to his end,
And when it comes say *Welcome Friend.*

Sydnaean showers
Of sweet discourse, whose powers
Can Crowne old Winters head with flowers,

Soft silken Houres,
Open sunnes; shady Bowers,
Bove all; Nothing within that lowres.

From 'Wishes. To his (supposed) Mistresse' by Richard Crashaw, 1646

'Of a faire woman: translated out of Casaneus his Catalogus gloriae mundi'

These thirty things that *Hellens* fame did raise,
A Dame should haue that seeks for beuties praise:
Three bright, three blacke, three red, 3. short, 3. tall,
Three thick, three thin, three close, 3. wide, 3. small:
Her skin, and teeth, must be cleare, bright, and neat,
Her browes, eyes, priuy parts, as blacke as Ieat:
Her cheekes, lips, nayles, must haue vermillian hiew,
Her hands, hayre, height, must haue ful length to view.
Her teeth, foote, eares, all short, no length allowes,
Large brests, large hips, large space between the browes,
A narrow mouth, small waste, streight [   ]
Her fingers, hayre, and lips, but thin and slender:
Thigh, belly, neck, should be full smooth and round,
Nose, head and teats, the least that can be found.
    Sith few, or none, perfection such attaine,
    But few or none are fayre, the case is plaine.

From the *Epigrams* of Sir John Harington (1561–1612)

The Ten Properties a Horse Shares with a Woman

The fyrst is, to be mery of chere, the seconde, to be well paced, the thyrde is to have a brode foreheed, the fourth, to have brode buttockes, the fyfthe, to be harde of warde, the syxte, to be easy to lepe uppon, the vii to be good at a longe journeye, the viii to be well sturrynge under a man, the ix to be alwaye besye with the mouthe, the tenth, ever to be chowynge on the brydell.

From *The Boke of Husbandry* by Anthony Fitzherbert

'Love Dislikes Nothing'

Whatsoever thing I see,
Rich or poore although it be;
'Tis a Mistresse unto mee.

Be my Girle, or faire or browne,
Do's she smile, or do's she frowne:
Still I write a Sweet-heart downe.

Be she rough, or smooth of skin;
When I touch, I then begin
For to let Affection in.

Be she bald, or do's she weare
Locks incurl'd of other haire;
I shall find enchantment there.

Be she whole, or be she rent,
So my fancie be content,
She's to me most excellent.

Be she fat, or be she leane,
Be she sluttish, be she cleane,
I'm a man for ev'ry Sceane.

From *Hesperides* by Robert Herrick, 1648

'I Can Love Both Fair and Brown'

I can love both faire and browne,
Her whom abundance melts, and her whom wants betraies,
Her who loves lonenesse best, and her who maskes and plaies,
Her whom the country form'd, and whom the town,
Her who believes, and her who tries,
Her who still weepes with spungie eyes,
And her who is dry corke, and never cries;
I can love her, and her, and you and you,
I can love any, so she be not true.

From 'The Indifferent' by John Donne (1572–1631)

The Catalogue Aria

Leporello: Madamina, il catalogo e questo
Delle belle che amò il padron mio,
Un catalogo egli è che he fatto io –
Osservato, leggete con me.

In Italia seicento e quaranta,
In Germania duecento e trent'una,
Cento in Francia, in Turchia novantuna,
Ma in Ispagna son gia mille e trè!

V'han fra queste contadine,
Cameriere, Cittadine,
V'han contesse, baronesse,
Marchesene, principesse,
E v'han donne d'ogni grado,
D'ogni forma, d'ogni età.
Nella bionda egli ha usanza
Di lodar la gentilezza,
Nella bruna la costanza,
Nella bianca la dolcezza
Vuol d'inverno la grassotta,
Vuol d'estate la magrotta,
E la grande maestosa,
La piccina è ognor vezzosa!

[151]

Delle vecchie fà conquista
Pel piacer di porle in lista,
Sua passion predominante
È la giovin principiante,
Non si picca se sia ricca,
Se sia brutta, se sia bella,
Purchè porti la gonnella,
Voi sapete, quel che fà.

From Lorenzo da Ponte's libretto to Mozart's *Don Giovanni*, 1787

I Have Had Them All

– So Lauderdale has been telling a story! – I suppose this is my reward for presenting him at the Countess Benzone's – & shewing him – what attention I could. – Which 'piece' does he mean? – since last year I have run the Gauntlet; – is it the Tarruscelli – the Da Mosti – the Spineda – the Lotti – the Rizzato – the Eleanora – the Carlotta – the Giulietta – the Alvisi – the Zambieri – The Eleanora da Bezzi – (who was the King of Naples' Gioaschino's mistress – at least one of them) – the Theresina of Mazzurati – the Glettenheimer – & her Sister – the Liugia & her mother – the Fornaretta – the Santa – the Caligari – the Portiera – the Bolognese figurante – the Tentora and her sister – cum multi aliis? – some of them are Countesses – & some of them Cobblers wives – some noble – some middling – some low – & all whores – which does the damned old 'Ladro – & porco fottuto' mean? – I have had them all & thrice as many to boot since 1817 –

From a letter by Lord Byron from Venice, 19 January 1819

So Many Beaus, Such a Number of Plumeys

Elaria: Thy Eyes are always laughing, Bellemante.
Bellemante: And so would yours had they been so well imployed as mine, this Morning. I have been at the Chapel; and seen so many Beaus, such a number of Plumeys, I cou'd not tell which I shou'd look on most, sometimes my heart was charm'd with the gay Blonding, then with the Melancholy Noir, annon the amiable brunet, sometimes the bashful, then again the bold; the little now, anon the lovely tall! In fine, my Dear, I was embarass'd on all sides, I did nothing but deal my heart *tout au toore*.

From *The Emperor of the Moon* by Aphra Behn, 1687

[152]

The Ingredients of Boys and Girls

What are little boys made of?
Frogs and snails and puppy-dogs' tails,
That's what little boys are made of.
What are little girls made of?
Sugar and spice and all things nice,
That's what little girls are made of.

Traditional

'Upon Some Women'

Thou who wilt not love, doe this;
Learne of me what Woman is.
Something made of thred and thrumme;
A meere Botch of all and some.
Pieces, patches, ropes of haire;
In-laid Garbage ev'ry where.
Out-side silk, and out-side Lawne;
Sceanes to cheat us neatly drawne.
False in legs, and false in thighes;
False in breast, teeth, haire, and eyes:
False in head, and false enough;
Onely true in shreds and stuffe.

From Hesperides by Robert Herrick, 1648

Blind Love

Love is blind, as the saying is, Cupid's blind, and so are all his followers.
Quisquis amat ranam, ranam putat esse Dianam. Every lover admires his
mistress, though she be very deformed of herself, ill-favoured, wrinkled,
pimpled, pale, red, yellow, tanned, tallow-faced, have a swollen juggler's
platter face, or a thin, lean, chitty face, have clouds in her face, be crooked,
dry, bald, goggle-eyed, blear-eyed, or with staring eyes, she looks like a
squis'd cat, hold her head still awry, heavy, dull, hollow-eyed, black or
yellow about the eyes, or squint-eyed, sparrow-mouthed, Persian hook-
nosed, have a sharp fox-nose, a red nose, China flat, great nose, *nare simo*

[153]

patuloque, a nose like a promontory, gubber-tushed, rotten teeth, black, uneven, brown teeth, beetle-browed, a witch's beard, her breath stink all over the room, her nose drop winter and summer, with a Bavarian poke under her chin, a sharp chin, lave-eared, with a long crane's neck, which stands awry too, *pendulus mammis*, 'her dugs like two double jugs,' or else no dugs, in that other extreme, bloody-fallen fingers, she have filthy, long unpared nails, scabbed hands or wrists, a tanned skin, a rotten carcass, crooked back, she stoops, is lame, splay-footed, 'as slender in the middle as a cow in the waist,' gouty legs, her ankles hang over her shoes, her feet stink, she breed lice, a mere changeling, a very monster, an oaf imperfect, her whole complexion savours, an harsh voice, incondite gesture, vile gait, a vast virago, or an ugly tit, a slug, a fat fustilugs, a truss, a long lean rawbone, a skeleton, a sneaker (*si qua latent meliora puta*), and to thy judgment looks like a mard in a lanthorn, whom thou couldst not fancy for a world, but hatest, loathest, and wouldest have spit in her face, or blow thy nose in her bosom, *remedium amoris* to another man, a dowdy, a slut, a scold, a nasty, rank, rammy, filthy, beastly quean, dishonest peradventure, obscene, base, beggarly, rude, foolish, untaught, peevish, Irus' daughter, Thersites' sister, Grobian's scholar; if he loves her once, he admires her for all this, he takes no notice of any such errors or imperfections of body or mind,

Ipse hæc
Delectant, veluti Balbinum polypus Agnæ;
he had rather have her than any woman in the world.

From *The Anatomy of Melancholy* by Robert Burton, 1621

Men

SCUM will kill all men who are not in the Men's Auxiliary of SCUM. Men in the Men's Auxiliary are those men who are working diligently to eliminate themselves, men who, regardless of their motives, do good, men who are playing ball with SCUM. A few examples of the men in the Men's Auxiliary are: men who kill men, biological scientists who are working on constructive programs, as opposed to biological warfare; journalists, writers, editors, publishers and producers who disseminate and promote ideas that will lead to the achievement of SCUM's goals; faggots who, by their shimmering, flaming example, encourage other men to de-man themselves and thereby make themselves relatively inoffensive; men who consistently give things away – money, things, services; men who tell it like it is (so far not one ever has), who put women straight, who reveal the truth about themselves, who give the mindless male females[1] correct sentences to parrot, who tell them a woman's primary goal in life should be to squash the male sex (to aid men in this endeavor SCUM will conduct Turd Sessions, at which every male present will give a speech beginning with the sentence: 'I am a turd, a lowly, abject turd,' then proceed to list all the ways in which he is. His reward for so doing will be the opportunity to fraternize after the session for a whole, solid hour with the SCUM who will be present. Nice, clean-living male women[2] will be invited to the sessions to help clarify any doubts and misunderstandings they may have about the male sex); makers and promoters of sex books and movies, etc., who are hastening the day when all that will be shown on the screen will be Suck and Fuck (males, like the rats following the Pied Piper, will be lured by Pussy to their doom, will be overcome and submerged by and will eventually drown in the passive flesh that they are); drug pushers and advocates, who are hastening the dropping out of men.

Being in the Men's Auxiliary is a necessary but not a sufficient condition for making SCUM's escape list; it's not enough to do good; to save their worthless asses men must also avoid evil. A few examples of the most obnoxious or harmful types are: rapists, politicians and all who are in their service (campaigners, members of political parties, etc.); lousy singers and musicians; Chairmen of Boards; Breadwinners; landlords; owners of greasy spoons and restaurants that play Musak; 'Great Artists'; cheap pikers; cops; tycoons; scientists working on death and destruction programs or for private industry (practically all scientists); liars and phonies; disc jockeys; men who intrude themselves in the slightest way on any strange female; real estate men; stock brokers; men who speak when they have nothing to say; men who loiter idly on the street and mar the landscape with their presence; double dealers; flim-flam artists; litterbugs; plagiarizers; men who in the slightest way harm any female; all men in the advertising industry; dishonest writers, journalists, editors, publishers, etc.; censors on both the public and private level; all members of the armed forces, including draftees (LBJ and McNamara give orders, but servicemen carry them out) and particularly pilots (if the Bomb drops, LBJ won't drop it; a pilot will). In the case of a man whose behaviour falls into both the good and bad categories, an overall subjective evaluation of him will be made to determine if his behaviour is, in the balance, good or bad.

From the SCUM *(Society for Cutting Up Men) Manifesto*
by Valerie Solanas, 1967

1 and 2: according to the SCUM argument, those women compelled by their fathers to adopt the male vices of shallowness, passivity, domesticity, insecurity, bestiality and cowardice. (Editor's note)

A Prayer

Now Ladies, when you find your *Inclinations strong upon you to a married Life,* you may (as we tell you in our **Athenian-Oracle**) use the following Form, if you ben't better furnish'd –

From a *Prophane Libertine,* from one *Affectedly Pious,* from a *Profuse Almoner,* from an *Uncharitable Wretch,* from a *Wavering Religioso;* and an *Injudicious Zealot* – **Deliver me!** From one of a *Starcht Gravity,* or of *Ridiculous Levity;* from an *Ambitious Statesman,* from a *Restless Projector,* from one that *loves any thing besides me,* but what is very *Just* and *Honourable* – **Deliver me!** From an *Extacy'd Poet,* from a *Modern Wit,* from a *Base Coward* and a *Rash Fool,* from a *Pad* and a *Pauper* – **Deliver me;** From a *Venus Darling,* from a *Bacchus Proselite,* from a *Travelling Half,* from a *Domestick Animal;* from all *Masculine Plagues* not yet recounted – **Deliver me!** But –

Give me one whose *Love* has more of *Judgment* than *Passion,* who is *Master of himself,* or at least an *Indefatigable Schollar* in such a Study, who has an *equal Flame,* a *Parallel Inclination,* a *Temper and Soul* so like mine, that as two Tallies we may appear more *Perfect* by *Union.* – Give me one of as *Genteel* an Education as a little expence of time will permit, with an *indifferent Fortune,* rather independent of the servile Fate of *Pallaces,* and yet one whose *Retirement* is not so much from the *Publick* as into *himself:* One (if possible) above *Flattery* and *Affronts,* and yet as careful in preventing the Injury as able to repair it: One, the *Beauty* of whose *Mind* exceeds that of his *Face,* yet not *Deformed* so as to be distinguishable from others even unto a *Ridicule.* – Give me one that has learnt to live much in a little time, one that is no great Familiar in Converse with the World, nor no little one with himself: One (if Two such *Happinesses* may be granted at one time to our Sex) who with these *uncommon endowments of Mind* may (*naturally*) have a *Sweet, Mild, Easie Disposition,* or at least one who by his Practice and frequent Habit has made himself so before he is made mine; but as the *Master-perfection* and chiefest *Draught,* let him be truly *Virtuous* and *Pious;* that is to say, Let me be truly *Happy* in my *Choice.*

From *The Athenian Spy,* 1704

A Wedding

More carriages at the gate, and lo the rest of the characters. Whom Lady Tippins, standing on a cushion, surveying through the eye-glass, thus checks off: 'Bride; five-and-forty if a day, thirty shillings a yard, veil fifteen pound, pocket-handkerchief a present. Bridesmaids; kept down for fear of outshining bride, consequently not girls, twelve-and-sixpence a yard, Veneering's flowers, snub-nosed one rather pretty but too conscious of her stockings, bonnets three pounds ten. Twemlow; blessed release for the dear man if she really was his daughter, nervous even under the pretence that she is, well he may be. Mrs Veneering; never saw such velvet, say two thousand pounds as she stands, absolute jeweller's window, father must have been a pawnbroker, or how could these people do it? Attendant unknowns; pokey.'

From *Our Mutual Friend* by Charles Dickens, 1864–5

Items *in the Married Man's Book*

To friend and to foe,
To all that I know,
That to Marriage Estate do prepare,
Remember your days
In several ways
Are troubled with sorrow and care.

For he that doth look
In the married man's book,
And read but his *Items* all over,
Shall finde them to come,
At length to a Sum,
Shall empty Purse, Pocket, and Coffer.

In the pastimes of love,
When their labours do prove,
And the Fruit beginneth to kick,
For this, and for that,
And I know not for what,
The woman must have, or be sick.

There's *Item* set down,
For a Loose-bodied Gown,
In her longing you must not deceive her;
For a Bodkin, a Ring,
Or the other fine thing,
For a Whisk, a Scarf, or a Beaver.

[157]

Deliver'd and well,
Who is't cannot tell,
That while the Childe lies at the Nipple,
There's *Item* for wine,
And Gossips so fine,
And Sugar to sweeten their Tipple.

There's *Item* I hope,
For water and Sope,
There's *Item* for Fire and Candle,
For better or worse,
There's *Item* for Nurse,
The Babe to dress and to dandle.

When swadled in lap,
There's *Item* for Pap,
And *Item* for Pot, Pan, and Ladle;
A Corral with Bells,
Which custom compells,
And *Item* ten Groats for a Cradle;

With twenty odd Knacks,
Which the little one lacks,
And thus doth thy pleasure bewray thee:
But this is the sport,
In Countrey and Court,
Then let not these pastimes betray thee.

From *The New Academy of Complements*, 1669

Five

SELF-ACCOUNTING

Oh! when to this Accompt, this cast upp Summe,
this Reckoning made, this Audit of my woe,
I call my thoughts . . .

MARY SIDNEY, COUNTESS OF PEMBROKE

'. . . I've been a costermonger, a lot-seller, a nut-seller, a
secret-paper-seller (with straws, you know, sir), a cap-seller,
a street-printer, a cakeman, a clown, an umbrella-maker, a
toasting-fork maker, a sovereign seller, and a ginger-beer
seller. I hardly know what I haven't been . . .'

A LONDON STREET HAWKER OF THE 1850S

I like hourglasses, maps, eighteenth-century typography,
etymologies, the taste of coffee, and Robert Louis
Stevenson's prose . . .

JORGE LUIS BORGES

Vertues are listed in the rank of invisible things.

THOMAS TRAHERNE

'. . . though, I know, to divide him inventorially would dozy
th'arithmetic of memory . . .'

Hamlet

The Means to Attain the Happy Life

My friend, the things that do attain
    The happy life be these, I find:
The riches left, not got with pain;
    The fruitful ground, the quiet mind;

The equal friend; no grudge, no strife;
    No charge of rule, nor governance;
Without disease the healthy life;
    The household of continuance;

The mean dièt, no dainty fare;
    Wisdom joinëd with simpleness;
The night dischargëd of all care,
    Where wine the wit may not oppress;

The faithful wife, without debate;
    Such sleeps as may beguile the night:
Content thyself with thine estate,
    Neither wish death, nor fear his might.

Henry Howard, Earl of Surrey (c.1517–47)

A Mind Content

Sweet are the thoughts that savour of content;
    The quiet mind is richer than a crown;
Sweet are the nights in careless slumber spent;
    The poor estate scorns fortune's angry frown:
Such sweet content, such minds, such sleep, such bliss,
Beggars enjoy, when princes oft do miss.

The homely house that harbours quiet rest;
    The cottage that affords no pride nor care;
The mean that 'grees with country music best;
    The sweet consort of mirth and music's fare;
Obscurëd life sets down a type of bliss:
A mind content both crown and kingdom is.

From *Greene's Farewell to Folly* by Robert Greene, 1591

The Things that Make the Happier Life

The Things that make the happier life, are these,
Most pleasant Martial; Substance got with ease,
Not labour'd for, but left thee by thy Sire;
A Soyle, not barren; a continewall fire;
Never at Law; seldome in office gown'd;
A quiet mind; free powers; and body sound;
A wise simplicity; freindes alike-stated;
Thy table without art, and easy-rated:
Thy night not dronken, but from cares layd wast;
No sowre, or sollen bed-mate, yet a Chast;
Sleepe, that will make the darkest howres swift-pac't;
Will to bee, what thou art; and nothing more:
Nor feare thy latest day, nor wish therfore.

Translated from Martial's Epigram XLVII, Book 10, by Ben Jonson

A Man of Qualities

Dogberry: . . . I am a wise fellow; and, which is more, an officer; and, which is more, a householder; and, which is more, as pretty a piece of flesh as any is in Messina; and one that knows the law, go to; and a rich fellow enough, go to; and a fellow that hath had losses; and one that hath two gowns, and everything handsome about him . . .

From *Much Ado About Nothing*, Act IV Scene ii, by William Shakespeare, 1598–9

The High Perfections of Our Transitory Days

The high *Perfections*, wherewith heav'n do's please
To crowne our transitory dayes, are these;
Goods well possest, and not possessing thee:
A faithfull *Friend*; equall in love, degree:
Lands fruitfull, and not conscious of a *Curse*:
A boastlesse *hand*; a Charitable *purse*:
A smiling *Conscience*; A contented *Mind*;
A sober *knowledge*, with true *Wisdome*, joynd;

A *Brest*, well-temper'd; *Dyet*, without Art,
Surfeit, or want; A wisely-simple *Heart*;
Pastimes ingenious, lawfull, manly, sparing;
A *Spirit* not contentious, rash, but daring:
A *Body* healthfull, sound, and fit for labour;
A *House* well order'd; and an equall *Neighbour*:
A prudent *Wife*, and constant to the roofe;
Sober, but yet not sad, and faire enough;
Sleepe seasonable, moderate, and secure;
Actions heroicke, constant, blamelesse, pure;
A *Life*, as long as faire; and when expir'd,
A glorious *Death*, unfear'd, as undesir'd.

From Book 4 of *Divine Fancies* by Francis Quarles, 1632

'The Will'

Before I sigh my last gaspe, let me breath,
Great love, some Legacies; Here I bequeath
Mine eyes to *Argus*, if mine eyes can see,
If they be blinde, then Love, I give them thee;
My tongue to Fame; to'Embassadours mine eares;
    To women or the sea, my teares.
Thou, Love, hast taught me heretofore
By making mee serve her who'had twenty more,
That I should give to none, but such, as had too much before.

My constancie I to the planets give;
My truth to them, who at the Court doe live;
Mine ingenuity and opennesse,
To Jesuites; to Buffones my pensiveness;
My silence to'any, who abroad hath beene;
    My mony to a Capuchin.
Thou Love taught'st me, by appointing mee
To love there, where no love receiv'd can be,
Onely to give to such as have an incapacitie.

My faith I give to Roman Catholiques;
All my good works unto the Schismaticks
Of Amsterdam: my best civility
And Courtship, to an Universitie;

[162]

My modesty I give to souldiers bare;
    My patience let gamesters share.
Thou Love taughtst mee, by making mee
  Love her that holds my love disparity,
Onely to give to those that count my gifts indignity.

    I give my reputation to those
    Which were my friends; Mine industrie to foes;
    To Schoolemen I bequeath my doubtfulnesse;
    My sicknesse to Physitians, or excesse;
    To Nature, all that I in Ryme have writ;
        And to my company my wit.
    Thou Love, by making mee adore
  Her, who begot this love in mee before,
Taughtst me to make, as though I gave, when I did but restore.

    To him for whom the passing bell next tolls,
    I give my physick bookes; my written rowles
    Of Morall counsels, I to Bedlam give;
    My brazen medals unto them which live
    In want of bread; To them which passe among
        All forrainers, mine English tongue.
    Thou, Love, by making mee love one
  Who thinkes her friendship a fit portion
For yonger lovers, dost my gifts thus disproportion.

    Therefore I'll give no more; But I'll undoe
    The world by dying; because love dies too.
    Then all your beauties will bee no more worth
    Than gold in Mines, where none doth draw it forth;
    And all your graces no more use shall have
        Than a Sun dyall in a grave.
    Thou Love taughtst mee, by making mee
  Love her, who doth neglect both mee and thee,
To'invent, and practise this one way, to'annihilate all three.

                                John Donne (1572–1631)

Sudden Catastrophes of Sickness

Is this the honour which man hath by being a little world, that he hath these earthquakes in himself, sudden shakings; these lightnings, sudden flashes; these thunders, sudden noises; these eclipses, sudden offuscations and darkening of his senses; these blazing stars, sudden fiery exhalations; these rivers of blood, sudden red waters?

From *Devotions upon Emergent Occasions* by John Donne, 1624

A Compound Melancholy

Jaques: I have neither the scholar's melancholy, which is emulation; nor the musician's, which is fantastical; nor the courtier's, which is proud; nor the soldier's, which is ambitious; nor the lawyer's, which is politic; nor the lady's, which is nice; nor the lover's, which is all these; but it is a melancholy of mine own, compounded of many simples, extracted from many objects, and, indeed, the sundry contemplation of my travels; in which my rumination often wraps me in a most humorous sadness.

From *As You Like It*, Act IV Scene i,
by William Shakespeare, c.1599

A Diverse Self

Sometimes I give my soule one visage and sometimes another, according unto the posture or side I lay her in. If I speake diversly of my selfe it is because I looke diversly upon my selfe. All contrarieties are found in her, according to some turne or removing, and in some fashion or other; shamefast, bashfull, insolent, chaste, luxurious, peevish, pratling, silent, fond, doting, labourious, nice, delicate, ingenious, slow, dull, froward, humourous, debonaire, wise, ignorant, false in words, true-speaking, both liberall, covetous, and prodigall. All these I perceive in some measure or other to bee in mee, according as I stirre or turne my selfe; And whosoever shall heedfully survey and consider himselfe, shall finde this volubility and discordance to be in himselfe, yea and in his very judgement. I have nothing to say entirely, simply, and with soliditie of my selfe, without confusion, disorder, blending, mingling, and in one word, Distinguo is the· most universall part of my logike.

From the essay 'Of the Inconstancie of Our Actions' by Michel de Montaigne (1533–92), translated from the French by John Florio, 1603

A Mere Spectator of Diverse Fortunes

A mere spectator of other men's fortunes and adventures, and how they act their parts, which methinks are diversely presented unto me, as from a common theatre or scene. I hear new news every day, and those ordinary rumours of war, plagues, fires, inundations, thefts, murders, massacres, meteors, comets, spectrums, prodigies, apparitions, of towns taken, cities besieged in France, Germany, Turkey, Persia, Poland, etc., daily musters and preparations, and such-like, which these tempestuous times afford, battles fought, so many men slain, monomachies, shipwrecks, piracies, and sea-fights, peace, leagues, stratagems, and fresh alarums. A vast confusion of vows, wishes, actions, edicts, petitions, lawsuits, pleas, laws, proclamations, complaints, grievances are daily brought to our ears. New books every day, pamphlets, currantoes, stories, whose catalogues of volumes of all sorts, new paradoxes, opinions, schisms, heresies, controversies in philosophy, religion, etc. Now come tidings of weddings, maskings, mummeries, entertainments, jubilees, embassies, tilts and tournaments, trophies, triumphs, revels, sports, plays: then again, as in a new shifted scene, treasons, cheating tricks, robberies, enormous villainies in all kinds, funerals, burials, deaths of princes, new discoveries, expeditions; now comical, then tragical matters. To-day we hear of new lords and officers created, to-morrow of some great men deposed, and then again of fresh honours conferred; one is let loose, another imprisoned; one purchaseth, another breaketh; he thrives, his neighbour turns bankrupt; now plenty, then again dearth and famine; one runs, another rides, wrangles, laughs, weeps, etc. Thus I daily hear, and such-like, both private and public news; amidst the gallantry and misery of the world – jollity, pride, perplexities and cares, simplicity and villainy; subtlety, knavery, candour and integrity, mutually mixed and offering themselves – I rub on *privus privatus*; as I still have lived, so I now continue, *statu quo prius*, left to a solitary life and mine own domestic discontents: saving that sometimes, *ne quid mentiar*, as Diogenes went into the city and Democritus to the haven to see fashions, I did for my recreation now and then walk abroad, look into the world, and could not choose but make some little observation, *non tam sagax observator, ac simplex recitator*, not as they did, to scoff or laugh at all, but with a mixed passion.

From the Preface, 'Democritus to the Reader', of *The Anatomy of Melancholy* by Robert Burton, 1621

'The Virgin'

The things that make a Virgin please,
She that seeks, will find them these;
A Beauty, not in Art to debt,
Rather agreeable than great;
An Eye, wherein at once do meet,
The beams of kindness, and of wit;
An undissembled Innocence,
Apt not to give, nor take offense:
A Conversation, at once, free
From Passion, and from Subtlety;
A Face that's modest, yet serene,
A sober, and yet lively Meen;
The vertue which does her adorn,
By honour guarded, not by scorn;
With such wise lowliness indu'd,
As never can be mean, or rude;
That prudent negligence enrich,
And Time's her silence and her speech;
Whose equal mind does alwaies move,
Neither a foe, nor slave to Love;
And whose Religion's strong and plain,
Not superstitious, nor profane.

Katherine Philips ('Orinda', 1631–64)

'On Sin'

Unhappy man! *Whose every breath*
is Sin: *Whose every Sin is death:*
Sin, first, Originall; Then our actuall *Sin:*
Our *Sins* that sally forth: Our *Sins* that lurk within:
Our wilfull *Sins*; and worlds of *Sins*, by chance;
Our conscious *Sins*; our *Sins* of darker Ignorance,
Our oft-repeated *Sins*: *Sins* never reckon'd:
Gainst the first Table *Sins*: *Sins* done against the second:
Our pleading *Sins*; our *Sins* without a cause;
Our gospel-*Sins*; rebellious *Sins* against thy laws:
Our *Sins* against our vowes; fresh *Sins* agin:

[166]

Sin of infirmity; and high presumptious *Sin*:
    Thus like our *Lines*, our Lives begin,
    Continue, and conclude in *Sin*.

        From Book 2 of *Divine Fancies* by Francis Quarles, 1632

Was Ever Heart Like Mine?

Still I complain; I am complaining still.
    Oh! woe is me! Was ever Heart like mine?
A Sty of Filth, a Trough of Washing-Swill
    A Dunghill Pit, a Puddle of mere Slime.
    A Nest of Vipers, Hive of Hornets; Stings.
    A Bag of Poyson, Civit-Box of Sins.

        From *Preparatory Meditations*, first series, no. 40,
        by Edward Taylor of Massachusetts, 1690–1

Mine Heart's a Park or Chase of Sins

Mine Heart's a Park or Chase of sins: Mine Head
    'S a Bowling Alley. Sins play Ninehole here.
Phansy's a Green: sin Barly breaks in't led.
    Judgment's a pingle. Blindeman's Buff's plaid there.
    Sin playes at Coursey Parke within my Minde.
    My Wills a Walke in which it aires what's blinde.

        From *Preparatory Meditations*, second series, no. 18,
        by Edward Taylor of Massachusetts, 1696

Some Necessary Implements

Trimalchio: . . . Since my father's death
    First thing I did I cashiered his old servants,
    And, to avoid confusion and expense,
    I left the country to revel it here,
    I' th' view of the world, and in the sight of
                    beauties;

And have confined myself unto some certain
Appendices, some necessary implements,
My single page, my groom, my coach, my foot-boy,
And my two penitentiary whores.

Agurtes: And these
                Are all your inventory?

From *Holland's Leaguer* by Shakerly Marmion, 1632

Modest Requirements

Beaugard: Look you, Sir: Though you have been a very ungratious Father,
upon condition that you'll promise to leave off Gaming, and stick to your
Whoring and Drinking, I will treat with you.
Father: The truth on't is, I have been to blame, *Jack*! But thou shalt find me
hereafter very obedient; that is, provided I have my Terms: which are these.
Beaugard: Come on, then.
Father: Three Bottles of Sack, *Jack*, *per diem*, without Deduction, or false
Measure: Two Pound of Tobacco *per* Month; and that of the best too.
Courtine: Truly this is but reasonable.
Father: Buttock-Beef and *March*-Beer at Dinner, you Rogue: A young
Wench of my own chusing, to wait on no body but me always: Money in
my Pocket: An old Pacing Horse, and an Elbow-Chair.
Beaugard: Agreed . . .

From *The Atheist* by Thomas Otway, 1684

Thoughts Several Be

As I sate *Musing* by my selfe alone,
My *Thoughts* on severall things did work upon.
Some did large *Houses* build, and *Stately Towers*,
Making *Orchards*, *Gardens*, and fine *Bowers*:
And *some* in *Arts*, and *Sciences* delight,
Some wars in Contradiction, *Reasons* fight.
And some, as *Kings*, do governe, rule a *State*;
Some as *Republickes*, which all *Monarches* hate.
Others, as *Lawyers*, pleading at the *Bar*,
Some privie Counsellors, and *Judges* are.

[168]

Some Priests, which do preach *Peace,* and *Godly life,*
Others *Tumultuous* are, and full of *strife.*
Some are *debauch'd,* do *wench, swagger,* and *sweare,*
And some poore *Thoughts* do tremble out of feare.
Some jealous are, and all things do suspect,
Others so *Carelesse,* every thing neglect.
Some Nymphes, Shepheards, and *Shepheardesses,*
Some so *kind,* as one another kisses.
All *sorts* of *Lovers,* and their *Passions,*
Severall waies of *Court-ship,* and fine *Fashions.*
Some take *strong Townes,* and *Battels* win,
Few do loose, but all must yeild to him.
Some are *Heroick, Generous,* and *Free,*
And some so base, do crouch with *Flattery.*
Some dying are, and in the *Grave* halfe lye,
And some *Repenting,* which for *sorrow* cry.
The *Mind* oppres'd with *Griefe, Thoughts Mourners* bee,
All cloath'd in *Black,* no light of *Joy* can see.
Some with *Despaire* do rage, are almost mad,
And some so merry, nothing makes them sad.
And many more, which were too long to tell,
Thoughts severall bee, in severall places dwell.

From 'A *Dialogue* between *Melancholy,* and *Mirth*', in *Poems and Fancies*
by Margaret Cavendish, Duchess of Newcastle, 1653

The Wild Ranging of the Mind

And yet in this wild ranging of the mind, a man may oft-times perceive the
way of it, and the dependance of one thought upon another. For in a
Discourse of our present civill warre, what could seem more impertinent,
than to ask (as one did) what was the value of a Roman Penny? Yet the
Cohærence to me was manifest enough. For the Thought of the warre,
introduced the Thought of the delivering up the King to his Enemies; The
Thought of that, brought in the Thought of the delivering up of Christ; and
that again the Thought of the 30 pence, which was the price of that treason:
and thence easily followed that malicious question; and all this in a moment
of time; for Thought is quick.

From *Leviathan* by Thomas Hobbes, 1651

Searching the Mind

Sometimes a man knows a place determinate, within the compass whereof he is to seek; and then his thoughts run over all the parts thereof, in the same manner, as one would sweep a room, to find a jewell; or as a Spaniel ranges the field, till he find a sent; or as a man should run over the Alphabet, to start a rime.

From *Leviathan* by Thomas Hobbes, 1651

A Very Impartial Statement of My Case

I now began to consider seriously my condition, and the circumstances I was reduced to, and I drew up the state of my affairs in writing, not so much to leave them to any that were to come after me, for I was like to have but few heirs, as to deliver my thoughts from daily poring on them, and afflicting my mind; and as my reason began now to master my despondency, I began to comfort my self as well as I could, and to set the good against the evil, that I might have something to distinguish my case from worse, and I stated it very impartially, like debtor and creditor, the comforts I enjoyed against the miseries I suffered, thus:

EVIL	GOOD
I am cast upon a horrible desolate island, void of all hope of recovery.	*But I am alive, and not drowned as all my ship's company was.*
I am singled out and separated, as it were, from all the world to be miserable.	*But I am singled out too from all the ship's crew to be spared from death; and He that miraculously saved me from death, can deliver me from this condition.*
I am divided from mankind, a solitaire, one banished from humane society.	*But I am not starved and perishing on a barren place, affording no sustenance.*
I have not clothes to cover me.	*But I am in a hot climate, where if I had clothes I could hardly wear them.*

I am without any defence or means to resist any violence of man or beast.	*But I am cast on an island, where I see no wild beasts to hurt me, as I saw on the coast of Africa; and what if I had been shipwrecked there?*
I have no soul to speak to, or relieve me.	*But God wonderfully sent the ship in near enough to the shore, that I have gotten out so many necessary things as will either supply my wants, or enable me to supply my self even as long as I live.*

Upon the whole, here was an undoubted testimony, that there was scarce any condition in the world so miserable, but there was something negative or something positive to be thankful for in it; and let this stand as a direction from the experience of the most miserable of all conditions in this world, that we may always find in it something to comfort our selves from, and to set in the description of good and evil, on the credit side of the accompt.

From *The Life and Strange Surprizing Adventures of Robinson Crusoe* by Daniel Defoe, 1719

God Hath Sent Me to Sea for Pearls

For I am not without authority in my jeopardy, which I derive inevitably from the glory of the name of the Lord.

For I bless God whose name is Jealous – and there is a zeal to deliver us from everlasting burnings.

For in my existimation is good even amongst the slanderers and my memory shall arise as a sweet savour unto the Lord.

For I bless the PRINCE of PEACE and pray that all the guns may be nail'd up, save such are for the rejoicing days.

For I have abstained from the blood of the grape and that even at the Lord's table.

For I have glorified God in GREEK and LATIN, the consecrated languages spoken by the Lord on earth.

For I meditate the peace of Europe amongst family bickerings and domestic jars.

For the HOST is in the WEST – the Lord shall make us thankful unto salvation.

For I preach the very GOSPEL of CHRIST without comment & with this weapon shall I slay envy.

For I bless God in the rising generation, which is on my side.

For I have translated in the charity, which makes things better & I shall be translated myself at the last.

For he that walked upon the sea, hath prepared the floods with the Gospel of peace.

For the merciful man is merciful to his beast, and to the trees that give them shelter.

For he hath turned the shadow of death into the morning, the Lord is his name.

For I am come home again, but there is nobody to kill the calf or to pay the musick.

For the hour of my felicity, like the womb of Sarah, shall come at the latter end.

For I shou'd have avail'd myself of waggery, had not malice been multitudinous.

For there are still serpents that can speak – God bless my head, my heart & my heel.

For I bless God that I am of the same seed with Ehud, Mutius Scævola, and Colonel Draper.

For the word of God is a sword on my side – no matter what other weapon a stick or a straw.

For I have adventur'd myself in the name of the Lord, and he hath mark'd me for his own.

For I bless God for the Postmaster general & all conveyancers of letters under his care especially Allen and Shelvock.

For my grounds in New Canaan shall infinitely compensate for the flats & maynes of Staindrop Moor.

For the praise of God can give to a mute fish the notes of a nightingale.

For I have seen the White Raven & Thomas Hall of Willingham & am myself a greater curiosity than both.

For I look up to heaven which is my prospect to escape envy by surmounting it.

For if Pharaoh had known Joseph, he would have blessed God & me for the illumination of the people.

For I pray God to bless improvements in gardening till London be a city of palm-trees.

For I pray to give his grace to the poor of England, that Charity be not offended & that benevolence may increase.

For in my nature I quested for beauty, but God, God hath sent me to sea for pearls.

For there is a blessing from the STONE of JESUS which is founded upon hell to the precious jewell on the right hand of God.

For the nightly Visitor is at the window of the impenitent, while I sing a psalm of my own composing.

For there is a note added to the scale, which the Lord hath made fuller, stronger & more glorious.

For I offer my goat as he browses the vine, bless the Lord from chambering and drunkeness.

For there is a traveling for the glory of God without going to Italy or France.

For I bless the children of Asher for the evil I did them & the good I might have received at their hands.

For I rejoice like a worm in the rain in him that cherishes and from him that tramples.

For I am ready for the trumpet & alarm to fight to die & to rise again.

For the banish'd of the Lord shall come about again, for so he hath prepared for them.

For sincerity is a jewel which is pure and transparent, eternal and inestimable.

For my hands and feet are perfect as the sublimity of Naphtali and the felicity of Asher.

For the numbers and names of animals are as the names and number of the stars.

For I pray the Lord Jesus to translate my MAGNIFICAT into verse and represent it.

For I bless the Lord Jesus from the bottom of Royston Cave to the top of King's Chapel.

For I am a little fellow, which is intitled to the great mess by the benevolence of God my father.

For I this day made over my inheritance to my mother in consideration of her infirmities.

For I this day made over my inheritance to my mother in consideration of her age.

For I this day made over my inheritance to my mother in consideration of her poverty.

For I bless the thirteenth of August, in which I had the grace to obey the voice of Christ in my conscience.

For I bless the thirteenth of August, in which I was willing to run all hazards for the sake of the name of the Lord.

For I bless the thirteenth of August, in which I was willing to be called a fool for the sake of Christ.

For I lent my flocks and my herds and my lands at once unto the Lord.

For nature is more various than observation tho' observers be innumerable.

For Agricola is *Georgos*.

For I pray God to bless POLLY in the blessing of Naomi and assign her to the house of DAVID.

For I am in charity with the French who are my foes and Moabites because of the Moabitish woman.

For my Angel is always ready at a pinch to help me out and to keep me up.

For CHRISTOPHER must slay the Dragon with a PAEON's head.

For they have separated me and my bosom, whereas the right comes by setting us together.

For Silly fellow! Silly fellow! is against me and belongeth neither to me nor my family.

For he that scorneth the scorner hath condescended to my low estate.

For Abiah is the father of Joab and Joab of all Romans and English Men.

For they pass by me in their tour, and the good Samaritan is not yet come.

For I bless God in the behalf of TRINITY COLLEGE in CAMBRIDGE & the society of PURPLES in LONDON.

For I have a nephew CHRISTOPHER to whom I implore the grace of God.

For I pray God bless the CAM – Mr. HIGGS & Mr. and Mrs. WASHBOURNE as the drops of the dew.

For I pray God bless the king of Sardinia and make him an instrument of his peace.

For I am possessed of a cat, surpassing in beauty, from whom I take occasion to bless Almighty God.

For I pray God for the professors of the University of Cambridge to attend & to amend.

For the Fatherless Children and widows are never deserted of the Lord.

From *Jubilate Agno* by Christopher Smart, 1759–63

Eighteenth Century Pursuits

Amusements that the following *Men of Fashion* principally delight in:

Abingdon, Earl of	Flute playing.
Aylesford, Earl of	Pistol shooting.
Berkeley, Earl of	Hare hunting.
Bessborough, Earl of	Virtu.
Buckinghamshire, Earl of	An old coat.
Camden, Lord	Agriculture.
Cornwallis, Earl	Military glory.

Cumberland, Duke of	Fresh water.
Dartmouth, Earl of	The tabernacle.
Devonshire, Duke of	Retirement.
Dorset, Duke of	Cricket.
Draper, Sir William	Tennis.
Effingham, Earl of	A dirty scirt.
Egmont, Earl of	Fox hunting.
Egremont, Earl of	Street riding.
Fox, Mr.	Popular tumult.
Grosvenor, Lord	The turf.
Hamilton, 'Lord'	Skaiting.
Hillsborough, Earl of	A nap.
Howe, Viscount	Naval practice.
Keppel, Viscount	A warm cot.
Lade, Sir John, Bart.	Gig driving.
Malden, Lord	Violoncello.
Montfort, Lord	Menageries.
Norfolk, Duke of	Toping.
North, Lord	A festive board.
Orford, Earl of	Coursing.
Pembroke, Earl of	The menage.
Rigby, Mr.	Conviviality.
Sandwich, Earl of	Ancient music.
Townshend, Viscount	Caricature.
Westcote, Lord	A parenthesis.
Weymouth, Viscount	Burgundy.
Wynn, Sir W. W., Bart.	Acting.

From the *Morning Herald*, 6 August 1782

Mr Burns's Protean Genitalia

But – as I always am on every occasion – I have been prudent and cautious to an astounding degree; I swore her, privately and solemnly, never to attempt any claim on me as a husband, even though anybody should persuade her she had such a claim, which she has not, neither during my life, nor after my death. She did all this like a good girl, and I took the opportunity of some dry horselitter, and gave her such a thundering scalade that electrified the very marrow of her bones. O, what a peacemaker is a guid weel-willy p––le! It is the mediator, the guarantee, the umpire, the bond of union, the solemn league and covenant, the plenipotentiary, the

Aaron's rod, the Jacob's staff, the prophet Elisha's pot of oil, the Ahasuerus' sceptre, the sword of mercy, the philosopher's stone, the horn of plenty, and Tree of Life between Man and Woman.

From a letter by Robert Burns to Robert Ainslie, 3 March 1788

Twenty Rules for Overcoming Low Spirits

DEAR LADY GEORGIANA, – Nobody has suffered more from low spirits than I have done – so I feel for you. 1st. Live as well as you dare. 2nd. Go into the shower-bath with a small quantity of water at a temperature low enough to give you a slight sensation of cold, 75°. or 80°. 3rd. Amusing books. 4th. Short views of human life – not further than dinner or tea. 5th. Be as busy as you can. 6th. See as much as you can of those friends who respect and like you. 7th. And of those acquaintances who amuse you. 8th. Make no secret of low spirits to your friends, but talk of them freely – they are always worse for dignified concealment. 9th. Attend to the effects tea and coffee produce upon you. 10th. Compare your lot with that of other people. 11th. Don't expect too much from human life – a sorry business at the best. 12th. Avoid poetry, dramatic representations (except comedy), music, serious novels, melancholy, sentimental people, and everything likely to excite feeling or emotion, not ending in active benevolence. 13th. *Do good*, and endeavour to please everybody of every degree. 14th. Be as much as you can in the open air without fatigue. 15th. Make the room where you commonly sit gay and pleasant. 16th. Struggle by little and little against idleness. 17th. Don't be too severe upon yourself, or underrate yourself, but do yourself justice. 18th. Keep good blazing fires. 19th. Be firm and constant in the exercise of rational religion. 20th. Believe me, dear Lady Georgiana, Very truly yours, – SYDNEY SMITH.

Letter from Sydney Smith to Lady Morpeth, 1820

'Il Proprio Ritratto' (The Self-Portrait)

Solcata ho fronte, occhi incavati intenti;
crin fulvo, emunte guance, ardito aspetto;
labbri tumidi, arguti, al riso lenti,
capo chino, bel collo, irsuto petto;
membra esatte; vestir semplice eletto;
ratti i passi, il pensier, gli atti, gli accenti:

[176]

prodigo, sobrio; umano, ispido, schietto;
avverso al mondo, avversi a me gli eventi.

Mesto i più giorni e solo; ognor pensoso,
alle speranze incredulo e al timore;
il pudor mi fa vile; e prode l'ira;
cauta in me parla la ragion; ma il core,
ricco di vizi e di virtù, delira –
Morte, tu mi darai fama e riposo.

Ugo Foscolo (1778–1827)

'The Calmest Thoughts'

After dark vapours have oppress'd our plains
   For a long dreary season, comes a day
   Born of the gentle South, and clears away
From the sick heavens all unseemly stains.
The anxious month, relieving from its pains,
   Takes as a long-lost right the feel of May,
   The eyelids with the passing coolness play,
Like rose leaves with the drip of summer rains.
The calmest thoughts come round us – as of leaves
   Budding, – fruit ripening in stillness, – autumn suns
Smiling at eve upon the quiet sheaves, –
Sweet Sappho's cheek, – a sleeping infant's breath, –
   The gradual sand that through an hour-glass runs, –
A woodland rivulet, – a Poet's death.

John Keats, 1817

A Curiously Fanciful Exemplification
of the Association of Ideas

I had been talking of the association of Ideas, and endeavouring to convince
an Idolator of Hume & Hartley, that this was strictly speaking a law only of
the memory & imagination, of the *Stuff out* of which we make our
conceptions & perceptions, not of the thinking faculty, by which we make
them – that it was as the force of gravitation to leaping to any given point –
without gravitation this would be impossible, and yet equally impossible to

[177]

leap except by a *power* counteracting first, and then using the *force* of gravitation. That Will, strictly synonimous with the individualizing Principle, the *'I'* of every rational Being, was this governing and applying Power – And yet to shew him that I was neither ignorant, nor idle in observing, the vast extent and multifold activity of the *Associative Force* I entered into a curious and tho fanciful yet strictly true and actual, exemplification. Many of my Instances recalled to my mind my little poem on *Lewti*, the Circassian (and by this same force joined with the assent of the will most often, tho' often too vainly because weakly opposed by it, I inevitably by some link or other return to you, or (say rather) bring some fuel of thought to the ceaseless Yearning for you at my Inmost, which like a steady fire attracts constantly the air which constantly feeds it) I began strictly and as a matter of fact to examine that subtle Vulcanian Spider-web Net of Steel – strong as Steel yet subtle as the Ether, in which my soul flutters inclosed with the Idea of your's – to pass rapidly as in a catalogue thro' the Images only, exclusive of the thousand Thoughts that possess the same force, which never fail instantly to awake into vivider flame the for ever and ever Feeling of you/ – The fire/ Mary, you & I at Gallow-Hill/ – or if flamy, reflected in children's round faces – ah whose children? – a dog – that dog whose restless eyes oft catching the light of the fire used to watch your face, as you leaned with your head on your hand and arm, & your feet on the *fender*/ the fender thence/ – Fowls at Table – the last dinner at Gallow Hill, when you drest the two fowls in that delicious white Sauce which when very ill is the only idea of food that does not make me sicker/ all natural Scenery – ten thousand links, and if it pleases me, the very spasm & drawing-back of a pleasure which is half-pain, you not being there – Cheese – at Middleham, too salt/ horses, my ride to Scarborough – asses, to that large living 2 or 3 miles from Middleham/ All books – my Study at Keswick/ – the Ceiling or Head of a Bed – the green watered Mazarine! – A Candle in its socket, with its alternate fits & dying flashes of lingering Light – *O God! O God!* – Books of abstruse Knowlege – the Thomas Aquinas & Suarez from the Durham Library/ – a [?peony/fiery] – faced cottage Girl – little Jane/ all articles of female dress – music – the opening of a Street door – when you first came to Keswick – of a Bed room door – with what thoughts you would nightly open your own, when I was far away – & that sweet blessed Letter/ Letters, yea, the very paper on which one might be written – or from the habit of half-unconsciously writing your name or its Symbol invented by me to express it – all Travels/ my yearning Absence/ all books of natural History – O if I had been blest & had lived with you in the country, the continual food of conversation by watching & explaining – the Heavens/ your name in those bright Stars, or an M or W recalling those Stars – Aurora borealis – at Keswick by the corner parlour window/

Waterfalls – that at Scale Force when D. laughed at me & at you thro' me, as the Lover – History – how you were interested at Buttermere by my account of the Cid – *a Promise – pictures* – any eye fixed kindly on me when I am talking – my face in the . . .

From Samuel Taylor Coleridge's *Notebooks*, March 1810

Coleridge's Conversation

– Last Sunday I took a Walk towards highgate and in the lane that winds by the side of Lord Mansfield's park I met Mr Green our Demonstrator at Guy's in conversation with Coleridge – I joined them, after enquiring by a look whether it would be agreeable – I walked with him a[t] his alderman-after dinner pace for near two miles I suppose In those two Miles he broached a thousand things – let me see if I can give you a list – Nightingales, Poetry – on Poetical sensation – Metaphysics – Different genera and species of Dreams – Nightmare – a dream accompanied by a sense of touch – single and double touch – A dream related – First and second consciousness – the difference explained between will and Volition – so m[an]y metaphysicians from a want of smoking the second consciousness – Monsters – the Kraken – Mermaids – southey believes in them – southeys belief too much diluted – A Ghost story – Good morning – I heard his voice as he came towards me – I heard it as he moved away – I had heard it all the interval – if it may be called so.

From a letter by John Keats to George and Georgiana Keats, Feb–May 1819

Opium Hallucinations by Association

Under the connecting feeling of tropical heat and vertical sun-lights, I brought together all creatures, birds, beasts, reptiles, all trees and plants, usages and appearances, that are found in all tropical regions, and assembled them together in China or Indostan. From kindred feelings, I soon brought Egypt and all her gods under the same law. I was stared at, hooted at, grinned at, chattered at, by monkeys, by paroquets, by cockatoos. I ran into pagodas: and was fixed, for centuries, at the summit, or in secret rooms; I was the idol; I was the priest; I was worshipped; I was sacrificed. I fled from the wrath of Brama through all the forests of Asia: Vishnu hated me: Seeva laid wait for me. I came suddenly upon Isis and Osiris: I had done a deed, they said, which the ibis and the crocodile trembled at. I was buried, for a thousand years, in stone coffins, with mummies and sphinxes, in narrow chambers at the heart of eternal pyramids. I was kissed, with cancerous kisses, by crocodiles; and laid, confounded with all unutterable slimy things, amongst reeds and Nilotic mud.

From *The Confessions of an English Opium Eater* by Thomas de Quincey, 1821

A Night Voyage to Corsica

The night voyage, though far from pleasant, has not been as bad as might have been anticipated. He is fortunate, who, after ten hours of sea passage can reckon up no worse memories than those of a passive condition of suffering – of that dislocation of mind and body, or inability to think straightforward, so to speak, when the outer man is twisted, and rolled, and jerked, and the movements of thought seem more or less to correspond with those of the body. Wearily go by

'The slow sad hours that bring us all things ill,'

and vain is the effort to enliven them as every fresh lurch of the vessel tangles practical or pictorial suggestions with untimely scraps of poetry, indistinct regrets and predictions, couplets for a new *Book of Nonsense*, and all kinds of inconsequent imbecilities – after this sort –

Would it not have been better to have remained at Cannes, where I had not yet visited Theoule, the Saut de Loup, and other places?

Had I not said, scores of times, such and such a voyage was the last I would make?

To-morrow, when 'morn broadens on the borders of the dark,' shall I see Corsica's 'snowy mountain-tops fringing the (Eastern) sky'?

Did the sentinels of lordly Volaterra see, as Lord Macaulay says they did, 'Sardinia's snowy mountain-tops,' and not rather these same Corsican tops, 'fringing the southern sky'?

Did they see any tops at all, or if any, which tops?

Will the daybreak ever happen?

Will 2 o'clock ever arrive?

Will the two poodles above stairs ever cease to run about the deck?

Is it not disagreeable to look forward to two or three months of travelling quite alone?

Would it not be delightful to travel, as JAS is about to do, in company with a wife and child?

Does it not, as the years advance, become clearer that it is very odious to be alone?

Have not many very distinguished persons, Oenone among others, arrived at this conclusion?

Did she not say, with evident displeasure –

> 'And from that time to this I am alone,
> And I shall be alone until I die'? –

Will those poodles ever cease from trotting up and down the deck?

Is it not unpleasant, at fifty-six years of age, to feel that it is increasingly probable that a man can never hope to be otherwise than alone, never, no, never more?

Did not Edgar Poe's raven distinctly say, 'Nevermore'?

Will those poodles be quiet? 'Quoth the raven, nevermore.'

Will there be anything worth seeing in Corsica?

Is there any romance left in that island? is there any sublimity or beauty in its scenery?

Have I taken too much baggage?

Have I not rather taken too little?

Am I not an idiot for coming at all? –

Thus, and in such a groove, did the machinery of thought go on, gradually refusing to move otherwise than by jerky spasms, after the fashion of mechanical Ollendorff exercises, or verb-catechisms of familiar phrases –

Are there not Banditti?

Had there not been Vendetta?

Were there not Corsican brothers?

Should I not carry clothes for all sorts of weather?

Must THOU not have taken a dress coat?

Had HE not many letters of introduction?

Might WE not have taken extra pairs of spectacles?

Could YOU not have provided numerous walking boots? . . .

May THEY not find cream cheeses?

Should there not be innumerable moufflons?

Ought not the cabin lamps and glasses to cease jingling?

Might not the poodles stop worrying? –

thus and thus, till by reason of long hours and monotonous rolling and shaking, a sort of comatose insensibility, miscalled sleep, takes the place of all thought, and so the night passes.

From *Journal of a Landscape Painter in Corsica* by Edward Lear, 9 April 1868

Three Rooms

(i)

The place through which he made his way at leisure, was one of those receptacles for old and curious things which seem to crouch in odd corners of this town, and to hide their musty treasures from the public eye in jealousy and distrust. There were suits of mail standing like ghosts in armour, here and there; fantastic carvings brought from monkish cloisters; rusty weapons of various kinds; distorted figures in china, and wood, and iron, and ivory; tapestry, and strange furniture that might have been designed in dreams. The haggard aspect of the little old man was wonderfully suited to the place; he might have groped among old churches, and tombs, and deserted houses, and gathered all the spoils with his own hands. There was nothing in the whole collection but was in keeping with himself; nothing that looked older or more worn than he.

(ii)

The milk arrived, and the child producing her little basket, and selecting its best fragments for her grandfather, they made a hearty meal. The furniture of the room was very homely of course – a few rough chairs and a table, a corner cupboard with their little stock of crockery and delf, a gaudy tea-tray, representing a lady in bright red, walking out with a very blue parasol, a few common, coloured scripture subjects in frames upon the wall and chimney, an old dwarf clothes-press and an eight-day clock, with a few bright saucepans and a kettle, comprised the whole. But everything was clean and neat, and as the child glanced around, she felt a tranquil air of comfort and content to which she had long been unaccustomed.

(iii)

There was not much to look at. A rickety table, with spare bundles of papers, yellow and ragged from long carriage in the pocket, ostentatiously displayed upon its top; a couple of stools set face to face on opposite sides of this crazy piece of furniture; a treacherous old chair by the fire-place, whose withered arms had hugged full many a client and helped to squeeze him dry; a second-hand wig-box, used as a depository for blank writs and declarations and other small forms of law, once the sole contents of the head which belonged to the wig which belonged to the box, as they were now of the box itself; two or three common books of practice; a jar of ink, a pounce-box, a stunted hearth-broom, a carpet trodden to shreds but still clinging with the tightness of desperation to its tacks – these, with the yellow wainscot of the walls, the smoke-discoloured ceiling, the dust and cobwebs, were among the most prominent decorations of the office of Mr Sampson Brass.

From *The Old Curiosity Shop* by Charles Dickens, 1840–1

Reflections on the Goods at the Old Clothes Exchange

These bales are each worth from 50 *l.* to 300 *l.*, though seldom 300 *l.*, and it is curious to reflect from how many classes the pile of old garments has been collected – how many privations have been endured before some of these habiliments found their way into the possession of the old clothes-man – what besotted debauchery put others in his possession – with what cool calculation others were disposed of – how many were procured for money, and how many by tempting offers of flowers, glass, crockery, spars, table-covers, lace, or millinery – what was the clothing which could first be spared when rent was to be defrayed or bread to be bought, and what was treasured until the last – in what scenes of gaiety or gravity, in the opera-house or the senate, had the perhaps departed wearers of some of that heap of old clothes figured – through how many possessors, and again through what new scenes of middle-class or artizan comfort had these dresses passed, or through what accidents of 'genteel' privation and destitution – and lastly through what necessities of squalid wretchedness and low debauchery.

From *London Labour and the London Poor* by Henry Mayhew, 1861–2

Frank Buckland's Rooms in Christ Church

In Fell's Buildings Frank had his rooms on the ground floor during his college course, and pursued his zoological and surgical studies with equal energy and originality: he made use of the court as a menagerie; continually adding to his collection specimens zoological and anatomical, living and dead. Amongst the former were a young bear named Tiglath Pileser, Jacko the monkey, an eagle, a jackal, besides marmots, guinea-pigs, squirrels and dormice, an adder and many harmless snakes and slow-worms, tortoises, green frogs, and a chameleon. Skeletons and stuffed specimens were numerous, and often anatomical preparations were in progress in the court. The live pets had a tendency to stray.

From *The Life of Frank Buckland* by George C. Bompas, 1885

The Spoils of Youth

Or else, there's no wife in the case,
But the portrait's queen of the place,
Alone mid the other spoils
Of youth, – masks, gloves and foils,
And pipe-sticks, rose, cherry-tree, jasmine,
    And the long whip, the tandem-lasher,
And the cast from a fist ('not, alas! mine,
    'But my master's, the Tipton Slasher'),
And the cards where pistol-balls mark ace,
And a satin shoe used for cigar-case,
And the chamois-horns ('shot in the Chablais')
    And prints – Rarey drumming on Cruiser,
    And Sayers, our champion, the bruiser,
And the little edition of Rabelais:
Where a friend, with both hands in his pockets,
    May saunter up close to examine it,
    And remark a good deal of Jane Lamb in it,
    'But the eyes are half out of their sockets;
    'That hair's not so bad, where the gloss is,
    'But they've made the girl's nose a proboscis:
    'Jane Lamb, that we danced with at Vichy!
    'What, is she not Jane? Then, who is she?'

From 'A Likeness' by Robert Browning (1812–89)

'The Best'

What's the best thing in the world?
June-rose, by May-dew impearl'd;
Sweet south-wind, that means no rain;
Truth, not cruel to a friend;
Pleasure, not in haste to end;
Beauty, not self-deck'd and curl'd
Till its pride is over-plain;
Light, that never makes you wink;
Memory, that gives no pain;
Love, when, *so*, you're loved again.

What's the best thing in the world?
– Something out of it, I think.

Elizabeth Barrett Browning (1806–61)

'Alchimie du Verbe'

À moi. L'histoire d'une de mes folies.

Depuis longtemps je me vantais de posséder tous les paysages possibles, et trouvais dérisoires les célébrités de la peinture et de la poésie moderne.

J'aimais les peintures idiotes, dessus de portes, décors, toiles de saltim-banques, enseignes, enluminures populaires; la littérature démodée, latin d'église, livres érotiques sans orthographe, romans de nos aïeules, contes de fées, petits livres de l'enfance, opéras vieux, refrains niais, rhythmes naïfs.

Je rêvais croisades, voyages de découvertes dont on n'a pas de relations, républiques sans histoires, guerres de religion étouffées, révolutions de moeurs, déplacements de races et de continents: je croyais à tous les enchantements.

J'inventai la couleur des voyelles! – *A* noir, *E* blanc, *I* rouge, *O* bleu, *U* vert. – Je réglai la forme et le mouvement de chaque consonne, et, avec des rhythmes instinctifs, je me flattai d'inventer un verbe poétique accessible, un jour ou l'autre, à tous les sens. Je réservais la traduction.

Ce fut d'abord une étude. J'écrivais des silences, des nuits, je notais l'inexprimable. Je fixais des vertiges.

From Une Saison en Enfer by Arthur Rimbaud, 1873

A Holocaust

Miss Fowler, in moments of irritation, had called Mary deadly methodical. She put on her oldest waterproof and gardening-hat and her ever-slipping galoshes, for the weather was on the edge of more rain. She gathered fire-lighters from the kitchen, a half-scuttle of coals, and a faggot of brushwood. These she wheeled in the barrow down the mossed paths to the dank little laurel shrubbery where the destructor stood under the drip of three oaks. She climbed the wire fence into the Rector's glebe just behind, and from his tenant's rick pulled two large armfuls of good hay, which she spread neatly on the fire-bars. Next, journey by journey, passing Miss Fowler's white face at the morning-room window each time, she brought down in the towel-covered clothes-basket, on the wheelbarrow, thumbed and used Hentys, Marryats, Levers, Stevensons, Baroness Orczys, Garvices, schoolbooks, and atlases, unrelated piles of the *Motor Cyclist*, the *Light Car*, and catalogues of Olympia exhibitions; the remnants of a fleet of sailing-ships from nine-penny cutters to a three-guinea yacht; a prep-school dressing-gown; bats from three-and-sixpence to twenty-four shillings; cricket and tennis balls; disintegrated steam and clockwork locomotives with their twisted rails; a grey and red tin model of a submarine; a dumb gramophone and cracked records; golf-clubs that had to be broken across the knee, like his walking-sticks, and an assegai; photographs of private and public school cricket and football elevens, and his OTC on the line of march; kodaks, and film-rolls; some pewters, and one real silver cup, for boxing competitions and Junior Hurdles; sheaves of school photographs; Miss Fowler's photograph; her own which he had borne off in fun and (good care she took not to ask!) had never returned; a play box with a secret drawer; a load of flannels, belts, and jerseys, and a pair of spiked shoes unearthed in the attic; a packet of all the letters Miss Fowler and she had ever written to him, kept for some absurd reason through all these years; a five-day attempt at a diary; framed pictures of racing motors in full Brooklands career, and load upon load of undistinguishable wreckage of tool-boxes, rabbit hutches, electric batteries, tin soldiers, fret-saw outfits, and jig-saw puzzles. ,.

Miss Fowler at the window watched her come and go, and said to herself, 'Mary's an old woman. I never realised it before.'

From 'Mary Postgate' by Rudyard Kipling (1865–1936)

The Death of Roland

De plusurs choses à remembrer li prist,
De tantes teres cume li bers cunquist,
De dulce France, des humes de sun lign,
De Carlemagne sun seignor ki l'nurrit.

Then began he to call many things to remembrance, – all the lands which his valour conquered, and pleasant France, and the men of his lineage, and Charlemagne his liege lord who nourished him.

From the *Chanson de Roland*, eleventh century, translated from the Old French by Matthew Arnold, 1880

[186]

The Death of Victoria

She herself, as she lay blind and silent, seemed to those who watched her to be divested of all thinking – to have glided already, unawares, into oblivion. Yet, perhaps, in the secret chambers of consciousness, she had her thoughts, too. Perhaps her fading mind called up once more the shadows of the past to float before it, and retraced, for the last time, the vanished visions of that long history – passing back and back, through the cloud of years, to older and ever older memories – to the spring woods at Osborne, so full of primroses for Lord Beaconsfield – to Lord Palmerston's queer clothes and high demeanour, and Albert's face under the green lamp, and Albert's first stag at Balmoral, and Albert in his blue and silver uniform, and the Baron coming in through a doorway, and Lord M. dreaming at Windsor with the rooks cawing in the elm-trees, and the Archbishop of Canterbury on his knees in the dawn, and the old King's turkey-cock ejaculations, and Uncle Leopold's soft voice at Claremont, and Lehzen with his globes, and her mother's feathers sweeping down towards her, and a great old repeater-watch of her father's in its tortoise-shell case, and a yellow rug, and some friendly flounces of sprigged muslin, and the trees and the grass at Kensington.

From *Queen Victoria* by Lytton Strachey, 1921

The Death of Prince Fabrizio

Tancredi. Yes, much on the credit side came from Tancredi; that sympathy of his, all the more precious for being ironic; the aesthetic pleasure of watching him manoeuvre amid the shoals of life, the bantering affection whose touch was so right. Then dogs; Fufi, the fat pug of his childhood, the impetuous poodle Tom, confidant and friend, Speedy's gentle eyes, Bendicò's delicious nonsense, the caressing paws of Pop, the pointer at that moment searching for him under bushes and garden chairs and never to see him again; then a horse or two, these already more distant and detached. There were the first few hours of returns to Donnafugata, the sense of tradition and the perennial expressed in stone and water, of time congealed; a few care-free shoots, a cosy massacre or two of hares and pheasants, some good laughs with Tumeo, a few minutes of compunction at the convent amid odours of musk and sugared almonds. Anything else? Yes, there were other things: but these were only grains of gold mixed with earth: moments of satisfaction when he had made some biting reply to a fool, of content when he had realised that in Concetta's beauty and character was prolonged the true Salina strain; a few seconds of frenzied passion; the surprise of Arago's letter spontaneously congratulating him on the accuracy of his difficult calculations about Huxley's comet. And – why not? – the public thrill at being given a medal at the Sorbonne, the exquisite sensation of one or two fine silk cravats, the smell of some morocco leathers, the gay voluptuous air of a few women passed in the street, of one glimpsed even yesterday at the station of Catania, in a brown travelling dress and suède gloves, mingling amid the crowds and seeming to search for his exhausted face through the dirty compartment window. What a noise that crowd was making! 'Sandwiches!' '*Il Corriere dell' Isola.*' And then the panting of the tired breathless train . . . and that appalling sun as they arrived, those lying faces, the crashing cataracts . . .

From *The Leopard* by Giuseppe Tomasi di Lampedusa, 1958, translated from the Italian by Archibald Colquhoun

Jacob's Room

Jacob's room had a round table and two low chairs. There were yellow flags in a jar on the mantelpiece; a photograph of his mother; cards from societies with little raised crescents, coats of arms, and initials; notes and pipes; on the table lay paper ruled with a red margin – an essay, no doubt, – 'Does History consist of the Biographies of Great Men?' There were books enough; very few French books; but then any one who's worth anything reads just what he likes, as the mood takes him, with extravagant enthusiasm. Lives of the Duke of Wellington, for example; Spinoza; the works of Dickens; the *Faery Queen*; a Greek dictionary with the petals of poppies pressed to silk between the pages; all the Elizabethans. His slippers were incredibly shabby, like boats burnt to the water's rim. Then there were photographs from the Greeks, and a mezzotint from Sir Joshua – all very English. The works of Jane Austen, too, in deference, perhaps, to some one else's standard. Carlyle was a prize. There were books upon the Italian painters of the Renaissance, a *Manual of the Diseases of the Horse*, and all the usual text-books. Listless is the air in an empty room, just swelling the curtain; the flowers in the jar shift. One fibre in the wicker arm-chair creaks, though no one sits there.

From *Jacob's Room* by Virginia Woolf, 1922

A Litany of Holy Memories

I would like to make a litany of all the things that bind me to the memory of holiness – of peaks. It would run – 'The Chilterns – Hampton Court – Hello Ragtime – Raymond Buildings' and a few more names. And it would begin and end with 'Cathleen'. It's a funny sort of mixed chain to hang on to heaven by: but very human. Repeat it, when you want to know values clearly.

From a letter by Rupert Brooke to Cathleen Nesbitt, October 1913

'Things That Arouse a Fond Memory of the Past'

Dried hollyhock. The objects used during the Display of Dolls. To find a piece of deep violet or grape-coloured material that has been pressed between the pages of a notebook.

It is a rainy day and one is feeling bored. To pass the time, one starts looking through some old papers. And then one comes across the letters of a man one used to love.

Last year's paper fan. A night with a clear moon.

From *The Pillow Book of Sei Shonagon*, tenth century, translated from the Japanese by Ivan Morris

These I Have Loved

These I have loved:
       White plates and cups, clean-gleaming,
Ringed with blue lines; and feathery, faery dust;
Wet roofs, beneath the lamp-light; the strong crust
Of friendly bread; and many-tasting food;
Rainbows; and the blue bitter smoke of wood;
And radiant raindrops couching in cool flowers;
And flowers themselves, that sway through sunny hours,
Dreaming of moths that drink them under the moon;
Then, the cool kindliness of sheets, that soon
Smooth away trouble; and the rough male kiss
Of blankets; grainy wood; live hair that is
Shining and free; blue-massing clouds; the keen

[189]

Unpassioned beauty of a great machine;
The benison of hot water; furs to touch;
The good smell of old clothes; and other such –
The comfortable smell of friendly fingers,
Hair's fragrance, and the musty reek that lingers
About dead leaves and last year's ferns . . .

                                                  Dear names,
And thousand other throng to me! Royal flames;
Sweet water's dimpling laugh from tap or spring;
Holes in the ground; and voices that do sing;
Voices in laughter, too; and body's pain,
Soon turned to peace; and the deep-panting train;
Firm sands; the little dulling edge of foam
That browns and dwindles as the wave goes home;
And washen stoves, gay for an hour; the cold
Graveness of iron; moist black earthen mould;
Sleep; and high places; footprints in the dew;
And oaks; and brown horse-chestnuts, glossy-new;
And new-peeled sticks; and shining pools on grass; –
All these have been my loves.

From 'The Great Lover' by Rupert Brooke, 1914

Le Roi Soleil, Le Pélican Lassé

La viande aussi, le pain, l'abbé, la messe, mes frères, les légumes, les fruits, un malade, le docteur, l'abbé, un mort, l'abbé, la messe des morts, les feuilles vivantes, Jésus-Christ tombe pour la première fois, le Roi Soleil, le pélican lassé, le plus petit commun multiple, le général Dourakine, le Petit Chose, notre bon ange, Blanche de Castille, le petit tambour Bara, le Fruit de nos entrailles, l'abbé, tout seul ou avec un petit camarade, le renard, les raisins, la retraite de Russie, Clanche de Bastille, l'asthme de Panama et l'arthrite de Russie, les mains sur la table, J.-C. tombe pour la nième fois, il ouvre un large bec et laisse tomber le fromage pour réparer des ans l'irréparable outrage, le nez de Cléopâtre dans la vessie de Cromwell et voilà la face du monde changée, ainsi on grandissait, on allait à la messe, on s'instruisait et quelque fois on jouait avec l'âne dans le jardin.

From 'Souvenirs de Famille, ou L'Ange Garde-Chiourme'
by Jacques Prévert, 1930

'Beautiful Lofty Things'

Beautiful lofty things: O'Leary's noble head;
My father upon the Abbey stage, before him a raging crowd:
'This Land of Saints,' and then as the applause died out,
'Of plaster Saints'; his beautiful mischievous head thrown back.
Standish O'Grady supporting himself between the tables
Speaking to a drunken audience high nonsensical words;
Augusta Gregory seated at her great ormolu table,
Her eightieth winter approaching: 'Yesterday he threatened my life.
I told him that nightly from six to seven I sat at this table,
The blinds drawn up'; Maude Gonne at Howth station waiting a
    train,
Pallas Athene in that straight back and arrogant head:
All the Olympians; a thing never known again.

From *Last Poems* by W. B. Yeats, 1936–9

Merlyn's Cottage

It was the most marvellous room that he had ever been in.

There was a real corkindrill hanging from the rafters, very lifelike and horrible with glass eyes and scaly tail stretched out behind it. When its master came into the room it winked one eye in salutation, although it was stuffed. There were thousands of brown books in leather bindings, some chained to the bookshelves and others propped against each other as if they had had too much to drink and they did not really trust themselves. These gave out a smell of must and solid brown-ness which was most secure. Then there were stuffed birds, popinjays, and maggot-pies and kingfishers, and peacocks with all their feathers but two, and tiny birds like beetles, and a reputed phoenix which smelt of incense and cinnamon. It could not have been a real phoenix, because there is only one of these at a time. Over by the mantelpiece there was a fox's mask, with GRAFTON, BUCKINGHAM TO DAVENTRY, 2 HRS 20 MINS written under it, and also a forty-pound salmon with AWE, 43 MIN., BULLDOG written under it, and a very life-like basilisk with CROWHURST OTTER HOUNDS in Roman print. There were several boars' tusks and the claws of tigers and libbards mounted in symmetrical patterns, and a big head of Ovis Poli, six live grass snakes in a kind of aquarium, some nests of the solitary wasp nicely set up in a glass cylinder, an ordinary beehive whose inhabitants went in and out of the window unmolested, two young hedgehogs in cotton wool, a pair of badgers which immediately began to cry Yik-Yik-Yik-Yik in loud voices as soon as the magician appeared, twenty boxes which contained stick caterpillars and six of the puss-moth, and even an oleander that was worth sixpence – all feeding on the appropriate leaves – a guncase with all sorts of weapons which would not be invented for half a thousand years, a rod-box ditto, a chest of drawers full of salmon flies which had been tied by Merlyn himself, another chest whose drawers were labelled Mandragora, Mandrake, Old Man's Beard, etc., a bunch of turkey feathers and goose-quills for making pens, an astrolabe, twelve pairs of boots, a dozen purse-nets, three dozen rabbit wires, twelve corkscrews, some ants' nests between two glass plates, ink-bottles of every possible colour from red to violet, darning-needles, a gold medal for being the best scholar at Winchester, four or five recorders, a nest of field-mice all alive-o, two skulls, plenty of cut glass, Venetian glass, Bristol glass and a bottle of Mastic varnish, some satsuma china and some cloisonné, the fourteenth edition of the Encyclopedia Brittanica (marred as it was by the sensationalism of the popular plates), two paint-boxes (one oil, one water-colour), three globes of the known geographical world, a few fossils, the stuffed head of a cameleopard, six pismires, some glass retorts with cauldrons, bunsen burners, etc., and a complete set of cigarette cards depicting wild fowl by Peter Scott.

From *The Sword in the Stone* by T. H. White, 1939, revised 1958

The Prince Rummages

What about the closet? Its gilt key turned reluctantly. All three shelves and the space beneath were stuffed with disparate objects: a palette with the dregs of many sunsets: a cupful of counters; an ivory backscratcher; a thirty-twomo edition of *Timon of Athens* translated into Zemblan by his Uncle Conmal, the Queen's brother; a seaside *situla* (toy pail); a sixty-five-carat blue diamond accidentally added in his childhood, from his late father's knickknackatory, to the pebbles and shells in that pail; a finger of chalk; and a square board with a design of interlaced figures for some long-forgotten game.

From *Pale Fire* by Vladimir Nabokov, 1962

'People's Surroundings'

They answer one's questions,
a deal table compact with the wall;
in this dried bone of arrangement
one's 'natural promptness' is compressed, not crowded out;
one's style is not lost in such simplicity.

The palace furniture, so old-fashioned, so old-fashionable;
Sèvres china and the fireplace dogs –
bronze dromios with pointed ears, as obsolete as pugs;
one has one's preferences in the matter of bad furniture,
and this is not one's choice.

The vast indestructible necropolis
of composite Yawman-Erbe separable units;
the steel, the oak, the glass, the Poor Richard publications
containing the public secrets of efficiency
on paper so thin that 'one thousand four hundred and twenty pages
        make one inch,'
exclaiming, so to speak, When you take my time, you take something
        I had meant to use;

the highway hid by fir-trees in rhododendron twenty feet deep,
the peacocks, hand-forged gates, old Persian velvet,
roses outlined in pale black on an ivory ground,
the pierced iron shadows of the cedars,
Chinese carved glass, old Waterford, lettered ladies;
landscape gardening twisted into permanence;

straight lines over such great distances as one finds in Utah or in
        Texas,
where people do not have to be told
that a good brake is as important as a good motor;
where by means of extra sense-cells in the skin
they can, like trout, smell what is coming –
those cool sirs with the explicit sensory apparatus of common sense,
who know the exact distance between two points as the crow flies;
there is something attractive about a mind that moves in a straight
        line –
the municipal bat-roost of mosquito warfare;

[193]

the American string quartet;
these are questions more than answers,

and Bluebeard's Tower above the coral-reefs,
the magic mouse-trap closing on all points of the compass,
capping like petrified surf the furious azure of the bay,
where there is no dust, and life is like a lemon-leaf,
a green piece of tough translucent parchment,
where the crimson, the copper, and the Chinese vermilion of the
 poincianas
set fire to the masonry and turquoise blues refute the clock;
this dungeon with odd notions of hospitality,
with its 'chessmen carved out of moonstones,'
its mocking-birds, fringed lilies, and hibiscus,
its black butterflies with blue half circles on their wings,
tan goats with onyx ears, its lizards glittering and without thickness,
like splashes of fire and silver on the pierced turquoise of the lattices
and the acacia-like lady shivering at the touch of a hand,
lost in a small collision of the orchids –
dyed quicksilver let fall,
to disappear like an obedient chameleon in fifty shades of mauve and
 amethyst.
Here where the mind of this establishment has come to the
 conclusion
that it would be impossible to revolve about oneself too much,
sophistication has, 'like an escalator,' 'cut the nerve of progress.'

In these non-committal, personal-impersonal expressions of
 appearance,
the eye knows what to skip;
the physiognomy of conduct must not reveal the skeleton;
'a setting must not have the air of being one,'
yet with X-ray-like inquisitive intensity upon it, the surfaces go back;
the interfering fringes of expression are but a stain on what stands
 out,
there is neither up nor down to it;
we see the exterior and the fundamental structure –
captains of armies, cooks, carpenters,
cutlers, gamesters, surgeons and armorers,
lapidaries, silkmen, glovers, fiddlers and ballad-singers,
sextons of churches, dyers of black cloth, hostlers and
 chimney-sweeps,

[194]

queens, countesses, ladies, emperors, travelers and mariners,
dukes, princes and gentlemen,
in their respective places –
camps, forges and battlefields,
conventions, oratories and wardrobes,
dens, deserts, railway stations, asylums and places where engines are
          made,
shops, prisons, brickyards and altars of churches –
in magnificent places clean and decent,
castles, palaces, dining-halls, theaters and imperial audience-chambers.

Marianne Moore (1887–1972)

Ambered and Cumbered with Other Matter

And so, the thought of love would be ambered over with snow and winter; with log fires burning; with Russian women, gold swords, and the bark of stags; with old King James' slobbering and fireworks and sacks of treasure in the holds of Elizabethan sailing ships. Every single thing, once he tried to dislodge it from its place in his mind, he found thus cumbered with other matter like the lump of glass which, after a year at the bottom of the sea, is grown about with bones and dragon-flies, and coins and the tresses of drowned women.

From *Orlando: A Biography* by Virginia Woolf, 1928

Des Cases dans le Cerveau

Il y a des cases dans le cerveau, avec inscriptions:
    A étudier au jour favorable. – A n'y penser jamais. – Inutile à approfondir. – Contenu non examiné. – Affaire sans issue. – Trésor connu et qui ne pourrait être attaqué que dans une second existence. – Urgent. – Dangereux. – Délicat. – Impossible. – Abandonné. – Réservé. – A d'autres! – Mon fort. – Difficile, etc.

There are boxes in the mind with labels on them: To study on a favourable occasion; Never to be thought about; Useless to go into further; Contents unexamined; Pointless business; Urgent; Dangerous; Delicate; Impossible; Abandoned; Reserved for others; My business; etcetera.

Paul Valéry, 1941, translated from the French by Alasdair Gray

Instead I Made Lists

It was not an unhappy time. I went away and there were fewer people. I found I was good-and-tired. I could lie around and was glad to, sleeping or dozing sometimes twenty hours a day and in the intervals trying resolutely not to think – instead I made lists – made lists and tore them up, hundreds of lists: of cavalry leaders and football players and cities, and popular tunes and pitchers, and happy times and hobbies and houses lived in and how many suits since I left the army and how many pairs of shoes (I didn't count the suit I bought in Sorrento that shrunk, nor the pumps and dress shirt and collar that I carried around for years and never wore, because the pumps got damp and grainy and the shirt and collar got yellow and starch-rotted). And lists of women I'd liked, and of the times I had let myself be snubbed by people who had not been my betters in character or ability.

From *The Crack-up* by F. Scott Fitzgerald, 1936

'Inventory'

Four be the things I am wiser to know:
Idleness, sorrow, a friend, and a foe.

Four be the things I'd been better without:
Love, curiosity, freckles, and doubt.

Three be the things I shall never attain:
Envy, content, and sufficient champagne.

Three be the things I shall have till I die:
Laughter and hope and a sock in the eye.

Dorothy Parker (1893–1967)

Pleasures Like the Zoo

The pleasure of dappled things, the beauty of adaptation to purpose, the glory of extravagance, classic elegance or romantic nonsense and grotes-querie – all these we get from the Zoo. We react to these with the same delight as to new potatoes in April speckled with chopped parsley or to the lights at night on the Thames of Battersea Power House, or to cars sweeping their shadows from lamp-post to lamp-post down Haverstock Hill or to brewer's drays or to lighthouses and searchlights or to a newly cut lawn or to a hot towel or a friction at the barber's or to Moran's two classic tries at Twickenham in 1937 or to the smell of dusting-powder in a warm bathroom or to the fun of shelling peas into a china bowl or of shuffling one's feet through dead leaves when they are crisp or to the noise of rain or to the crackling of a newly lit fire or the jokes of a street-hawker or the silence of snow in moonlight or the purring of a powerful car.

From *Zoo* by Louis MacNeice, 1938

'Elegant Things'

A white coat worn over a violet waistcoat.
Duck eggs.
Shaved ice mixed with liana syrup and put in a new silver bowl.
A rosary of rock crystal.
Wistaria blossoms. Plum blossoms covered with snow.
A pretty child eating strawberries.

From *The Pillow Book of Sei Shonagon*, tenth century, translated from the Japanese by Ivan Morris

A Tabletop by Holbein

The Bay of Spezia, mulberry groves, sheds where the silkworms fatten, but here, the sun in golden sheets and slats on the floor, young Revely's study was all Archimedes and Sicily, or a tabletop by Holbein with instruments in brass and walnut, calipers, rules, maps, calculations in silverpoint and red ink. Under a map in French colours, slate blues and provincial yellows, poppy reds, cabbage greens, a sepia line from Genoa across the Lunae Portus to Pisa, there sat in harmonic disarray a wooden bowl of quicksilver (a cup of Tuscan moonlight, a dish for gnomes to sup down in the iron roots of mountains where the earthquake demons swill lava and munch gold), cogged wheels, a screw propeller, drawings of frigates, steamboats, a machinery of gears and levers coloured blue and yellow, lighthouses with cyclopean lamps, plans of harbours and moorings, a lump of rosin, a china cup full of ink, a half-burnt match, a box of watercolours, a block of ivory, a volume of Laplace, a book of conic sections, spherics, logarithms, Saunderson's *Algebra*, Simms' *Trigonometry*, and most beautiful of all this Archi-magian gear, tilted in its fine calibrations, gleaming index and glass, the newly unpacked theodolite.

From *57 Views of Fujiyama* by Guy Davenport, 1981

The Geographical Agility of Thought

The mote of dust or small insect seen for an instant in a bend or pale of light, may remind us of the bird that winged swiftly through the lighted mote-hall, and that I suppose cannot but remind us of the northern Witan and that may recall the city of York and that again Canterbury and that the 'blisful briddes', and that again Tabard Street, E.C.1, and that London Bridge, and that the South Bank and its present abstract artefacts, and that again Battersea, and that the forcing of the river at the Claudian invasion, and that the 'Battersea shield', and that that other abstract art of the La Tène Celts in the British Museum in Bloomsbury, w.c.1.

From the Preface to *The Anathemata* by David Jones, 1952

Miss Wells's Room

Miss Wells's room was tiny, decorated, perched in and temporary. Black Victorian bookcases, with machine-cut Gothic beading of the kind that ruined the young Alfred Tennyson, supported a bitty collection of objects. Cut glass candlesticks, tin teacaddy with Gloire de Dijon roses, Japanese silk pincushion, conical Benares brass vase with two peacock feathers, three biscuit barrels (rotund glass, floral china and wicker, wooden keg with brass knobs), Florentine leather sewing bag, scissors with enamelled handles representing a crane stalking, a miniature Spode cup, six sugar-pink grey-tinged Woolworths tea-cups, a pile of apostle spoons, half a loaf of bread, half a pot of lemon curd, a pile of bills weighed down with a plaster of Paris hand, an ebony and silver crucifix, a crocheted beret, a bundle of lisle stockings, a bottle of ink, a jam-jar of red pencils, pussywillow and a Palm Sunday cross from the Holy Land . . .

From *The Virgin in the Garden* by A. S. Byatt, 1978

Classified, déclassé, aspiring to a higher class, they see themselves as unclassifiable, 'excluded,' 'dropped out,' 'marginal,' anything rather than categorized, assigned to a class, a determinate place in social space. And yet all their practices, cultural, sporting, educational, sexual, speak of classification – but in the mode of denial, as one sees from a few headings taken from the index of a 'resource' guide to adolescent counter-culture: akido, agit-prop, alternative press, anthroposophy, anti-gymnastics, anti-nuclear, anti-psychiatry, anti-radiation, anti-scientism, anti-vaccination, astrology, basket-making, biodynamics, bio-energy, biological farming, body, Charlie Hebdo, childhood, communes, creativity, dance, diet, drugs, ecology, encounters, esoterica, extra-terrestrial, folk, freedom, free flight, futuristics, gays, Gestalt therapy, gliding, go, green, hallucinogens, hiking, grass, homeopathy, imagination, immigrants, independent cinema, invention, judo, kyudo, Larzac, life, macrobiotics, madness, magnetism, nomads, non-verbal communication, non-violence, one-night stands, ongoing education, oriental medicine, parallel, parapsychology, parascientific popularization, physiotherapy, plants, pottery, prisons, psi-phenomena, regionalism, repression, science fiction, struggles, telepathy, therapy, trailers, transcendental meditation, travel, trekking, vegetarianism, weaving, yoga, Zen. An inventory of thinly-disguised expressions of a sort of dream of social flying, a desperate effort to defy the gravity of the social field.

From *Distinction* by Pierre Bourdieu, 1985

'J'aime, je n'aime pas –
I like, I don't like'

I like: salad, cinnamon, cheese, pimento, marzipan, the smell of new-cut hay (why doesn't someone with a 'nose' make such a perfume), roses, peonies, lavender, champagne, loosely held political convictions, Glenn Gould, too-cold beer, flat pillows, toast, Havana cigars, Handel, slow walks, pears, white peaches, cherries, colours, watches, all kinds of writing pens, desserts, unrefined salt, realistic novels, the piano, coffee, Pollock, Twombly, all romantic music, Sartre, Brecht, Verne, Fourier, Eisenstein, trains, Médoc wine, having change, *Bouvard et Pécuchet*, walking in sandals on the lanes of southwest France, the bend of the Adour seen from Doctor L's house, the Marx brothers, the mountains at seven in the morning leaving Salamanca, etc.

I don't like: white Pomeranians, women in slacks, geraniums, straw-berries, the harpsichord, Miró, tautologies, animated cartoons, Arthur Rubinstein, villas, the afternoon, Satie, Bartók, Vivaldi, telephoning, children's choruses, Chopin's concertos, Burgundian branles and Renaissance dances, the organ, Marc-Antoine Charpentier, his trumpets and kettle-drums, the politico-sexual, scenes, initiatives, fidelity, spontaneity, evenings with people I don't know, etc.

I like, I don't like: this is of no importance to anyone; this, apparently, has no meaning. And yet all this means: *my body is not the same as yours*. Hence, in this anarchic foam of tastes and distastes, a kind of listless blur, gradually appears the figure of a bodily enigma, requiring complicity or irritation. Here begins the intimidation of the body, which obliges others to endure me *liberally*, to remain silent and polite confronted by pleasures or rejections which they do not share.

From Roland Barthes by Roland Barthes, 1975

The Promised Life

Sometimes they thought that the lives they would lead would be as magical, as flexible, as whimsical as American comedy films or title sequences by Saul Bass; and miraculous, luminous visions of pristine snow-covered fields crossed by lines of ski-tracks, of blue seas, sun, verdant hills, of logs crackling in stone hearths, of spectacular motorways, of pullmans and palatial hotels caressed them, as if they were promises.

From *Things. A Story of the Sixties* by Georges Perec, 1965, translated from the French by David Bellos

What a Man Needs

John looks about him with enjoyment.
What a man needs, he thinks, is health;
Well-paid, congenial employment;
A house; a modicum of wealth;
Some sunlight; coffee and the papers;
Artichoke hearts adorned with capers;
A Burberry trenchcoat; a Peugeot;
And in the evening, some Rameau
Or Couperin; a home-cooked dinner;

A Stilton, and a little port;
And so to a duvet. In short,
In life's brief game to be a winner
A man must have ... oh yes, above
All else, of course, someone to love.

From *The Golden Gate* by Vikram Seth, 1986

Demands

1.

I said 12 Hankis, were are they?
I said 6 eggcups   ,,   ,,   ,,
Or where is at least one for me?
I said 2 pairs of sheets for double
bed. We need them.
Game of all kinds. I need Butter Bacon Potatoes Ham
Pheasant Grouse Duck Ptamigan Liars Cheats Breakers Marmalade

2.

No egg cups
No handkis
No sheets
You have been at my
whisky you swine.
Please leave it in here
in future. At least I can
witness your nefarious
practices.
So get your priorities straight
Spagheti. Ravioli. Potatoes. Butter
Bacon Eggcups Ham.
Endives.
Spring Onions
Garlic.
Spinach.
It is all my fault. I am a
shit..
Thank you.

3.

List.
Made by his Holiness Pope Roger the 1'st; in the
year A.D. 1973.
Thou shalt: procure my *Ronson* to be mended
Thou shalt *not* commit adultery.
Get those things mentioned by E. David like Coriander
Saffron &c. & *garlic*.
Buy some more torches.
Dog chain.
Fergis sandels &c.
Outfit for *yourself* from Boutique.
More anchovies.
Jaffa juice. Roses lime juice
Some tins of that HAM
Small bot. of Brilliantine. Doesn't matter unless you are in boots.
Sell up all arable land and strike Bottalack off The
map. That includes Harry. And me.
Buy rent or loan that grey horse.
Do not frequent the public houses in the town.
Go equiped with money. I must still have a credit
at PZ if not Jaco must arrange one.
Get a goose, brace of pheasants & so on (they've got to be
well hung)
Perambulator for transporting his holiness to
local.
A rivederci.

4.

Give me back my Observer. Beast.
List
All the usual
Mylanta.
Refills for stove.
Ronsonol, or better, get another
Ronson, like that one, in London.
Nitchevo. Get a packet of matches
Not that silly Cowgirl that Ben sells.
Cornish Match
This is a pretty hairy exedition you're going on.
All the breast as Al says.

[202]

Should be fun. Don't get too
exhausted before the show.
Try & rest up somewhere. Get Bo some
books & Me some new Tintins &c, &c,
I love you. (No, I want my Observer)

5.

Get some jam.
And beetroot
Most things damage the stomack
anyway.
There is a reek of common humanity
coming across the radio.
When you next buy spinach, get
epinaros en branches, not the finely
ground variety. Don't get any more
asperges, revolting.
Get more ginger nuts & don't let
the children get at them.
If you can find a ripe Camembert or
Bel Paese buyy them.
Terrine de perdraux à la Japonais
Barkus is willing.
Mackerel
Raie au beurre noir
Think nothing of it.
Squid.
Octopus.
Whitebait. Here here,
Well we've had a sumptuous meal
now. It only remains to tidy up the mess.
Done two cards
All wishfull thinking.

6.

Biscuits.
Water. Petit beure. Osborn.
Olive oil.
Put cheques in bank
More Radishes & Carrots uncooked.

Preferably young ones.
You can have Patum Peperium
I don't like it.
Only Italian Ravioli Spaghetti & that long saucage which kept me
going for a month Tell the man to get some more.
Fuck the gnomes of Zurick
& everything Swiss.
Soho Italiano.
Ring Stewart at Kinchy Hall
& ask where he bought that wine.
Keep the Labels so you can
get some more.
Walking Stick
Got through another night thank God
5 a.m.

7.

Spade.
Sugar
More French butter
More of those pink saucesges.
Those tins of ham.
Ring Jaco & ask him if there's any dough.
At all at all.
Give me my gherkins back.
Cunning little woman thinks, 'Give him a
list to make, that will keep him happy for
an hour.'
Eggs Eggs c.f. Kipling 'boots boots boots'
Ring Jaco.

From the *Night Letters* of Roger Hilton (1911–75)

'A Hunger'

Black beans, white sunlight.
These have sufficed.

Approval of mothers, of brothers,
of strangers – a plunge of the hands
in sifted flour, over the wrists.
It gives pleasure.

And being needed. Being loved for that.
Being forgiven.

What mountains there are
to border solitude and provide
limits, blue or
dark as raisins.

But hunger: a hunger there is
refuses. Refuses the earth.

Denise Levertov

Valentine's Day Resolutions

'Aren't you mixing this up with New Year's?'
  'Nah. That's nickel-dime stuff. Smoking-eating-drinking resolutions.
These are the – you know – the hardcore, maybe-this-time, kiss-today-
goodbye, some-enchanted-evening resolutions.'
  He reached into the pocket of his Pendleton and handed her a sheet of
paper:

MICHAEL TOLLIVER'S DIRTY THIRTY FOR '77
  1. I will not call anyone nellie or butch, unless that is his name.
  2. I will not assume that women who like me are fag hags.
  3. I will stop expecting to meet Jan-Michael Vincent at the tubs.
  4. I will inhale poppers only through the mouth.
  5. I will not spend more than half an hour in the shower at the Y.
  6. I will stop trying to figure out what colour my handkerchief would be if
     I wore one.

7. I will buy a drink for a Fifties Queen sometime.
8. I will not persist in hoping that attractive men will turn out to be brainless and boring.
9. I will sign my real name at The Glory Holes.
10. I will ease back into religion by attending concerts at Grace Cathedral.
11. I will not cruise at Grace Cathedral.
12. I will not vote for *anyone* for Empress.
13. I will make friends with a straight man.
14. I will not make fun of the way he walks.
15. I will not tell him about Alexander the Great, Walt Whitman or Leonardo da Vinci.
16. I will not vote for politicians who use the phrase 'Gay Community'.
17. I will not cry when Mary Tyler Moore goes off the air.
18. I will not measure it, no matter who asks.
19. I will not hide the A-200.
20. I will not buy a Lacoste shirt, a Marimekko pillow, a secondhand letterman's jacket, an All-American Boy T-shirt, a razor blade necklace or a denim accessory of any kind.
21. I will learn to eat alone and like it.
22. I will not fantasise about firemen.
23. I will not tell anyone at home that I just haven't found the right girl yet.
24. I will wear a suit on Castro Street and feel comfortable about it.
25. I will not do impressions of Bette Davis, Tallulah Bankhead, Mae West or Paul Lynde.
26. I will not eat more than one It's-It in a single evening.
27. I will find myself acceptable.
28. I will meet somebody nice, away from a bar or the tubs or a roller-skating rink, and I will fall hopelessly but conventionally in love.
29. But I won't say I love you before he does.
30. The hell I won't.

From *More Tales of the City* by Armistead Maupin, 1980

'What to Say When You Talk to Yourself'

In the corner, doubled up, black PVC,
my travelling bag: my four cream walls: my single key:
my wardrobe: my mirror: my coloured underwear:
my sponge bag: my dirty laundry watching me:
my comb, my gel and my spikes of hair:

my box of matches: my sparks:
my wallet and my BR clerks:
my grilles: my Standard Class return
to Paddington: my black remarks:
my fondness for watching things burn:

my rainy pavements, all night
barnacled with yellow light:
my nostalgia for the beach:
my empty rooms: my long sight
and my skinny, boxer's reach:

my arrivals, my departures: my grey, wax-faced
commuters on the Circle Line: my sense of waste:
my animosities: my lungs: my sliding door
hiccoughing at Swindon: my freshly-soled and -laced
black boots, fit for pacing my bedroom floor,

and one brittle rose
sandwiched in the prose
of Jonathan Swift:
my forehead, my nose,
my ears and my gift

for hanging pictures well: my rigid way with words:
my desserts: my tasteless ties: my love of birds
with Paxo: big eyes and lips: my skew-whiff smile
dying on my face: my dark, unbroken turds
slipped into the water like a crocodile.

Stephen Knight, 1988

Six

SOMETHING UNDERSTOOD

*Sacred and Profane Renaissance
Lists*

Sweetly Empty Woods

O sweet woods, the delight of solitariness!
O how much I do like your solitariness!
Here nor treason is hid, veilèd in innocence,
Nor envy's snaky eye finds any harbour here,
Nor flatterers' venomous insinuations,
Nor cunning humorists' puddled opinions,
Nor courteous ruin of proffered usury,
Nor time prattled away, cradle of ignorance,
Nor causeless duty, nor cumber of arrogance,
Nor trifling title of vanity dazzleth us,
Nor golden manacles stand for a paradise.
Here wrong's name is unheard, slander a monster is.
Keep thy sprite from abuse, here no abuse doth haunt:
What man grafts in a tree dissimulation?

From 'Solitariness' in the *Arcadia*
by Sir Philip Sidney (1554–86)

'False Love'

Farewell false love, the oracle of lies,
   A mortal foe and enemy to rest,
An envious boy, from whom all cares arise,
   A bastard vile, a beast with rage possessed,
     A way of error, a temple full of treason,
     In all effects contrary unto reason.

A poisoned serpent covered all with flowers,
   Mother of sighs, and murderer of repose,
A sea of sorrows from whence are drawn such showers,
   As moisture lend to every grief that grows,
     A school of guile, a net of deep deceit,
     A gilded hook, that holds a poisoned bait.

A fortress foiled, which reason did defend,
   A Syren song, a fever of the mind,
A maze wherein affection finds no end,
   A ranging cloud that runs before the wind,

A substance like the shadow of the sun,
A goal of grief for which the wisest run.

A quenchless fire, a nurse of trembling fear,
A path that leads to peril and mishap,
A true retreat of sorrow and despair,
An idle boy that sleeps in pleasure's lap,
A deep mistrust of that which certain seems,
A hope of that which reason doubtful deems.

Sith then thy trains my younger years betrayed
And for my faith ingratitude I find.
And sith repentance hath my wrongs bewrayed
Whose course was ever contrary to kind.
False love, desire and beauty frail adieu!
Dead is the root whence all these fancies grew.

Sir Walter Raleigh (1552?–1618)

An Inscription

Grass of levity,
Span in brevity,
Flowers' felicity,
Fire of misery,
Winds' stability,
Is mortality.

Dated 1609, in St Mary Magdalene, Milk Street, London

All These the Lord Did Frame

The azured vault, the crystal circles bright,
The gleaming fiery torches powdered there;
The changing round, the shining beamy light,
The sad bearded fires, the monsters fair;
The prodigies appearing in the air;
The rearding thunders and the blustering winds;
The fowls in hue and shape and nature rare,
The pretty notes that winged musicians finds;

[211]

In earth, the savoury flowers, the metalled minds,
The wholesome herbs, the hautie pleasant trees,
The silver streams, the beasts of sundry kinds,
The bounded roars and fishes of the seas, –
    All these, for teaching man, the Lord did frame
    To do his will whose glory shines in thame.

By King James I, in *The Lepanto*, 1591

'Time'

Time wasteth years, and months, and hours,
    Time doth consume fame, honour, wit, and strength,
Time kills the greenest herbs and sweetest flowers,
    Time wears out youth and beauty's looks at length,
        Time doth convey to ground both foe and friend,
        And each thing else but love, which hath no end.

Time maketh every tree to die and rot,
    Time turneth oft our pleasures into pain,
Time causeth wars and wrongs to be forgot,
    Time clears the sky, which first hung full of rain,
        Time makes an end of all humane desire,
        But only this, which sets my heart on fire.

Time turneth into nought each princely state,
    Time brings a flood from new resolved snow,
Time calms the sea where tempest was of late,
    Time eats whate'er the moon can see below;
        And yet no time prevails in my behove,
        Nor any time can make me cease to love.

From *Hekatompathia* by Thomas Watson, 1582

'Time'

In time the strong and stately turrets fall,
   In time the rose and silver lilies die,
In time the monarchs captive are, and thrall,
   In time the seas and rivers are made dry;
The hardest flint in time doth melt asunder;
   Still living fame in time doth fade away;
The mountains proud we see in time come under;
   And earth, for age, we see in time decay.
The sun in time forgets for to retire
   From out the east where he was wont to rise;
The basest thoughts we see in time aspire,
   And greedy minds in time do wealth despise.
      Thus all, sweet Fair, in time must have an end,
      Except thy beauties, virtues, and thy friend.

From *Licia* by Giles Fletcher, 1593

Maidenhood

The perfectest of all created things;
The purest gold that suffers no allay;
The sweetest flower that on th'earth's bosom springs;
The pearl unbored, whose prize no price can pay.

The crystal glass that will no venom hold;
The mirror wherein angels love to look;
Diana's bathing fountain, clear and cold;
Beauty's fresh rose, and virtue's living book.

Of love and fortune both the mistress born;
The sovereign spirit that will be thrall to none;
The spotless garment that was never worn;
The princely eagle that still flies alone.

From 'A Contention betwixt a Wife, a Widow, and a Maid'
by Sir John Davies, 1602

A Valet, a Pillar, a Cloudburst of Water

From the metal poppy
this good blast of trance
arriving as a shock, private cloudburst blazing down,
worst in a boarding-house greased tub, or a barrack with
      competitions,
best in a stall, this enveloping passion of Australians:
tropics that sweat for you, torrent that braces with its heat,
inflames you with its chill, action sauna, reverse bidet,
sleek vertical coruscating ghost of your inner river,
reminding all your fluids, streaming off your points, awakening
the tacky soap to blossom and ripe autumn, releasing the
      squeezed gardens,
smoky valet smoothing your impalpable overnight pyjamas off,
pillar you can step through, force-field absolving love's
      efforts,
nicest yard of the jogging track, speeding aeroplane minutely
steered with two controls, or trimmed with a knurled wheel . . .

From 'Shower' by Les A. Murray

'Sic Vita'

Like to the falling of a Starre;
Or as the flights of Eagles are;
Or like the fresh springs gawdy hew;
Or silver drops of morning dew;
Or like a wind that chafes the flood;
Or bubbles which on water stood;
Even such is man, whose borrow'd light
Is streight call'd in, and paid to night.

The wind blows out; the Bubble dies;
The Spring entomb'd in Autumn lies;
The Dew dries up; the Starre is shot;
The Flight is past; and Man forgot.

Henry King (1592–1669)

Sleep

Sleepe, Death's allye, oblivion of teares,
　Silence of passions, balme of angry sore,
Suspence of loves, securitie of feares,
　Wrath's lenitive, heart's ease, storme's calmest shore;
Senses' and soules' reprievall from all cumbers,
Benumning sense of ill, with quiet slumbers.

From 'St Peter's Complaint' by Robert Southwell, 1595

Life

La vie est du futur un souhait agréable
Et regret du passé, un désir indompté
De goûter et tâter ce qu'on n'a pas goûté,
De ce qu'on a goûté un dégoût incurable;

Un vain ressouvenir de l'état désirable
Des siècles jà passés, du futur souhaité
Un espoir incertain, frivolement jeté
Sur le vain fondement d'une attente muable;

Une horreur de soi-même, un souhait de sa mort,
Un mépris de sa vie, un gouffre de remords,
Un magasin de pleurs, une mer de tempête:

Où plus nous approchons du rivage lointain,
Plus nous nous regrettons et lamentons en vain
Que le vent ait si tôt notre course parfaite.

Jean-Baptiste Chassignet (c. 1570–1635)

Fear

Ah, Feare! abortive impe of drouping mind;
   Selfe-overthrow, false friend, roote of remorse:
Sighted, in seeing evils; in shunning blind:
   Foil'd without field, by fancie not by force;
Ague of valour; phrensie of the wise;
   True honour's staine; love's frost, the mint of lies.

From 'St Peter's Complaint' by Robert Southwell, 1595

The Life of Man

A blast of wind, a momentary breath,
   A watery bubble symbolized with air,
   A sun-blown rose, but for a season fair,
A ghostly glance, a skeleton of death;
A morning dew, pearling the grass beneath,
   Whose moisture sun's appearance doth impair;
   A lightning glimpse, a muse of thought and care,
A planet's shot, a shade which followeth,
A voice which vanisheth so soon as heard,
   The thriftless heir of time, a rolling wave,
A show, no more in action than regard,
   A mass of dust, world's momentary slave,
     Is man, in state of our old Adam made,
     Soon born to die, soon flourishing to fade.

From the *Spiritual Sonnets* by Barnaby Barnes, 1595

Christian Names

If that any among us have named their children *Remedium amoris*, *Imago sæculi*, or with such like names, I know some will thinke it more then a vanitie, as they doe but little better of the new names, *Free-gift*, *Reformation*, *Earth*, *Dust*, *Ashes*, *Delivery*, *More fruite*, *Tribulation*, *The Lord is neare*, *More triall*, *Discipline*, *Joy againe*, *From above*: which have lately beene given by some to their children with no evill meaning, but upon some singular and precise conceit.

From *Remaines concerning Britaine* by William Camden, 1614

'Why? What Are Men?'

Why? what are men? But quicken'd lumps of earth?
A FEAST FOR WORMES; A bubble full of mirth;
A Looking-glasse for griefe; A flashe; A minute;
A painted Toombe, with putrifaction in it;
A mappe of Death; A burthen of a song;
A winter's Dust; A worme of fiue foot long:
Begot in sinne; In darknesse nourisht; Borne
In sorrow; Naked; Shiftlesse; and forlorne:
His first voice (heard) is crying for reliefe;
Alas! he comes into a world of griefe:
His Age is sinfull; and his Youth is vaine;
His Life's a punishment; his death's a paine;
His Life's an houre of Ioy; a world of Sorrow;
His death's a winter's night, that findes no morrow:
Man's life's an Houre-glasse, which being run,
Concludes that houre of Ioy, and so is dun . . .

From the 'Meditatio prima' of *A Feast for Wormes*
by Francis Quarles, 1626

The Purified Soul

... No hope deceives it, and no doubt divides it;
No grief disturbs it, and no errour guides it;
No fear distracts it, and no rage inflames it;
No guilt condemns it, and no folly shames it;
No sloth besots it, and no lust inthralls it;
No scorn afflicts it, and no passion gawls it:
It is a carknet of immortall life;
An Ark of peace; the lists of sacred strife;
A purer piece of endlesse transitory;
A shrine of Grace, a little throne of Glory:
A Heav'n-born Of-spring of a new-born birth;
An earthly Heav'n; an ounce of Heav'nly earth.

From Book 2, number 15 of the *Emblemes* by Francis Quarles, 1643

Diversely Holy Darkness

Dear night! this worlds defeat;
The stop to busie fools; cares check and curb;
The day of Spirits; my souls calm retreat
    Which none disturb!
Christs progress, and his prayer time;
The hours to which high Heaven doth chime.

Gods silent, searching flight:
When my Lords head is fill'd with dew, and all
His locks are wet with the clear drops of night;
    His still, soft call;
His knocking time; The souls dumb watch,
When Spirits their fair kindred catch.

From 'The Night' in *Silex Scintillans* by Henry Vaughan, 1650

'Son-dayes'

Bright shadows of true Rest! some shoots of blisse,
          Heaven once a week;
The next worlds gladnes prepossest in this;
          A day to seek
Eternity in time; the steps by which
We Climb above all ages; Lamps that light
Man through his heap of dark days; and the rich,
And full redemption of the whole weeks flight.

The Pulleys unto headlong man; times bower;
          The narrow way;
Transplanted Paradise; Gods walking houre;
          The Cool o'th' day;
The Creatures *Jubile*; Gods parle with dust;
Heaven here; Man on those hills of Myrrh, and flowres;
Angels descending; The Returns of Trust;
A Gleam of glory, after six-days-showres.

The Churches love-feasts; Times Prerogative,
          And Interest
Deducted from the whole; The Combs, and hive,
          And home of rest.
The milky way Chalkt out with Suns; a Clue
That guides through erring hours; and in full story
A taste of Heav'n on earth; the pledge, and Cue
Of a full feast; And the Out Courts of glory.

From *Silex Scintillans* by Henry Vaughan, 1650

'Prayer (i)'

Prayer the Churches banquet, Angels age,
    Gods breath in man returning to his birth,
    The soul in paraphrase, heart in pilgrimage,
The Christian plummet sounding heav'n and earth;
Engine against th'Almightie, sinners towre,
    Reversed thunder, Christ-side-piercing spear,
    The six-daies world transposing in an houre,

[219]

A kinde of tune, which all things heare and fear;
Softnesse, and peace, and joy, and love, and blisse,
   Exalted Manna, gladnesse of the best,
   Heaven in ordinarie, man well drest,
The milkie way, the bird of Paradise,
   Church-bels beyond the starres heard, the souls bloud,
   The land of spices; something understood.

From *The Temple* by George Herbert, 1633

That Which I Love When I Love My God

But yet when I loue thee, what kind of thing is it that I loue? Not the beauty
of bodyes, not the order of tyme; not the cleernes of this light which our
eyes are so glad to see; not the harmony of sweet songes in Musique; not the
fragrancy of flowres, and other unctuous and aromatical odours; not
Manna, nor any thing of sweet and curious tast; not carnall creaturs which
may delightfuly be imbraced by flesh and bloud: They are not these thinges
which I loue in louing God. And yet I loue a kind of *Light*, a kind of *voyce*, a
kind of *odour*, a kind of *food*, and a kind of *imbracing*, when I loue my God;
The *light*, the *voyce*, the *odour*, the *food* and the *imbracing* of my inward man.
Where that shins to my soule, which is not circumscribed by any place; that
sounds to myne eare which is not stolne, and snatcht away by tyme; that
yieldeth smell which is not scattered by ayre; that sauours in tast, which is
not consumed by our eating; that remayns enioyed, which is not diuorced
by satiety; This is that which I loue when I loue my God.

From the *Confessions* of St Augustine, translated from the Latin
by Sir Tobias Matthew, 1620

Prayer and Anger

The first thing that hinders the prayers of a good man from obtaining its
effect is a violent anger, a violent storm in the spirit of him that prayes. For
anger sets the house on fire, and all the spirits are busie upon trouble, and
intend propulsion, defence, displeasure or revenge; it is a short madnesse,
and an eternall enemy to discourse, and sober counsels, and fair conversation; it intends its own object with all the earnestnesse of perception, or
activity of designe, and a quicker motion of a too warm and distempered
bloud; it is a feaver in the heart, and a calenture in the head, and a fire in the

[220]

face, and a sword in the hand, and a fury all over; and therefore can never suffer a man to be in a disposition to pray. For prayer is an action and a state of entercourse, and desire, exactly contrary to this character of anger. Prayer is an action of likenesse to the holy Ghost, the Spirit of gentlenesse and dove-like simplicity; an imitation of the holy Jesus, whose Spirit is meek up to the greatnesse of the biggest example, and a conformity to God whose anger is alwaies just, and marches slowly, and is without transportation, and often hindred, and never hasty, and is full of mercy; prayer is the peace of our spirit, the stilnesse of our thoughts, the evennesse of recollection, the seat of meditation, the rest of our cares, and the calme of our tempest; prayer is the issue of a quiet minde, of untroubled thoughts, it is the daughter of charity, and the sister of meeknesse; and he that prays to God with an angry, that is, with a troubled and discomposed spirit, is like him that retires into a battle to meditate, and sets up his closet in the out quarters of an army, and chooses a frontier garrison to be wise in.

From *XXV Sermons Preached at Golden-Grove* by Jeremy Taylor, 1653

God's Gatherings and Humanity's Divisions

All my Fathers Angels stand *gathered* together about his Throne: No Bread is made, but of graines of Corne *gathered* together: no building is raysed, but of a number of stones glued and *gathered* together. There is no perfect societie or Citty, but of a number of men *gathered* together. Geese (which are the simplest of al foules) *gather* themselues together, goe together, flie together. Bees in one Hiue holde their consistory *together*. The starres in Heauen doe shine *together*. What is a man, if the parts of his body be disparted, and not incorporated and essentiate *together*? What is the Sea, but an assembly or *gathering together* of waters, and so the Earth, a congestion or heaping vp of grosse matter *together*? A Wood or Forrest, but an hoste of Trees encampt *together*? A generall counsaile or Parliament, but a congregation or *gathering together* of special wise-men, to consult about Religion or Lawes? *O what a good thing is it* (saith *Dauid*) *for Bretheren to liue or be gathered together in vnity!* ... Nor *Dauid*, nor all the euills of diuision, nor al the instances of Angels, Bread, buildings, societies, Geese, Bees, starres, Men, Seas, counsails, Parliaments, may conform these vngratious degenerates.

From *Christs Teares Over Ierusalem* by Thomas Nashe, 1593

Angels in the Plural

I consider thy plentiful goodness, O my God, in employing angels more than one in so many of thy remarkable works. Of thy Son, thou sayest, *Let all the angels of God worship him*; if that be in heaven, upon earth he says, *that he could command twelve legions of angels*; and when heaven and earth shall be all one, at the last day, thy Son, O God, *the Son of man, shall come in his glory, and all the holy angels with him*. The angels that celebrated his birth to the shepherds, the angels that celebrated his second birth, his resurrection, to the Maries, were in the plural, angels associated with angels. In Jacob's ladder, they who ascended and descended, and maintained the trade between heaven and earth, between thee and us, they who have the commission, and charge to guide us in all our ways, they who hastened Lot, and in him, us, from places of danger and temptation, they who are appointed to instruct and govern us in the church here, they who are sent to punish the disobedient and refractory, they that are to be mowers and harvestmen after we are grown up in one field, the church, at the day of judgement, they that are to carry our souls whither they carried Lazarus, they who attend at the several gates of the new Jerusalem, to admit us there; all these who administer to thy servants, from the first to their last, are angels, angels in the plural, in every service angels associated with angels.

From *Devotions upon Emergent Occasions* by John Donne, 1624

From The Litany

From all evil and mischief, from sin, from the crafts and assaults of the devil, from thy wrath, and from everlasting damnation,
Good Lord, deliver us.
From all blindness of heart; from pride, vain-glory, and hypocrisie; from envy, hatred, and malice, and all uncharitableness,
Good Lord, deliver us.
From fornication, and all other deadly sin; and from all the deceits of the world, the flesh, and the devil,
Good Lord, deliver us.
From lightning and tempest; from plague, pestilence, and famine; from battle, and murder, and from sudden death,
Good Lord, deliver us.
From all sedition, privy conspiracy, and rebellion; from all false doctrine,

heresie, and schism; from hardness of heart, and contempt of thy Word and Commandment,
Good Lord, deliver us.

From *The Book of Common Prayer*, 1662

Better Ways to Read the Word

... but better schollers they, that have their lessons without book, and can reade God (not by roate) but plainly and perfectly, on the backside, and outside of the book, as well as in the inside: that can take this Primer in their hands; and hold it heeles upward, and then reade him there: that can spell every word backwards, and then tell what it is: that can reade him from the left hand to the right, as if they were reading *English*, or from the right to the left, as if they were reading *Hebrew*: that can read God as plainly in the *Octavo* of a late converted JEW, as in a Church Bible in *Folio*: that can reade him within book, and without book, and as well without book, as within book: that can reade him downwards and upwards, upwards and downwards, from left to right, from right to left: that can reade him in the Sun, and in the Clouds, and as well in the Clouds, as in the Sun.

From *Some Sweet Sips, of Some Spirituall Wine* by Abiezer Coppe, 1649

What and Who God Can Speak Through

And it is neither Paradox, Hetrodox, Riddle, or ridiculous to good Schollers, who know the *Lord in deed*, (though perhaps they know never a letter in the Book) to affirm that God can speak, & gloriously preach to some through Carols, Anthems, Organs; yea, all things else, &c. Through Fishers, Publicans, Tanners, Tent-makers, Leathern-aprons, as well as through University men, – Long-gowns, Cloakes, or Cassocks; O *Strange*!

From *Some Sweet Sips, of Some Spirituall Wine* by Abiezer Coppe, 1649

Ardelia's Spiritual Progress

But all in vain are Pray'rs, extatick Thoughts,
Recover'd Moments, and retracted Faults,
Retirement, which the World *Moroseness* calls,
Abandon'd Pleasures in Monastick Walls:
These, but at distance, towards that purpose tend,
The lowly Means to an exalted End;
Which He must perfect, who allots her Stay,
And That, accomplish'd, will direct the way.
Pity her restless Cares, and weary Strife,
And point some Issue to escaping Life;
Which so dismiss'd, no Pen nor Human Speech
Th'ineffable Recess can ever teach:
Th'Expanse, the Light, the Harmony, the Throng,
The Bride's Attendance, and the Bridal Song,
The numerous Mansions, and th'immortal Tree,
No Eye, unpurg'd by Death, must ever see,
Or Waves which through that wond'rous City roll...

From 'A Fragment' by Anne Finch, Countess of Winchilsea (1661–1720)

Seven

HOSTILITIES

Polemic, Satire and Abuse

From *The Crab with the Golden Claws*
© Hergé, 1953

Pagans

You are fond of spectacles: expect the greatest of all spectacles, the last and eternal judgment of the universe. How shall I admire, how laugh, how rejoice, how exult, when I behold so many proud monarchs and fancied gods groaning in the lowest abyss of darkness; so many magistrates, who persecuted the name of the Lord, liquefying in fiercer fires than they ever kindled against the Christians; so many sage philosophers blushing in red-hot flames with their deluded scholars; so many celebrated poets trembling before the tribunal not of Minos but of Christ; so many tragedians, more tuneful in the expression of their own sufferings; so many dancers, lither of limb by far than in life; so many charioteers, reddened by wheels of flame; so many athletes to be seen, not in the gymnasium, but in the furnace . . .

From *De Spectaculis* by Tertullian (160–225)

Papists

In the meantime, he that shall but see their profane rites and foolish customs, how superstitiously kept, how strictly observed, their multitude of saints, images, that rabble of Romish deities, for trades, professions, diseases, persons, offices, countries, places: St. George for England; St. Denis for France; Patrick, Ireland; Andrew, Scotland; Jago, Spain, etc.; Gregory for students; Luke for painters; Cosmas and Damian for philosophers; Crispin, shoemakers; Katherine, spinners, etc.; Anthony for pigs; Gallus, geese; Wenceslaus, sheep; Pelagius, oxen; Sebastian, the plague; Valentine, falling sickness: Apollonia, toothache; Petronella for agues; and the Virgin Mary for sea and land, for all parties, offices: he that shall observe these things, their shrines, images, oblations, pendants, adorations, pilgrimages they make to them, what creeping to crosses, our Lady of Loretto's rich gowns, her donaries, the cost bestowed on images, and number of suitors; St. Nicholas' burg in France; our St. Thomas' shrine of old at Canterbury; those relics at Rome, Jerusalem, Genoa, Lyons, Pratum, St. Denis; and how many thousands come yearly to offer to them, with what cost, trouble, anxiety, superstition (for forty masses are daily said in some of their churches, and they rise at all hours of the night to mass, come barefoot, etc.), how they spend themselves, times, goods, lives, fortunes, in such ridiculous observations; their tales and figments, false miracles, buying and selling of pardons, indulgences for 40,000 years to come, their

[226]

processions on set days, their strict fastings, monks, anachorites, friar mendicants, Franciscans, Carthusians, etc.; their vigils and fasts, their ceremonies at Christmas, Shrovetide, Candlemas, Palm-Sunday, St. Blaise, St. Martin, St. Nicholas' day; their adorations, exorcisms etc., will think all those Grecian, pagan, Mahometan superstitions, gods, idols, and ceremonies, the name, time, and place, habit only altered, to have degenerated into Christians.

From *The Anatomy of Melancholy* by Robert Burton, 1621

Socialists

One sometimes gets the impression that the mere words 'Socialism' and 'Communism' draw towards them with magnetic force every fruit-juice drinker, nudist, sandal-wearer, sex-maniac, Quaker, 'Nature Cure' quack, pacifist and feminist in England.

From *The Road to Wigan Pier* by George Orwell, 1937

Animals

Break that Deer; Leach that Brawn; Rear that Goose; Lift that Swan; Sawce that Capon; Spoyl that Hen; Trush that Chicken; Unbrace that Mallard; Unlace that Cony; Dismember that Heron; Display that Crane; Disfigure that Peacock; Unjoynt that Bittern: Untach that Curlew: Allay that Pheasant: Wing that Partridge, with that Quail: Mince that Plover: Thigh that Pigeon: Border that Pastie: Thigh that Woodcock, also all manner of small fowl: Timber the fire: Tire the Egg: Chine that Salmon: String that Lamprey: Splat the Pike: Sauce that Plaice: Sauce that Tench; Splay that Bream: Side that Haddock: Tusk that Barbel: Culpon that Trout: Fin that Chevine: Transon that Eele: Tranch that Sturgeon: Underteach that Porpas: Tame that Crab: Barb that Lobster.

From *The Whole Body of Cookery Dissected* by William Rabisha, 1661

Man

Man is to man all kinds of beasts; a fawning dog, a roaring lion, a thieving fox, a robbing wolf, a dissembling crocodile, a treacherous decoy, and a rapacious vulture.

> From the essay 'The Dangers of an Honest Man in Company'
> by Abraham Cowley (1618–67)

Natural Detestations

My heart hath naturally detested foure things: The standing of the Apocrypha in the Bible; Forrainers dwelling in my Countrey, to crowd out native Subjects into the corners of the Earth; Alchymized coins; Tolerations of diverse Religions, or of one Religion in segregant shapes . . .

> From *The Simple Cobler of Agawam in America* by Nathaniel Ward, 1647

Squalid Things

The back of a piece of embroidery.
The inside of a cat's ear.
A swarm of mice, who still have no fur, when they come wriggling out of their nest.
The seams of a fur robe that has not yet been lined.
Darkness in a place that does not give the impression of being very clean.
A rather unattractive woman who looks after a large brood of children.
A woman who falls ill and remains unwell for a long time. In the mind of her lover, who is not particularly devoted to her, she must appear rather squalid.

> From *The Pillow Book of Sei Shonagon*, tenth century,
> translated from the Japanese by Ivan Morris

Villainous and Abominable Falstaff

Prince: Swearest thou, ungracious boy? henceforth ne'er look on me. Thou art violently carried away from grace: there is a devil haunts thee in the likeness of an old fat man; a tun of man is thy companion. Why dost thou converse with that trunk of humours, that bolting-hutch of beastliness, that swoln parcel of dropsies, that huge bombard of sack, that stuffed cloak-bag of guts, that roasted Manningtree ox with the pudding in his belly, that reverend vice, that grey iniquity, that father ruffian, that vanity in years? Wherein is he good but to taste sack and drink it? wherein neat and cleanly but to carve a capon and eat it? wherein cunning but in craft? wherein crafty but in villany? wherein villanous but in all things? wherein worthy but in nothing?

Falstaff: I would your grace would take me with you: whom means your grace?

Prince: That villanous abominable misleader of youth, Falstaff, that old white-bearded Satan.

> From *Henry IV Part 1*, Act II Scene iv,
> by William Shakespeare, 1598

Overbold Invectives

But I can prompt you with a demonstration wherin Invectiues haue been too bold. Do you remember what you writ in your Item for Earthquakes, *of double fac'd* Iani, *changeable Cameleons, Aspen leaues, painted sheathes, and sepulchers, Asses in Lions skinnes, dunghill cockes, slipperie eeles, dormise, &c?* Besides your testimoniall of Doctour *Perne*, wherein it pleased you, of your singular liberalitie and bountie, to bestowe vpon him this beautifull *Encomium*: *A busie and diʒʒie head, a braʒen fore head, a leaden braine, a wodden witte, a copper face, a stonie brest, a factious and eluish heart, a founder of nouelties, a confounder of his owne and his friendes good giftes, a morning booke-worme, an afternoon malt-worme, a right Iugler, as full of his sleightes, wiles, fetches, casts of legerdemaine, toyes to mocke Apes withall, odde shifts and knauish practises, as his skinne can holde.*

> From *Foure Letters Confuted* by Thomas Nashe, 1592

All Abusive Names He Was Called

Earwicker, that patternmind, that paradigmatic ear, receptoretentive as his of Dionysius, longsuffering although whitening under restraint in the sititout corner of his conservatory, behind faminebuilt walls, his thermos flask and ripidian flabel by his side and a walrus whiskerbristle for a tuskpick, compiled, while he mourned the flight of his wild guineese, a long

[229]

list (now feared in part lost) to be kept on file of all abusive names he was called (we have been compelled for the rejoicement of foinne loidies ind the humours of Milltown etcetera by Josephine Brewster in the collision known as Contrastations with Inkermann and so on and sononward, lacies in loo water, flee, celestials, one clean turv): *Firstnighter, Informer, Old Fruit, Yellow Whigger, Wheatears, Goldy Geit, Bogside Beauty, Yass We've Had His Badannas, York's Porker, Funnyface, At Baggotty's Bend He Bumped, Grease with the Butter, Opendoor Ospices, Cainandabler, Ireland's Eighth Wonderful Wonder, Beat My Price, Godsoilman, Moonface the Murderer, Hoary Hairy Hoax, Midnight Sunburst, Remove that Bible, Hebdromadary Publocation, Tummer the Lame the Tyrannous, Blau Clay, Tight before Teatime, Read Your Pantojoke, Acoustic Disturbance, Thinks He's Gobblasst the Good Dook of Ourguile, W D's Grace, Gibbering Bayamouth of Dublin, His Farther was a Mundzucker and She had him in a Growler, Burnham and Bailey, Artist, Unworthy of the Homely Protestant Religion, Terry Cotter, You're Welcome to Waterfood, signed the Ribbonmen, Lobsterpot Lardling, All for Arthur of this Town, Hooshed the Cat from the Bacon, Leathertogs Donald, The Ace and Deuce of Paupering, O'Reilly's Delights to Kiss the Man behind the Borrel, Magogagog, Swad Puddlefoot, Gouty Ghibeline, Loose Luther, Hatches Cocks' Eggs, Muddle the Plan, Luck before Wedlock, I Divorce Thee Husband, Tanner and a Make, Go to Hellena or Come to Connies, Pioball Puffpuff His Bride, Purged out of Burke's, He's None of Me Causin, Barebarean, Peculiar Person, Grunt Owl's Facktotem, Twelve Months Aristocrat, Lycanthrope, Flunkey Beadle Vamps the Tune Letting on He's Loney, Thunder and Turf Married into Clandorf, Left Boot Sent on Approval, Cumberer of Lord's Holy Ground, Stodge Arschmann, Awnt Yuke, Tommy Furlong's Pet Plagues, Archdukon Cabbanger, Last Past the Post, Kennealey Won't Tell Thee off Nancy's Gown, Scuttle to Cover, Salary Grab, Andy Mac Noon in Annie's Room, Awl Out, Twitchbratschballs, Bombard Street Bester, Sublime Porter, A Ban for Le King of the Burgaans and a Bom for Ye Sur of all the Ruttledges, O'Phelim's Cutprice, And at Number Wan Wan Wan, What He Done to Castlecostello, Sleeps with Feathers end Ropes, It is Known who Sold Horace the Rattler, Enclosed find the Sons of Fingal, Swayed in his Falling, Wants a Wife and Forty of Them, Let Him Do the Fair, Apeegeequanee Chimmuck, Plowp Goes his Whastle, Ruin of the Small Trader, He – – Milking-honeybeaverbrooker, Vee was a Vindner, Sower Rapes, Armenian Atrocity, Sickfish Bellyup, Edomite, – Man Devoyd of the Commoner Characteristics of an Irish Nature, Bad Humborg, Hraabhraab, Coocoohandler, Dirt, Miching Daddy, Born Burst Feet Foremost, Woolworth's Worst, Easyathic Phallusaphist, Guilteypig's Bastard, Fast in the Barrel, Boose in the Bed, Mister Fatmate, In Custody of the Polis, Boawwll's Alocutionist, Deposed.*

From *Finnegans Wake* by James Joyce, 1939

Nicknames

The history of politics, of religion, of literature, of morals, and of private life, is too often little less than the history of nicknames. What are one-half the convulsions of the civilized world – the frequent overthrow of states and kingdoms – the shock and hostile encounters of mighty continents – the battles by sea and land – the intestine commotions – the feuds of the Vitelli and Orsini, of the Guelphs and Ghibellines – the civil wars in England and the League in France – the jealousies and heart-burnings of cabinets and councils – the uncharitable proscriptions of creeds and sects, Turk, Jew, Pagan, Papist and Puritan, Quaker, and Methodist – the persecutions and massacres – the burnings, tortures, imprisonments, and lingering deaths, inflicted for a different profession of faith – but so many illustrations of the power of this principle?

From the essay 'On Nicknames' by William Hazlitt (1778–1830)

Surnames

If you please to compare the Roman names that seeme so stately, because you understand them not, you will disdaine them in respect of our meanest names; For what is *Fronto* but Beetle-browed? *Cæsius* but Cattes-eies? *Petus* but Pinke-eyed? *Cocles* One-eye, *Naso* Bottle-nose, *Galba* Maggot, as *Suetonius* interpreteth; *Silo* Apes-nose, *Ancus* Crooked arme, *Pansa* Broade-foote, *Strabo* Squint-eye, *Suillius* Swineheard, *Capito* Iobbernoll, *Calvus* Bald-pate, *Crispus* Curle-pate, *Flaccus* Loll-eares, or Flagge-eared, *Labeo* Blabber-lippe, *Scaurus* Knobd-heele, *Varus* Bow-legged, *Pedo* Long-shankes, *Marcellus* Hammer, for it commeth from *Marculus*, *Hortensius* Gardner, *Cilo* Petty-long-pate, *Chilo* Flap-lippes, or, as *Velius Longus* saith, *Improbioribus labris homo.*

From *Remaines concerning Britaine* by William Camden, 1614

An Argument for the Superiority of English

... neither can any tongue (as I am perswaded) deliver a matter with more varietie than ours, both plainely and by proverbs and Metaphors: for example, when wee would bee rid of one, we use to say, *bee going, trudge, packe, bee faring, hence, away, shift,* and by circumlocution; *Rather your roome*

then your company, lets see your backe, come againe when I bid you, when you are
called, sent for, intreated, willed, desired, invited, spare us your place, another in your
steed, a shippe of Salt for you, save your credite, you are next the doore, the doore is
open for you, there is no body holdeth you, no body tears your sleeve, &c.

From *The Excellencie of the English Tongue* by Richard Carew, 1614

A Pathetical Posy of Horrible New Expressions

The floures of your *Foure Letters* it may be I haue ouerlookt more narrowlie, and done my best deuoire to assemble them together into a patheticall posie, which I will here present to Maister Orator *Edge* for a Newyeares gift, leauing them to his *wordie* discretion to be censured, whether they be currant in inkehornisme or no.

Conscious mind: canicular tales: egregious an argument; when as egregious is neuer vsed in english but in the extreame ill part. Ingenuitie: Iouiall mind: valarous Authors: inckehorne aduentures: inckehorne pads: putatiue opinions: putatiue artists: energeticall persuasions: Rascallitie: materiallitie: artificiallitie: Fantasticallitie: diuine Entelechy: loud Mentery: deceitfull perfidy: addicted to Theory: the worlds great Incendiarie: sirenized furies: soueraigntie immense: abundant Cauteles: cautelous and aduentrous: cordiall liquor: Catilinaries and Phillipicks: perfunctorie discourses: Dauids sweetnes olimpique: the Idee high and deepe Abisse of excellence: The only Vnicorne of the Muses: the Aretinish mountain of huge exaggerations: The gratious law of Amnesty: amicable termes: amicable end: Effectuate: addoulce his melodie: Magy: polimechany: extensiuely emploid: precious Traynment: Nouellets: Notorietie: negotiation: mechanician.

Nor are these all, for euerie third line hath some of this ouer-rackt absonisme . . .

From *Foure Letters Confuted* by Thomas Nashe, 1592

Better Books to Burn

Had I fore-knowne of this thy least desire
T'have held a Triumph, or a feast of fire,
Especially in paper; that, that steame
Had tickled your large Nosthrill: many a Reame,
To redeeme mine, I had sent in; enough,
Thou should'st have cry'd, and all beene proper stuffe.
The *Talmud*, and the *Alcoran* had come,

With pieces of the *Legend*; The whole summe
Of errant Knight-hood, with the Dames, and Dwarfes;
The charmed Boates, and the inchanted Wharfes,
The Tristrams, Lanc'lots, Turpins, and the Peers,
All the madde Rolands, and sweet Oliveers;
To Merlins Marvailes, and his Caballs losse,
With the Chimæra of the Rosie-Crosse,
Their Seales, their Characters, Hermetique rings,
Their Jemme of Riches, and bright Stone, that brings
Invisibilitie, and strength, and tongues:
The art of kindling the true Coale, by lungs;
With Nicholas Pasquill's, Meddle with your match,
And the strong lines, that so the time doe catch,
Or Captaine Pamphlets horse, and foot; that sallie
Upon th'Exchange, still out of Popes-head-Alley,
The weekly Corrants, with Pauls Seale; and all
Th'admir'd discourses of the Prophet Ball:
These, had'st thou pleas'd either to dine, or sup,
Had made a meale for Vulcan to lick up.
But in my Deske, what was there to accite
So ravenous, and vast an appetite?

From 'An Execration upon Vulcan' by Ben Jonson, 1623

A Quick Catalogue of Non-Books

I have no repugnances. Shaftesbury is not too genteel for me, nor Jonathan Wild too low. I can read anything which I call *a book*. There are things in that shape which I cannot allow for such.

In this catalogue of *books which are no books – biblia a-biblia –* I reckon Court Calendars, Directories, Pocket Books, Draught Boards, bound and lettered on the back, Scientific Treatises, Almanacs, Statutes at Large: the works of Hume, Gibbon, Robertson, Beattie, Soame Jenyns, and generally, all those volumes which 'no gentleman's library should be without': the *Histories* of Flavius Josephus (that learned Jew), and Paley's *Moral Philosophy*. With those exceptions, I can read almost anything. I bless my stars for a taste so catholic, so unexcluding.

From 'Detached Thoughts on Books and Reading'
by Charles Lamb (1775–1834)

[233]

Prohibitions

1   There shall be no more novels in which a group of people, isolated by circumstances, revert to the 'natural condition' of man, become essential, poor, bare, forked creatures. All that may be written is one short story, the final one of the genre, the cork in the bottle. I'll write it for you. A group of travellers are shipwrecked, or airwrecked, somewhere, no doubt on an island. One of them, a large, powerful, dislikeable man, has a gun. He forces all the others to live in a sandpit of their own digging. Every so often, he takes one of his prisoners out, shoots him or her, and eats the carcass. The food tastes good, and he grows fat. When he has shot and eaten his final prisoner, he begins to worry what he will do for food; but fortunately a seaplane arrives at this point and rescues him. He tells the world that he was the sole survivor of the original wreck, and that he has sustained himself by eating berries, leaves and roots. The world marvels at his fine physical condition, and a poster bearing his photograph is displayed in the windows of vegetarian food shops. He is never found out.

You see how easy it is to write, how much fun it is? That's why I'd ban the genre.

2   There shall be no more novels about incest. No, not even ones in very bad taste.

3   No novels set in abattoirs. This is, I admit, a rather small genre at the moment; but I have recently noticed increasing use of the abattoir in short stories. It must be nipped in the bud.

4   There is to be a twenty-year ban on novels set in Oxford or Cambridge, and a ten-year ban on other university fiction. No ban on fiction set in polytechnics (though no subsidy to encourage it). No ban on novels set in primary schools; a ten-year ban on secondary-school fiction. A partial ban on growing-up novels (one per author allowed). A partial ban on novels written in the historic present (again, one per author). A total ban on novels in which the main character is a journalist or a television presenter.

5   A quota system is to be introduced on fiction set in South America. The intention is to curb the spread of package-tour baroque and heavy irony. Ah, the propinquity of cheap life and expensive principles, of religion and banditry, of surprising honour and random cruelty. Ah, the daiquiri bird which incubates its eggs on the wing; ah, the fredonna tree whose roots grow at the tips of its branches, and whose fibres assist the hunchback to impregnate by telepathy the haughty wife of the hacienda owner; ah, the opera house now overgrown by jungle. Permit me to rap on the table and murmur 'Pass!' Novels set in the Arctic and the Antarctic will receive a development grant.

6a   No scenes in which carnal connection takes place between a human being and an animal. The woman and the porpoise, for instance, whose tender coupling symbolises a wider mending of those gossamer threads which formerly bound the world together in peaceable companionship. No, none of that.

b   No scenes in which carnal connection takes place between man and woman (porpoise-like, you might say) in the shower. My reasons are primarily aesthetic, but also medical.

7   No novels about small, hitherto forgotten wars in distant parts of the British Empire, in the painstaking course of which we learn first, that the British are averagely wicked; and secondly, that war is very nasty indeed.

8   No novels in which the narrator, or any of the characters, is identified simply by an initial letter. Still they go on doing it!

9   There shall be no more novels which are really about other novels. No 'modern versions', reworkings, sequels or prequels, no imaginative completions of works left unfinished on their author's death. Instead, every writer is to be issued with a sampler in coloured wools to hang over the fireplace. It reads: Knit Your Own Stuff.

10   There shall be a twenty-year ban on God: or rather, on the allegorical, metaphorical, allusive, offstage, imprecise and ambiguous uses of God. The bearded head gardener who is always tending the apple tree; the wise old sea-captain who never rushes to judgment; the character you're not quite introduced to, but who is giving you a creepy feeling by Chapter Four . . . pack them off into storage, all of them. God is permitted only as a verifiable divinity who gets extremely cross at man's transgressions.

From *Flaubert's Parrot* by Julian Barnes, 1984

The State of the Nation

Now is Ingland all in fight;
Muche peple of consciens light;
Many knightes and litel of might;
Many lawes and litel right;
Many actes of parlament
And few kept with tru entent;
Litel charité and fain to plese;
Many a galant penylese;
And many a wonderful disgising
By unprudent and misavising;

Grete countenanse and smalle wages;
Many gentilemen and few pages;
Wide gownes and large sleves;
Wel besene and strong theves;
Much bost of their clothes,
But wel I wot they lake none othes.

Anon., c.1450

Tired With All These

Tired with all these, for restful death I cry;
　As to behold desert a beggar born,
And needy nothing trimmed in jollity,
　And purest faith unhappily forsworn,
And gil'l'd honour shamefully misplaced,
　And inaiden virtue rudely strumpeted,
And right perfection wrongfully disgraced,
　And strength by limping sway disabled,
And art made tongue-tied by authority,
　And folly, doctor-like, controlling skill,
And simple truth miscalled simplicity,
　And captive good attending captain ill.
　　Tired with all these, from these would I be gone,
　　Save that, to die, I leave my Love alone.

Sonnet LXVI by William Shakespeare

'A Prophesie when Asses shall grow Elephants'

1 When making harmful gunnes, vnfruitfull glasses,
　Shall quite consume our stately Oakes to ashes:
2 When Law fils all the land with blots and dashes,
3 When land long quiet, held concealed, passes.
4 When warre and truce playes passes and repasses,
5 When Monopolies are giu'n of toys and trashes:
6 When courtiers mar good clothes, with cut & slashes,
7 When Lads shal think it free to ly with Lasses,
8 When clergy romes to buy, sell, none abashes,
9 When fowle skins are made fair with new found washes,

10 When prints are set on work, with *Greens and Nashes*,
11 When Lechers learn to stir vp Lust with lashes,
    When plainnesse vanishes, vainenesse surpasses,
    Some shal grow Elephants, were knowne but Asses.

From the Epigrams of Sir John Harington (1561–1612)

'As Concerning Man'

To what intent or purpose was Man made,
Who is by Birth to misery betray'd?
Man in his tedeous course of life runs through
More Plagues than all the Land of *Egypt* knew:
Doctors, Divines, grave Disputations, Puns,
Ill looking Citizens and scurvy Duns;
Insipid Squires, fat Bishops, Deans and Chapters,
Enthusiasts, Prophecies, new Rants and Raptures;
Pox, Gout, Catarrhs, old Sores, Cramps, Rheums and Aches;
Half witted Lords, double chinn'd bawds with Patches;
Illiterate Courtiers, Chancery Suits for Life,
A teazing Whore, and a more tedeous Wife;
Raw Inns of Court men, empty Fops, Buffoons,
Bullies robust, round Aldermen, and Clowns;
Gown-men which argue, and discuss, and prate,
And vent dull Notions of a future State,
Sure of another World, yet do not know
Whether they shall be sav'd, or damn'd, or how.

   'Twere better then that Man had never been,
Than thus to be perplex'd: *God Save the Queen.*

Alexander Radcliffe (c.1656–after 1696)

An Awful Tally of Bad Behaviour

Father: . . . tell me her Name, or for thy Drunkenness, and burning of Houses; thy Whoredoms, and Adulteries; Blasphemy, and Profaneness; Thy Swearing, and Forswearing; Thy rubbing out Milk-scores, and lampblacking of Signs in *Covent-Garden*; Thy breaking of Windows, killing

Constables and Watchmen, Beadles, Taylors, Hackney-Coachmen and
Link-Boys; for all these –

[*Noises of squeaking from each side of the Stage, one from* Sylvia]

Heark there the screaming Fiends are at thy door already. Heark!

From The Atheist by Thomas Otway, 1684

A London Street-Scene

Young Drunkards reeling, Bayliffs dogging,
Old Strumpets plying, Mumpers progging,
Fat Dray-men squabling, Chair-men ambling,
Oyster-Whores fighting, School-Boys scrambling,
Street Porters running, Rascals batt'ling,
Pick-pockets crowding, Coaches rattling,
News bawling, Ballad-wenches singing,
Guns roaring, and the Church-Bells ringing . . .

From Hudibras Redidivus by Edward Ward, 1705–7

The Recreations of the Town

Being now arrived at the proper Age for producing themselves, they came
up to Town, and fell in love with the Ladies, but especially three, who about
that time were in chief Reputation: The Dutchess *d'Argent, Madame de Grand
Titres,* and the Countess *d'Orgueil.* On their first Appearance, our three
Adventurers met with a very bad Reception; and soon with great Sagacity
guessing out the Reason, they quickly began to improve in the good
Qualities of the Town: They Writ, and Raillyed, and Rhymed, and Sung,
and Said, and said Nothing; They Drank, and Fought, and Whor'd, and
Slept, and Swore, and took Snuff: They went to new Plays on the first
Night, haunted the *Chocolate*-Houses, beat the Watch, lay on Bulks, and got
Claps: They bilkt Hackney-Coachmen, ran in Debt with Shop-keepers, and
lay with their Wives: They kill'd Bayliffs, kick'd Fidlers down Stairs, eat at
Locket's, loytered at *Will*'s: They talk'd of the Drawing-Room and never
came there, Dined with Lords they never saw; Whisper'd a Dutchess, and
spoke never a Word; exposed the Scrawls of their Laundress for Billets-
doux of Quality: came ever just from Court and were never seen in it;
attended the Levee *sub dio;* Got a list of Peers by heart in one Company, and

with great Familiarity retailed them in another. Above all, they constantly attended those Committees of Senators who are silent in the *House*, and loud in the *Coffee-House*, where they nightly adjourn to chew the Cud of Politicks, and are encompass'd with a Ring of Disciples, who lye in wait to catch up their Droppings. The three Brothers had acquired forty other Qualifications of the like Stamp, too tedious to recount, and by consequence, were justly reckoned the most accomplish'd Persons in Town . . .

From *A Tale of a Tub* by Jonathan Swift, 1696

Unwelcome Guests

Therefore, as I would avoid reprimanding any body in my *Own* Apartment, I take this Opportunity, to intreat the Absence of all *Effeminate Fops*, that drink *Milk and Water*, wear *Cherry colour'd Stockings* & *Stitch'd Wastcoats*, & in a Counter-tenor Voice, complain of *Vapors* & the *Spleen*; impudent *Beau-Jews*, that talk obscenely in modest Womens Company, then stare 'em in the Face, & burst out a laughing, who, so far from being admitted into Civil Society, ought to be expell'd the Nation; all *Comick Gentlemen*, that act in Tragedies for their Diversion; *Designing Persons*, that make Assignations at publick *Drawing-Rooms*; and *Foreign Beaus*, that assume the Title of *Count*, that just make an outside Show, to engage some great Fortune, and when they have receiv'd her Money, Fly away with it into their own Country, – But in a more particular manner, the two famous *Sparks* who have been seven Years at the *Bar*, and yet never made any greater Figure there, than upon a Five-shilling-Motion given 'em by some Relation, yet their Faces are constantly observ'd at every *Lord-Mayor*'s, *Sherrif*'s, and *City Company*'s Feast, at every *Dancing-School* in Town, and every private *Hop*, where they have Interest to be admitted; they understand nothing but *Dancing*, talk of nothing but the *Union*, the *Brawl of Audenarde*, and the *Royal Portuguese*, and their Rapture is inexpressible, to perform a [ ] with Trumpets, and Kettle-Drums, and think themselves highly honoured if they can engage Mons. *Rigadoon* to accept of a ten Guinea Collation after the Ball's over.

From *The Female Tatler*, July 1709

And that I might not be disturb'd in my view, I put on my invisible Ring, and set my Glass to my Eye, and look'd *at once*, all over this *sinful* City, but, O wonderful! What did I see? Tradesmens-wives intreiging with Lawyers-clerks; Apprentice-boys a-bed with Chamber-maids; old grave Citizens with Bands, standing behind Counters, venturing their souls to get three half-pence, and venting their Lies by wholesale; common Jilts prostituting their Carkasses to Porters and Footmen, for Pots of Ale, and Noggins of Brandy; young Heirs dipping their Estates; powder'd *Beaus* pawning their watches; fine whores without any smocks; many Citts gnawing their Thumbs for want of Trade; Men of repute marching off; Old Men praising the Days of Queen *Bess*; young Traders cursing the Times for want of Business; meer Boys at Bawdy Houses; Men of grey Hairs keeping their Misses; the *Jacks* wishing for a Turn in Government; Men of Places sollacing themselves with the Thoughts of their present Felicity; Great Men afraid of *Duns*; Atheists afraid to die; younger Brothers put to their shifts to live; elder Brothers rattling it about in their Coach and Six; young Girls eat up with the Green-sickness; old Women without Teeth, wanting Husbands; some that had so much Money they knew not what to do with it; others ready to hang themselves for want of it; private Sinners in the Surgeon's powdering Tub; Town-Bullies pimping at Bawds Chamber-Doors; common Rakes engaged with the Watch; poor Men opprest for want of Friends and Money; rich Men at their Wits end how to get more *Mammon*; Misers breaking their rest for fear of losing their Golden Gods; and indeed, what did I not see? All was wonderful and amazing, and yet, at the same time, mixt with delight.

From *The Wandering Spy*, 1705

'The Place of the Damned'

All Folks who pretend to *Religion* and *Grace*,
Allow there's a HELL, but dispute of the Place;
But if HELL by *Logical* Rules be defin'd,
The Place of the *Damn'd*, – I'll tell you my Mind.
Wherever the Damn'd do Chiefly abound,
Most certainly there's the HELL to be found,
Damn'd *Poets*, Damn'd *Criticks*, Damn'd *Block-Heads*, Damn'd *Knaves*,
Damn'd *Senators* brib'd, Damn'd prostitute *Slaves*;

Damn'd *Lawyers* and *Judges*, Damn'd *Lords* and Damn'd *Squires*,
Damn'd *Spies* and *Informers*, Damn'd *Friends* and Damn'd *Lyars*;
Damn'd *Villains*, Corrupted in every *Station*,
Damn'd *Time-serving Priests* all over the *Nation*;
And into the Bargain, I'll readily give you,
Damn'd Ignorant *Prelates* and *Councellors Privy*.
Then let us no longer by *Parsons* be Flam'd,
For We know by these *Marks*, the place of the Damn'd;
And HELL to be sure is at *Paris* or *Rome*,
How happy for *Us*, that it is not at *Home*.

Jonathan Swift (1667–1745)

Unthinkable Alternatives to Eating the Children of Ireland

Therefore let no man talk to me of other Expedients: Of Taxing our Absentees at five Shillings a Pound: Of using neither Cloaths, nor Household Furniture, except what is of our own Growth and Manufacture: Of utterly rejecting the Materials and Instruments that promote Foreign Luxury: Of curing the Expensiveness of Pride, Vanity, Idleness, and Gaming in our Women: Of introducing a Vein of Parcimony, Prudence and Temperance: Of learning to love our Country, wherein we differ even from Laplanders, and the Inhabitants of Topinamboo: Of quitting our Animosities, and Factions, nor act any longer like the Jews, who were murdering one another at the very Moment their City was taken: Of being a little cautious not to sell our Country and Consciences for nothing: Of teaching Landlords to have at least one Degree of Mercy towards their Tenants. Lastly, Of putting a Spirit of Honesty, Industry, and Skill into our Shop-keepers, who, if a Resolution could now be taken to buy only our Native Goods, would immediately unite to cheat and exact upon us in the Price, the Measure, and the Goodness, nor could ever yet be brought to make one fair Proposal of just Dealing, though often and earnestly invited to it.

Therefore I repeat, let no Man talk to me of these and the like Expedients, till he hath at least some Glimpse of Hope, that there will ever be some hearty and sincere Attempt to put them in Practice.

From *A Modest Proposal* by Jonathan Swift, 1729

Gulliver's Happy Life Among the Houyhnhnms

... I enjoyed perfect Health of Body, and Tranquility of Mind; I did not feel the Treachery or Inconstancy of a Friend, nor the Injuries of a secret or open Enemy. I had no Occasion of bribing, flattering or pimping, to procure the Favour of any great Man, or of his Minion. I wanted no Fence against Fraud or Oppression: Here was neither Physician to destroy my Body, nor Lawyer to ruin my Fortune: No Informer to watch my Words and Actions, or forge Accusations against me for Hire: Here were no Gibers, Censurers, Backbiters, Pickpockets, Highwaymen, House-breakers, Attorneys, Bawds, Buffoons, Gamesters, Politicians, Wits, Spleneticks, tedious Talkers, Controvertists, Ravishers, Murderers, Robbers, Virtuoso's; no Leaders or Followers of Party and Faction; no Encouragers to Vice, by Seducement or Examples: No Dungeon, Axes, Gibbets, Whipping-posts, or Pillories; No cheating Shopkeepers or Mechanicks: No Pride, Vanity or Affectation: No Fops, Bullies, Drunkards, strolling Whores, or Poxes: No ranting, lewd, expensive Wives: No stupid, proud Pedants: No importunate, over-bearing, quarrelsome, noisy, roaring, empty, conceited, swearing Companions: No Scoundrels raised from the Dust upon the Merit of their Vices; or Nobility thrown into it on account of their Virtues: No Lords, Fidlers, Judges or Dancing-masters.

From *Gulliver's Travels* by Jonathan Swift, 1726

Gulliver Outlines War to the Houyhnhnms

I could not forbear shaking my Head and smiling a little at his Ignorance. And, being no Stranger to the Art of War, I gave him a Description of Cannons, Culverins, Muskets, Carabines, Pistols, Bullets, Powder, Swords, Bayonets, Sieges, Retreats, Attacks, Undermines, Countermines, Bombardments, Sea-fights; Ships sunk with a Thousand Men; twenty Thousand killed on each Side; dying Groans, Limbs flying in the Air: Smoak, Noise, Confusion, trampling to Death under Horses Feet; Flight, Pursuit, Victory; Fields strewed with Carcases left for Food to Dogs, and Wolves, and Birds of Prey; Plundering, Stripping, Ravishing, Burning and Destroying. And, to set forth the Valour of my own dear Countrymen, I assured him, that I had seen them blow up a Hundred Enemies at once in a Siege, and as many in a Ship; and beheld the dead Bodies drop down in Pieces from the Clouds, to the great Diversion of all the Spectators.

I was going on to more Particulars, when my Master commanded me Silence...

From Gulliver's Travels by Jonathan Swift, 1726

That Inextricable Labyrinth

What a jovial and a merry world would this be, may it please your worships, but for that inextricable labyrinth of debts, cares, woes, want, grief, discontent, melancholy, large jointures, impositions and lies!

From Tristram Shandy by Laurence Sterne, 1759–67

An Anonymous Satire, 1773

You I love my dearest life,
More than Georgey loves his wife;
More than ministers to rule,
More than North to play the fool,
More than Camden to grimace,
More than Barrington his place,
More than Clive his black jagueer,
More than Bute the Royal ear;
More than patriots their price,
More than Fox loves cards and dice,
More than cits the Court to spite,
More than Townshend not to fight,
More than Colebrook heaps of pelf,
More than Elliot loves himself,
More than Alderman his gut,
More than Hillsborough to strut,
More than cullies love a jilt,
More than Grosvenor horns well gilt;
More than Dartmouth loves field preachers,
More than Huntingdon her teachers,
More than Carlisle those who cheat him,
More than Long Tom those who treat him,
More than Pomfret a lead mine
More than Weymouth play and wine,
More than fools at wits to nibble,

More than Walpole loves to scribble,
More than Lyttleton to write,
More than blackleg March to bite,
More than country squires their dogs,
More than Mawbey loves his hogs,
More than demireps a spark,
More than Martin a sure mark;
More than Grafton loves his pimps,
More than the Devil loves his imps,
More than the Tories love the Stuarts,
More than Whigs love all true hearts,
Thus, my fair, I love you more
Than ever man loved fair before.

Anon., 1773

Novelties

To return to the Question of Evil – woe to the man, to whom it is an uninteresting Question – tho' many a mind, overwearied by it, may shun it with Dread/ and here, N.B. scourge with deserved and lofty Scorn those Critics who laugh at the discussion of Old Questions – God, Right & Wrong, Necessity & Arbitrement – Evil, &c – No! forsooth! – the Question must be new, *new spicy hot* Gingerbread, a French Constitution, a Balloon, change of Ministry, or which had the best of it in the Parliamentary Duel, Wyndham or Sheridan, or at the best, a chemical Theory, whether the new celestial Bodies shall be called Planets or Asteroids – &c – Something new, something *out* of themselves – for whatever is *in* them, is deep within them, must be *old as* elementary Nature. To find no contradiction in the union of old and novel – to contemplate the Ancient of Days with Feelings new as if they then sprang forth at his own Fiat – this marks the mind that feels the Riddle of the World, & may help to unravel it.

From Samuel Taylor Coleridge's Notebooks, *October 1803*

Adieu Sirocco, Sun, and Sweat

Adieu, ye joys of La Valette!
Adieu, sirocco, sun, and sweat!
Adieu, thou palace rarely enter'd!
Adieu, ye mansions where – I've ventured!

[244]

Adieu, ye cursed streets of stairs!
(How surely he who mounts you swears!)
Adieu, ye merchants often failing!
Adieu, thou mob for ever railing!
Adieu, ye packets – without letters!
Adieu, ye fools – who ape your betters!
Adieu, thou damned'st quarantine,
That gave me fever, and the spleen!
Adieu, that stage which makes us yawn, Sirs,
Adieu, his Excellency's dancers!
Adieu to Peter – whom no fault's in,
But could not teach a colonel waltzing;
Adieu, ye females fraught with graces!
Adieu, red coats, and redder faces!
Adieu, the supercilious air
Of all that strut 'en militaire'!
I go – but God knows when, or why,
To smoky towns and cloudy sky,
To things (the honest truth to say)
As bad – but in a different way.

Lord Byron, May 1811

'Sonnet: England in 1819'

An old, mad, blind, despised, and dying king, –
Princes, the dregs of their dull race, who flow
Through public scorn, – mud from a muddy spring, –
Rulers who neither see, nor feel, nor know,
But leech-like to their fainting country cling,
Till they drop, blind in blood, without a blow, –
A people starved and stabbed in the untilled field, –
An army, which liberticide and prey
Makes as a two-edged sword to all who wield, –
Golden and sanguine laws which tempt and slay;
Religion Christless, Godless – a book sealed;
A Senate, – Time's worst statute unrepealed, –
Are graves, from which a glorious Phantom may
Burst, to illumine our tempestuous day.

Percy Bysshe Shelley

Eighteen Shillings a Week!

Eighteen shillings a week! Just, most just, thy censure, upright Pecksniff! Had it been for the sake of a ribbon, star, or garter; sleeves of lawn, a great man's smile, a seat in parliament, a tap upon the shoulder from a courtly sword; a place, a party, or a thriving lie, or eighteen thousand pounds, or even eighteen hundred; – but to worship the golden calf for eighteen shillings a week! Oh pitiful, pitiful!

From *Martin Chuzzlewit* by Charles Dickens, 1843–4

The Lord High Executioner's Song

As some day it may happen that a victim must be found,
    I've got a little list – I've got a little list
Of social offenders who might well be underground,
    And who never would be missed – who never would be
        missed!
There's the pestilential nuisances who write for autographs –
All the people who have flabby hands and irritating laughs –
All children who are up in dates, and floor you with 'em flat –
All persons who in shaking hands, shake hands with you like *that* –
And all third persons who on spoiling *tête à têtes* insist –
    They'd none of 'em be missed – they'd none of 'em be missed!

CHORUS: He's got 'em on the list – he's got 'em on the list;
        And they'll none of 'em be missed, – They'll none of
        'em be missed.

There's the nigger serenader, and the others of his race,
    And the piano organist – I've got him on the list!
And the people who eat peppermint and puff it in your face,
    They never would be missed – they never would be missed!
Then the idiot who praises, with enthusiastic tone,
All centuries but this, and every country but his own;
And the lady from the provinces, who dresses like a guy,
And 'who doesn't think she waltzes, but would rather like to try';
And that singular anomaly, the lady novelist
    I don't think that she'd be missed – I'm *sure* she'd not be
        missed!

CHORUS: He's got her on the list – he's got her on the list;
    And I don't think that she'll be missed – I'm *sure* she'll
        not be missed!

And that *Nisi Prius* nuisance, who just now is rather rife,
    That Judicial humorist – I've got *him* on the list!
All funny fellows, comic men, and clowns of private life –
    They'd none of 'em be missed – they'd none of 'em be missed.
And apologetic statesmen of a compromising kind,
Such as – what d'ye call him – Thing 'em bob, and likewise Never
    Mind,
And 'St-'st-'st – and What's-his-name, and also You-know-who –
The task of filling up the blanks I'd rather leave to *you*.
But it really doesn't matter whom you put upon the list,
    For they'd none of 'em be missed – they'd none of 'em be
        missed!

CHORUS: You may put 'em on the list – you may put 'em on the
    list;
    And they'll none of 'em be missed – they'll none of 'em
    be missed!

From the libretto of *The Mikado* by W. S. Gilbert, 1885

'Of the Enemy'

Three kinds of enemy walk – the grandiose stunt – the melancholic stagger – the paranoic sidle.

Three kinds of enemy bearing – the condor stoop – the toad stupor – the robin's stance.

Three kinds of enemy face – the June bride – the favourite puss – the stone in the rain.

Three kinds of enemy eye – the lobster – the boot-button – the submarine.

Three kinds of enemy hand – the marsh – the claw – the dead yam.

Three kinds of enemy clothing – fisherman's pockets – Dickens' waist-coats – adhesive trousers.

Three enemy traits – refusal to undress in public – proficiency in modern languages – inability to travel back to the engine.

Three enemy occupations – playing cards – collecting – talking to animals.

Three terms of enemy speech – I mean – quite frankly – speaking as a scientist, etc.

Three signs of an enemy letter – underlining – parentheses in brackets – careful obliteration of cancelled expressions.

Three enemy questions – Am I boring you? – Could you tell me the time? – Are you sure you're fit enough?

Three enemy catchwords – insure now – keep smiling – safety first.

Three enemy don'ts – don't kiss your baby on the mouth – don't lean out of the carriage window – don't miss this.

Three signs of an enemy country – licensed hours – a national art – nursery schools.

Three signs of an enemy house – old furniture – a room called the Den – photographs of friends.

Three warnings of enemy attack – depression in the mornings – rheumatic twinges – blips on the face.

Three symptoms in convalescence – nail-biting – nightmares – short-sight.

Three results of an enemy victory – impotence – cancer – paralysis.

Three counter-attacks – complete mastery of the air – ancestor worship – practical jokes.

From *The Orators* by W. H. Auden, 1932

Vorticist Denunciations

I.

BLAST First (from politeness) ENGLAND
    CURSE ITS CLIMATE FOR ITS SINS AND INFECTIONS
      DISMAL SYMBOL, SET round our bodies,
        of effeminate lout within.
      VICTORIAN VAMPIRE, the LONDON cloud sucks
      the TOWN's heart.

A 1000 MILE LONG, 2 KILOMETER Deep
      BODY OF WATER even, is pushed against us
      from the Floridas, TO MAKE US MILD.
    OFFICIOUS MOUNTAINS keep back DRASTIC WINDS
SO MUCH MACHINERY TO PRODUCE
        THE CURATE of 'Eltham'
        BRITANNIC ÆSTHETE
        WILD NATURE CRANK

DOMESTICATED POLICEMAN
LONDON COLISEUM SOCIALIST-PLAYWRIGHT
DALY'S MUSICAL COMEDY
GAIETY CHORUS GIRL
TONKS

CURSE

the flabby sky that can manufacture no snow, but
can only drop the sea on us in a drizzle like a poem
by Mr Robert Bridges.

CURSE

the lazy air that cannot stiffen the back of the SERPENTINE,
or put Aquatic steel half way down the MANCHESTER CANAL.

————————

But ten years ago we saw distinctly both snow and
ice here.

May some vulgarly inventive, but useful person, arise,
and restore to us the necessary BLIZZARDS.

LET US ONCE MORE WEAR THE ERMINE
OF THE NORTH.

WE BELIEVE IN THE EXISTENCE OF THIS USEFUL LITTLE CHEMIST IN
OUR MIDST!

2.

OH BLAST FRANCE
pig plagiarism
BELLY
SLIPPERS
POODLE TEMPER
BAD MUSIC
SENTIMENTAL GALLIC GUSH
SENSATIONALISM
FUSSINESS.

PARISIAN PAROCHIALISM. Complacent young man,
so much respect for Papa
and his son! – Oh! – Papa
is wonderful: but *all* papas
are!

BLAST
APERITIFS (Pernods, Amers picon)
Bad change

[249]

Naively seductive Houri salon-
picture Cocottes
Slouching blue porters (can
carry a pantechnicon)
Stupidly rapacious people at
every step
Economy maniacs
Bouillon Kub (for being a bad
pun)
PARIS Clap-trap Heaven of amative German
professor.
Ubiquitous lines of silly little trees.
Arcs de Triomphe.
Imperturbable, endless prettiness.
Large empty cliques, higher up.
Bad air for the individual.

BLAST
MECCA OF THE AMERICAN
because it is not other side of Suez Canal, instead of an
afternoon's ride from London.

3.

CURSE
WITH EXPLETIVE OF WHIRLWIND
THE BRITANNIC ÆSTHETE
CREAM OF THE SNOBBISH EARTH
ROSE OF SHARON OF GOD-PRIG OF SIMIAN VANITY
SNEAK AND SWOT OF THE SCHOOLROOM
IMBERB (or Berbed when in Belsize) – PEDANT
PRACTICAL JOKER
DANDY
CURATE
BLAST all products of phlegmatic cold
Life of LOOKER-ON.
CURSE   SNOBBERY
(disease of femininity)
FEAR OF RIDICULE
(arch vice of inactive, sleepy)
PLAY
STYLISM
SINS AND PLAGUES

[250]

of this LYMPHATIC finished
(we admit in every sense
finished)
    VEGETABLE HUMANITY.

4.

BLAST

THE SPECIALIST
'PROFESSIONAL'
'GOOD WORKMAN'
'GROVE-MAN'
ONE ORGAN MAN
        BLAST THE

                AMATEUR
                SCIOLAST
                ART-PIMP
                JOURNALIST
                SELF MAN
                NO ORGAN MAN

5.

BLAST HUMOUR
Quack ENGLISH drug for stupidity and sleepiness.
Arch enemy of REAL, conventionalizing like
        gunshot, freezing supple
        REAL in ferocious chemistry
        of laughter.
    BLAST SPORT
HUMOUR'S FIRST COUSIN AND ACCOMPLICE.
        Impossibility for Englishman to be
        grave and keep his end up,
        psychologically.
        Impossible for him to use Humour
        as well as be *persistently*
        grave.
        Alas! necessity for big doll's show
        in front of mouth.
        Visitation of Heaven on
        English Miss
        gums, canines of FIXED GRIN
        Death's Head symbol of Anti-Life.

CURSE those who will hang over this
Manifesto with SILLY CANINES exposed.

From 'Manifesto-I' in *Blast* no. 1, edited by Wyndham Lewis, 1914

Cambridge

Now, however, it is not from Real England that I write. It is from the Hinder
Parts, the *faeces* or *crassamentum* or dregs, the Eastern Counties; a low
swamp, a confluence of mist and mire, a gathering place of Dankness, and
Mud, and Fever; where men's minds rot in the mirk like a leper's flesh, and
their bodies grow white and soft and malodorous and suppurating and
fungoid, and so melt in slime.
   I have a cold.

From a letter by Rupert Brooke to Jacques Raverat, 1908

'Everything'

... Leaves, words, tears
Tinned food, cats
Trams from time to time, queues for flour
Weevils, empty bottles, speeches
Elongated images on the TV
Colorado beetles, petrol
Pennants, the European Cup
Trucks with gas cylinders, well-known portraits
Export-reject apples
Newspapers, loaves
Blended oil, carnations
Receptions at the airport
Cico-cola, balloons
Bucharest salami, diet yoghurt
Gypsy women with Kents, Crevedia eggs
Rumours
The Saturday serial, coffee substitutes
The struggle of nations for peace, choirs
Production by the acre
Gerovital, the Victory Street lads

The Hymn to Romania, Adidas shoes
Bulgarian stewed fruit, jokes, ocean fish
Everything.

Ana Blandiana, 1984

NOTES ON THE ABOVE BY THE TRANSLATOR (1986)

The title is the first irony. 'Totul' (everything) is a catchphrase or verbal tic which punctuates every other sentence of Ceauşescu's speeches. He uses it either to insist that everything remains to be done by, or that the Party has done everything conceivable for, the people. 'Everything' is a fitting symbol for a bankrupt regime, the nature of which is to insist that it has the answer to everything.

1 *Leaves* can be seen on trees. There is no shortage of *words* or *tears*.

2 *Tinned*, not fresh food which is harder to find. Self-service or corner grocery stores used to offer row on row of dusty tins (fish, stewed or pickled vegetables) which would be long past their sell-by dates if they had them. They are thin on the shelves now.

Cats: the State enterprise *Ecarisajul* battles with some success against stray dogs, but has less luck with cats. Bucharest gossip has immortalised a certain cat which challenged the General Secretary's dogs, as he was surveying the district where his grandiose Civic Centre now nears completion. As he approached the Brâncoveanu Hospital, founded in the eighteenth century, his way was barred by an alley cat which proceeded to wound his two watchdogs in the ensuing scrap. He ordered the cat to be caught and brought to him. Naturally, this proved impossible, thereby vindicating the proverb 'A cat may look at a King'.

The good cat, alas, failed to save the historic quarter beyond the Piaţa Unirii market from destruction. Forty thousand residents were evacuated for the clearance of the site, fine old houses, churches, monastery, Brâncoveanu Hospital and all.

3 *Trams from time to time*, but they are so full you can't get on them.

Queues for flour and everything else: bread, sugar, eggs, bits of non-export or non-restaurant grade meat, vodka, you name it.

4 *Empty bottles* are kept, either to reclaim your deposit, or because unless you bring your own bottles you cannot buy various liquid goods, such as cooking oil. The energy shortage has either closed the bottle factories or reduced their output to a trickle. 'Empty bottles' is also a familiar street-cry by which gypsy women, collecting bottles for recycling, announce their passage. The prudent citizen always carries an empty bottle or two, just in case there is a queue worth joining somewhere along the way.

Speeches are never in short supply, and are never short.

5 *Elongated images on the* TV: things are enlarged and distorted by the poor quality of the sets or of their reception.

6 *Petrol*: strictly rationed and very expensive. Private use of cars is also banned during the worst months of winter, January to March, a restriction imposed shortly after the publication of this poem and now enforced annually.

7 *The European Cup*: football, at least, is politically uncontroversial. There may be little *panem* but there are *circenses*.

8 *Trucks with gas cylinders* are eagerly awaited by households which rely on butane gas cylinders for their stoves. The ration is one cylinder for every two months. Perhaps irrelevantly, the phrase also brings to mind the common sight in Bucharest streets of the buses which were adapted to run on gas: they sport huge cylindrical tanks which run the length of the bus's roof, marked GAZ. Unfortunately the engineers had been unable to find an economical method of converting the engines, so the roof-tanks are passengers.

Well-known portraits: you know who. Icons of the Big C. Compulsory in offices, factories, etc.

9 *Export-reject apples*: all food of decent quality is now exported. Romania has halved its foreign hard-currency debt in the last five or six years by exporting everything worth buying.

10 *Newspapers*: well, yes, in a manner of speaking. Their main use is as wrapping paper.

Loaves sell like hot cakes.

11 *Blended oil* is the euphemism for adulterated cooking oil.

Carnations abound, and are handy for

12 *Receptions at the airport*. These are frequent, since Ceauşescu likes to entertain, and require the clearance of main streets for the convoy of official cars which sweep visiting dignitaries into the capital, past the new mock marble (hardboard) arch, which dwarfs the old replica of the Arc de Triomphe, and on which is writ large: THE AGE OF NICOLAE CEAUŞESCU 1965–1985: A GOLDEN AGE ('Epocă de aur'), and finally down the boulevard which has been festively lined with dragooned schoolchildren waving *pennants* (line 7).

13 *Cico*, to give it its simple Romanian name, is an acidic, urine-coloured soft drink, universally available when all else fails. It is palatable.

14 *Bucharest* (or 'summer') *salami* is less so, but almost all the excellent Sibiu ('winter') salami goes for export. The Bucharest version is a generic name for a substance produced nationwide to a recipe given the official seal of approval by the General Secretary. Contents may include powdered bones, soya oil, scraps of meat and skin, and the offal or worse of various

animals, especially of coypu. Even shortages of toilet paper have been attributed to changes in the recipe. It imparts the characteristically acrid odour which greets the entrant to what used to be called delicatessens.

Diet yoghurt, i.e. ordinary yoghurt considered as a health-food, is good but you had to queue for it at the crack of dawn. It is now unobtainable.

Kent cigarettes are a second currency: why only Kents should have attained this status is a mystery. The *cachet* of Kent has no rival. They are also the secret police's favoured brand. On the black market, three cartons will fetch the average monthly salary; a single packet changes hands for 100 lei. The gypsy *mafiosi* are thought to be the main Kent smugglers. Kents are confiscated at Customs from Romanians returning home. As in ancient Greece, it was a custom at Romanian funerals for a coin to be placed in the dead person's mouth. The new custom is: a packet of Kents on the corpse's chest.

Crevedia eggs: eggs from the Crevedia state farm are supposed to be the best, and attract large queues when rumours of a supply circulate.

16 *Rumours* are the most reliable source of information about what's going on and where things might be obtained.

17 *The Saturday serial*: the weekly treat of imported TV: *Dallas, The Avengers, Columbo, Kojak*. From time to time the authorities have tried to drop these in favour of home-made patriotic drama, but they have succumbed to the pressure of public opinion.

Coffee substitutes: real coffee can only be obtained at the 'shops', the Romanian term for hard-currency stores in hotel lobbies (oil, sugar and flour are now on sale in 'shops'). The coffee-drinking population now has to make do with blends of acorn, chicory and so on, since coffee is too expensive and luxurious to import. Visitors from Hungary, where coffee is easily bought, are searched for smuggled coffee.

18 *The struggle of nations for peace* is the Conducator's rallying cry. The only political demonstrations permitted are those which he organises against the nuclear threat. This wins him friends abroad, or used to.

Choirs grace such occasions. They are also seen on TV when the screen is not occupied by football, the Saturday serial or – speeches.

19 *Production by the acre*: much mention of this stirs the peasantry to its patriotic duty of increasing produce.

20 *Gerovital* is Dr Ana Aslan's elixir, now marketed abroad in the State's pursuit of hard currency. It is regarded as a ludicrous emblem of the State's belief in the gullibility of Western consumers. (But it seems to fool a lot of Romanians.)

The Victory Street lads – or just 'the lads', 'the boys' – are the secret police's plain-clothes heavies, entrusted with guarding the President's route into the centre. They are thought to be an elite corps of hand-picked orphans.

Easy to spot them by their suits. There is no shortage of them, but they are expensive to buy.

21 *The Hymn to Romania* is the much-advertised, all-year-round 'festival', a series of amateurish artistic events – music, dance and theatre – whose purpose seems to be twofold: (i) to give constant, ritual praise to the Party and especially its leader, and (ii) to provide lowbrow, *kitsch* but patriotic performances as an antidote to the ideologically suspect, real professional thing.

Adidas shoes have been trendy in our label-conscious Western society. That guarantees their status in Romania, where they are manufactured under licence and are, naturally, in short supply. However, there is a nicely macabre twist to the term in colloquial usage, which has it that pigs' trotters – sometimes available as an alternative to the now rare (because exported) pork which used to be plentiful in restaurants, and less scarce than other meats at the butchers – are the slaughtered pigs' Adidases.

22 *Bulgarian stewed fruit* was permanently available in 1984, having been dumped on the Romanian market years before. It has all gone now.

Jokes galore. You cannot spend more than five minutes in conversation, even with an official, without hearing several of the latest. They are sometimes grimly funny.

Ocean fish, much promoted for its nutritional qualities, is a euphemism for stale frozen fish of suspect, greyish appearance and dubious gastric consequences.

23 *Everything*: and There Is No Alternative, just more of Everything.

Eight

FEASTS

The Recipe for Hell-Broth

First Witch: Thrice the brinded cat hath mew'd.
Second Witch: Thrice and once the hedge-pig whin'd.
Third Witch: Harpier cries: 'tis time, 'tis time.
First Witch: Round about the cauldron go;
In the poison'd entrails throw.
Toad that under cold stone
Days and nights hath thirty-one
Swelt'red venom sleeping got
Boil thou first i' th' charmed pot.
All: Double, double toil and trouble;
Fire burn, and cauldron bubble.
Second Witch: Fillet of a fenny snake,
In the cauldron boil and bake;
Eye of newt, and toe of frog,
Wool of bat, and tongue of dog,
Adder's fork, and blind-worm's sting,
Lizard's leg, and howlet's wing –
For a charm of pow'rful trouble,
Like a hell-broth boil and bubble.
All: Double, double toil and trouble;
Fire burn, and cauldron bubble.
Third Witch: Scale of dragon, tooth of wolf,
Witch's mummy, maw and gulf
Of the ravin'd salt-sea shark,
Root of hemlock digg'd i' th' dark,
Liver of blaspheming Jew,
Gall of goat, and slips of yew
Sliver'd in the moon's eclipse,
Nose of Turk, and Tartar's lips,
Finger of birth-strangled babe
Ditch-delivered by a drab –
Make the gruel thick and slab;
Add thereto a tiger's chaudron,
For th'ingredience of our cauldron.
All: Double, double toil and trouble;
Fire burn, and cauldron bubble.
Second Witch: Cool it with a baboon's blood,
Then the charm is firm and good.

From *Macbeth*, Act IV Scene i, by William Shakespeare, 1606

A Simpler Recipe for Hell-Broth

Prentice: What's the ingredience of your Perfume
Bell: All horrid things to burne i'th Roome
Hag: As Childrens heads
Bell: Mens leggs
Hag: Weomens Armes
Bell: And little Barnes
Hag: And these wee will you show
Prentice: Noe thanke you, I will take my leggs to goe.

From the first antemasque to an unperformed 'Pastorall'
by Jane Cavendish and Elizabeth Brackley, c.1644

Alchemical Ingredients

Surley: What else are your *Termes*,
Whereon no one o'your *Writers* grees with other?
Of your *Elixir*, your *Lac virginis*,
Your *Stone*, your *Med'cine*, and your *Chrysosperme*,
Your *Sal*, your *Sulphur*, and your *Mercurie*,
Your *Oyle of height*, your *Tree of life*, your *Blood*,
Your *Marchesite*, your *Tutie*, your *Magnesia*,
Your *Toade*, your *Crow*, your *Dragon*, and your *Panthar*,
Your *Sunne*, your *Moone*, your *Firmament*, your *Adrop*,
Your *Lato*, *Azoch*, *Zernich*, *Chibrit*, *Heauterit*,
And then your *Red man*, and your *white woman*;
With all your Broathes, your *Menstrues*, and *Materialls*,
Of Pisse, and Egge-shells, Womens termes, Mans blood,
Hayre o'the head, burnt Cloutes, Chalke, Merds, and Clay,
Poulder of bones, scalings of Iron, glasse,
And worlds of other strange *Ingredients*,
Would burst a man to name.

From *The Alchemist* by Ben Jonson, 1610

'Oberon's Feast'

A little mushroome table spred,
After short prayers, they set on bread;
A Moon-parcht grain of purest wheat,
With some small glit'ring gritt, to eate
His choyce bitts with; then in a trice
They make a feast lesse great than nice.
But all this while his eye is serv'd,
We must not thinke his eare was sterv'd:
But that there was in place to stir
His Spleen, the chirring Grashopper;
The merry Cricket, puling Flie,
The piping Gnat for minstralcy.
And now, we must imagine first,
The Elves present to quench his thirst
A pure seed-Pearle of Infant dew,
Brought and besweetned in a blew
And pregnant violet; which done,
His kitling eyes begin to runne
Quite through the table, where he spies
The hornes of paperie Butterflies,
Of which he eates, and tastes a little
Of that we call the Cuckoes spittle.
A little Fuz-ball-pudding stands
By, yet not blessed by his hands,
That was too coorse; but then forthwith
He ventures boldly on the pith
Of sugred Rush, and eates the sagge
And well bestrutted Bees sweet bagge:
Gladding his pallat with some store
Of Emits eggs; what wo'd he more?
But Beards of Mice, a Newt's stew'd thigh,
A bloated Earewig, and a Flie;
With the Red-capt worme, that's shut
Within the concave of a Nut,
Browne as his Tooth. A little Moth,
Late fatned in a piece of cloth:
With withered cherries; Mandrakes eares;
Moles eyes; to these, the slain-Stags teares:
The unctuous dewlaps of a Snaile;

The broke-heart of a Nightingale
Ore-come in musicke; with a wine,
Ne're ravished from the flattering Vine,
But gently prest from the soft side
Of the most sweet and dainty Bride,
Brought in a dainty daizie, which
He fully quaffs up to bewitch
His blood to height; this done, commended
Grace by his Priest; *The feast is ended.*

From *Hesperides* by Robert Herrick, 1648

Lily, Germander, and Sops-in-Wine

And can the physician make sick men well?
And can the magician a fortune divine?
Without lily, germander, and sops-in-wine,
     With sweet briar
     And bon-fire
     And strawberry wire
     And columbine.

From *Robin Good-fellow,* 1628

'Nature's Cook'

Death is the *Cook* of *Nature*; and we find
Meat drest severall waies to please her *Mind.*
Some *Meates shee* rosts with *Feavers, burning hot,*
And some *shee* boiles with *Dropsies* in a *Pot.*
Some for *Gelly* consuming by degrees,
And some with *Ulcers,* Gravie out to squeese.
Some *Flesh* as *Sage* she stuffs with *Gouts,* and *Paines,*
Others for tender *Meat* hangs up in *Chaines.*
Some in the *Sea* she *pickles* up to keep,
Others, as *Brawne* is sous'd, those in *Wine steep.*
Some with the *Pox,* chops *Flesh,* and *Bones* so small,
Of which *She* makes a *French Fricasse* withall.
Some on *Gridirons* of *Calentures* is broyl'd
And some is trodden on, and so quite spoyl'd.

But those are *bak'd*, when smother'd they do dye,
By *Hectick Feavers* some *Meat* She doth *fry*.
In *Sweat* sometimes *she stues* with *savoury smell*,
A *Hodge-Podge* of *Diseases* tasteth well.
Braines drest with *Apoplexy* to *Natures* wish,
Or swimmes with *Sauce* of *Megrimes* in a *Dish*.
And *Tongues* she dries with *Smoak* from *Stomacks* ill,
Which as the second *Course* she sends up still.
Then *Death* cuts Throats, for *Blood-puddings* to make,
And puts them in the *Guts*, which *Collicks* rack.
Some hunted are by *Death*, for *Deere* that's red,
Or *Stal-fed Oxen*, knocked on the *Head*.
Some for *Bacon* by *Death* are *Sing'd*, or scal'd,
Then powdered up with *Flegme*, and *Rhume* that's salt.

From *Poems and Fancies* by Margaret Cavendish, Duchess of
Newcastle, 1653

Wines to Drive Out Melancholy

. . . Ye shall have rumney and malmesine,
Both ypocrasse and vernage wine,
Mountrose and wine of Greke,
Both algarde and respice eke,
Antioche and bastarde,
Piment also and garnarde,
Wine of Greke and muscadell,
Both claré, piment, and rochell;
The red your stomake to defy,
And pottes of osey set you by . . .

Anon., medieval

Worrying Fruit

Morning and evening
Maids heard the goblins cry:
'Come buy our orchard fruits,
Come buy, come buy:

Apples and quinces,
Lemons and oranges,
Plump unpecked cherries,
Melons and raspberries,
Bloom-down-cheeked peaches,
Swart-headed mulberries,
Wild free-born cranberries,
Crab-apples, dewberries,
Pine-apples, blackberries,
Apricots, strawberries; –
All ripe together
In summer weather, –
Morns that pass by,
Fair eves that fly;
Come buy, come buy:
Our grapes fresh from the vine,
Pomegranates full and fine,
Dates and sharp bullaces,
Rare pears and greengages,
Damsons and bilberries,
Taste them and try:
Currants and gooseberries,
Bright fire-like barberries,
Figs to fill your mouth,
Citrons from the South,
Sweet to tongue and sound to eye;
Come buy, come buy.'

From 'Goblin Market' by Christina Rossetti, 1862

Unworrying Fruit

I should like now to promenade round you[r] Gardens – apple tasting –
pear-tasting – plum judging – apricot nibbling – peach sc[r]unching –
Nectarine-sucking and Melon carving – I have also a great feeling for
antiquated cherries full of sugar cracks – and a white currant tree kept for
company –

From a letter by John Keats to Fanny Keats, 28 August 1819

Covent Garden Market

At every turn there is a fresh odour to sniff at; either the bitter aromatic perfume of the herbalists' shops breaks upon you, or the scent of oranges, then of apples, and then of onions is caught for an instant as you move along. The broccoli tied up in square packets, the white heads tinged slightly red, as it were, with the sunshine, – the sieves of crimson love-apples, polished like china, – the bundles of glossy white leeks, their roots dangling like fringe, – the celery, with its pinky stalks and bright green tops, – the dark purple pickling-cabbages, – the scarlet carrots, – the white knobs of turnips, – the bright yellow balls of oranges, and the rich brown coats of the chesnuts – attract the eye on every side.

From *London Labour and the London Poor* by Henry Mayhew, 1861–2

A Creole Feast

The result was charming. The heavy scent of the garlands mingled with that of polish and beeswax. Together they arranged the great sheaves of flowers and chose the places for the branching candelabra. (Each candle was enclosed in the swelling and waisted cylinder of a glittering hurricane glass.) Next they inspected the cold table, with its hams and its quails in aspic, the giant lobsters and crabs, the ivory pyramids of *chou coco* and *chou palmiste* for each one of which a tall palm tree had been felled in order that the precious heart might be dislodged; the mounds of soursops and mangos, the pineapples and sapodillas and sweetsops and granadillas and avocado pears; the cold barracks for champagne, where on banks of ice from Nova Scotia, the magnums of Aï reclined in green and golden battalions; the arrays of rum and newly-cut yard-long swizzle sticks for the *punch martiniquais*; the ingredients for the sorbets and the Sangaree were methodically laid out along a dresser.

From *The Violins of Saint-Jacques* by Patrick Leigh Fermor, 1953

Hungry Imaginations

On a typical day during this backward march we would leave camp at about 6.40 a.m., and half an hour later we would have recovered our frost-bitten fingers, while the moisture on our clothes, melted in the sleeping bags, would have begun to ablate, after having first frozen hard. We would be beginning to march with some degree of comfort, and one of us would remark, 'Well, boys, what are we going to have for breakfast to-day?' We had just finished our breakfast as a matter of fact, consisting of half a pannikin of semi-raw horse-meat, one biscuit and a pannikin of tea, but the meal had not taken the keenness from our appetites. We used to try to persuade ourselves that our half-biscuit was not quite a half, and sometimes we managed to get a little bit more that way. The question would receive our most serious and careful consideration at once, and we would proceed to weave from our hungry imaginations a tale of a day spent in eating. 'Now we are on board ship,' one man would say. 'We wake up in a bunk, and the first thing we do is stretch out our hands to the side of the bunk and get some chocolate, some Garibaldi biscuits and some apples. We eat those in the bunk, and then we get up for breakfast. Breakfast will be at eight o'clock, and we will have porridge, fish, bacon and eggs, cold ham, plum pudding, sweets, fresh roll and butter, marmalade and coffee. At eleven o'clock we will have hot cocoa, open jam tarts, fried cods' roe and slices of heavy plum cake. That will be all until lunch at one o'clock. For lunch we will have Wild roll, shepherd's pie, fresh soda-bread, hot milk, treacle pudding, nuts, raisins and cake. After that we will turn in for a sleep, and we will be called at 3.45, when we will reach out again from the bunks and have dough-nuts and sweets. We will get up then and have big cups of hot tea and fresh cake and chocolate creams. Dinner will be at six, and we will have thick soup, roast beef and Yorkshire pudding, cauliflower, peas, asparagus, plum pudding, fruit, apple pie with thick cream, scones and butter, port wine, nuts, and almonds and raisins. Then at midnight we will have a really big meal, just before we go to bed. There will be melon, grilled trout and butter-sauce, roast chicken with plenty of livers, a proper salad with eggs and very thick dressing, green peas and new potatoes, a saddle of mutton, fried suet pudding, peaches *à la Melba*, egg curry, plum pudding and sauce, Welsh rarebit, Queen's pudding, angels on horseback, cream cheese and celery, fruit, nuts, port wine, milk and cocoa. Then we will go to bed and sleep till breakfast time. We will have chocolate and biscuits under our pillows, and if we want anything to eat in the night we will just have to get it.'

From *The Heart of the Antarctic* by Sir Ernest Shackleton, 1909

Rat's Picnic-Basket

'What's inside it?' asked the Mole, wriggling with curiosity.

'There's cold chicken inside it,' replied the Rat briefly; 'coldtonguecold-hamcoldbeefpickledgherkinssaladfrenchrollscresssandwidgespottedmeat-gingerbeerlemonadesodawater –'

'O stop, stop,' cried the Mole in ecstasies: 'This is too much!'

From *The Wind in the Willows* by Kenneth Grahame, 1908

Nine

MIXTURES AND COLLAGES

How things bind and blend themselves together!

JOHN RUSKIN

Confusum est quidquid usque in pulverem sectum est: 'Whatsoever is sliced into very powder is confused.'

MONTAIGNE

Images, descendez comme des confettis.

LOUIS ARAGON

Everything only connected by 'and' and 'and'.

ELIZABETH BISHOP

Types and Symbols of Eternity

            ... The immeasurable height
Of woods decaying, never to be decayed,
The stationary blasts of waterfalls,
And in the narrow rent at every turn
Winds thwarting winds, bewildered and forlorn,
The torrents shooting from the clear blue sky,
The rocks that muttered close upon our ears,
Black drizzling crags that spake by the way-side
As if a voice were in them, the sick sight
And giddy prospect of the raving stream,
The unfettered clouds and region of the Heavens,
Tumult and peace, the darkness and the light –
Were all like workings of one mind, the features
Of the same face, blossoms upon one tree;
Characters of the great Apocalypse,
The types and symbols of Eternity,
Of first, and last, and midst, and without end.

       From *The Prelude* by William Wordsworth, 1799–1805

A Laputan Summary

I'll not run over the Ground we have passed. that would be merely as bad as telling a dream – unless perhaps I do it in the manner of the Laputan printing press – that is I put down Mountains, Rivers, Lakes, dells, glens, Rocks, and Clouds, With beautiful enchanting, gothic picturesque fine, delightful, enchancting, Grand, sublime – a few Blisters &c – and now you have our journey thus far ...

       From a letter by John Keats to J. H. Reynolds, 11 and 13 July 1818

Entering Moscow

Farewell, Petrovsky Castle, witness
to humbled glory. Well! Don't stop!
Drive on! Here the wide gate's pillars
gleam white, now down Tverskaya Street
the potholes check the driver's speed.
Stalls flash by and peasant women,
small shuttered shops, street lamps, boys,
monasteries, gardens and mansion houses,
Bukhara merchants, orchards, sledges,
traders, peasants, unsightly shacks,
towers, avenues and Cossacks,
chemists and fashionable shops,
balconies, gates with carved lion guards
and, on the crosses, jackdaws in crowds.

From the seventh chapter of *Evgeny Onegin* by Alexandr Pushkin, 1833,
translated from the Russian by Thomas de Waal

The Chaotic Credulity of the Enlightenment

Figure all this boundless cunningly devised Agglomerate of royal-arches,
death's-heads, hieroglyphically painted screens, *Columbs* in the state of
innocence; with spacious masonic halls, dark, or in the favourablest
theatrical light-and-dark; Kircher's magic lantern, Belshazzar hand-
writings, of phosphorus: 'plaintive tones', gong-beatings; hoary beard of a
supernatural Grand Cophta emerging from the gloom; – and how it acts,
not only indirectly through the foolish senses of men, but directly on their
Imagination; connecting itself with Enoch and Elias, with Philanthropy,
Immortality, Eleutheromania, and Adam Weisshaupt's Illuminati, and so
downwards to the infinite Deep: figure all this; and in the centre of it, sitting
eager and alert, the skilfulest Panourgos, working the mighty chaos, into a
creation – of ready-money. In such a wide plastic ocean of sham and foam
had the Archquack now happily begun to envelop himself.

From the essay 'Count Cagliostro' by Thomas Carlyle, 1833

Browning Finds 'The Book' in the Piazza di San Lorenzo, on a Day of Buzzing and Blaze in June 1860

This book, – precisely on that palace step
Which, meant for lounging knaves o' the Medici,
Now serves re-venders to display their ware, –
'Mongst odds and ends of ravage, picture-frames
White through the worn gilt, mirror-sconces chipped,
Bronze angel-heads once knobs attached to chests,
(Handled when ancient dames chose forth brocade)
Modern chalk drawings, studies from the nude,
Samples of stone, jet, brecchia, porphyry
Polished and rough, sundry amazing busts
In baked earth, (broken, Providence be praised!)
A wreck of tapestry, proudly-purposed web
When reds and blues were indeed red and blue,
Now offered as a mat to save bare feet
(Since carpets constitute a cruel cost)
Treading the chill scagliola bedward: then
A pile of brown-etched prints, two *crazie* each,
Stopped by a conch a-top from fluttering forth
– Sowing the Square with works of one and the same
Master, the imaginative Sienese
Great in the scenic backgrounds – (name and face
None of you know, nor does he fare the worse:)
From these ... Oh, with a Lionard going cheap
If it should prove, as promised, that Joconde
Whereof a copy contents the Louvre! – these
I picked this book from. Five compeers in a flank
Stood left and right of it as tempting more –
A dogseared Spicilegium, the fond tale
O' the Frail One of the Flowers, by young Dumas,
Vulgarized Horace for the use of schools,
The Life, Death, Miracles of Saint Somebody,
Saint Somebody Else, his Miracles, Death and Life, –
With this, one glance at the lettered back of which,
And 'Stall!' cried I: a *lira* made it mine.

From *The Ring and the Book* by Robert Browning, 1868–9

Sir Walter Vivian's House

And me that morning Walter showed the house,
Greek, set with busts: from vases in the hall
Flowers of all heavens, and lovelier than their names,
Grew side by side; and on the pavement lay
Carved stones of the Abbey-ruin in the park,
Huge Ammonites, and the first bones of Time;
And on the table every clime and age
Jumbled together; celts and calumets,
Claymore and snowshoe, toys in lava, fans
Of sandal, amber, ancient rosaries,
Laborious orient ivory sphere in sphere,
The cursed Malayan crease, and battle-clubs
From the isles of palm: and higher on the walls,
Betwixt the monstrous horns of elk and deer,
His own forefathers' arms and armour hung.

From *The Princess* by Alfred Tennyson, 1847

London Impossibilities

A good cigar bought at a Betting Shop.

A playbill that spoke the truth.

A fresh-laid egg that was less than a month old.

A statue that was an ornament to the metropolis.

A glass of London porter that had not been doctored.

A shilling that had been refused by a box-keeper for a seat at the theatre.

A quiet street without an organ.

An omnibus that was not going to start directly.

A bargain, bought at an 'Awful Failure' shop, that did not turn out a do.

A policeman with spectacles, a blue-coat boy on horse-back; a chimney-sweep with an umbrella; a quaker with a bull-dog; a fountain that was not supremely ridiculous; a Leicester Square foreigner that looked happy; a Belgravian JEAMES in a hurry; a bishop carrying a baby; or a beadle in a balloon.

And lastly, a paving-stone of solid gold, the same as the streets of London are proverbially paved with.

From *Punch*, February 1855

[271]

Instantly Classical Gluttony in the City

Le soir, un peu fatiguée, vous voulûtes vous asseoir devant un café neuf qui formait le coin d'un boulevard neuf, encore tout plein de gravois et montrant déjà glorieusement ses splendeurs inachevées. Le café étincelait. Le gaz lui-même y déployait toute l'ardeur d'un début, et éclairait de toutes ses forces les murs aveuglants de blancheur, les nappes éblouissantes des miroirs, les ors des baguettes et des corniches, les pages aux joues rebondies traînés par les chiens en laisse, les dames riant au faucon perché sur leur poing, les nymphes et les déesses portant sur leur tête des fruits, des pâtés et du gibier, les Hébés et les Ganymèdes présentant à bras tendu la petite amphore à bavaroises ou l'obélisque bicolore des glaces panachées; toute l'histoire et toute la mythologie mises au service de la goinfrerie.

'Les Yeux des Pauvres', from *Le Spleen de Paris* XXVI
by Charles Baudelaire, 1864

Molony's Account of the Great Exhibition

With ganial foire
Thransfuse me loyre,
Ye sacred nympths of Pindus,
The whoile I sing
That wondthrous thing,
The Palace made of windows! ...

There's holy saints
And window paints
By Maydiayval Pugin;
Alhamborough Jones,
Did paint the tones,
Of yellow and gambouge in.

There's fountains there
And crosses fair;
There's water-gods with urrns;
There's organs three,
To play, d'ye see?
'God Save the Queen,' by turrns.

[272]

There's statues bright
Of marble white,
Of silver, and of copper;
And some in zinc,
And some, I think,
That isn't over proper.

There's staym ingynes,
That stands in lines,
Enormous and amazing,
That squeal and snort
Like whales in sport,
Or elephants a-grazing.

There's carts and gigs,
And pins for pigs,
There's dibblers and there's harrows,
And ploughs like toys
For little boys,
And iligant wheelbarrows.

For thim genteels
Who ride on wheels,
There's plenty to indulge 'em:
There's drosky's snug
From Paytersbug,
And vayhycles from Bulgium.

There's cabs on stands
And shandthrydanns;
There's waggons from New York here;
There's Lapland sleighs
Have crossed the seas,
And jaunting cyars from Cork here.

Amazed I pass
From glass to glass,
Deloighted I survey 'em;
Fresh wondthers grows
Before me nose
In this sublime Músayum!

Look, here's a fan
From far Japan,
A sabre from Damasco:
There's shawls ye get
From far Thibet,
And cotton prints from Glasgow.

There's German flutes,
Marocky boots,
And Naples macaronies;
Bohaymia
Has sent Bohay;
Polonia her polonies.

There's granite flints
That's quite imminse,
There's sacks of coals and fuels,
There's swords and guns,
And soap in tuns,
And gingerbread and jewels.

There's taypots there,
And cannons rare;
There's coffins filled with roses;
There's canvas tints,
Teeth insthrumints,
And shuits of clothes by Moses.

There's lashins more
Of things in store,
But thim I don't remimber;
Nor could disclose
Did I compose
From May time to Novimber! . . .

From 'The Crystal Palace', in *Lyra Hybernica*
by William Makepeace Thackeray, 1851

All of Beauty, All of Use

And, lo! the long laborious miles
Of Palace; lo! the giant aisles,
Rich in model and design;
Harvest-tool and husbandry,
Loom and wheel and enginery,
Secrets of the sullen mine,
Steel and gold, and corn and wine,
Fabric rough, or fairy-fine,
Sunny tokens of the Line,
Polar marvels, and a feast
Of wonder, out of West and East,
And shapes and hues of Art divine!

All of beauty, all of use,
That one fair planet can produce,
     Brought from under every star,
Blown from over every main,
And mixt, as life is mixt with pain,
     The works of peace with works of war.

From the 'Ode Sung at the Opening of the International Exhibition'
of 1862, for four hundred voices, by Alfred Tennyson

The Crowd in the Crystal Palace

A unit unperceived,
I sink into the living stream again! –
Nave, transept, aisles and galleries,
Pacing untired: insatiate!
– Amazing spectacle!
Touchstone of character! capacity! and knowledge!
Spectacle, now lost in the Spectators: then spectators,
in the spectacle!
Rich: poor: gentle: simple: wise: foolish: young: old:
learned: ignorant: thoughtful: thoughtless: haughty: humble:
frivolous: profound:
Every grade of intellect: every shade of character!
Here, is a voluble smatterer: suddenly discomfited by

[275]

the chance question of a curious child: and rather than own ignorance, will tell him falsely!

There, a bustling piece of earth: one of the earth, earthy: testing everything by money value!

Here is a stale bundle of prejudices, hard bound together: to whom everything here is topsy-turvy, and discoloured, seen through jaundiced eyes!

Here comes one, serenely unconscious that he is a fool!

There is one suddenly startled by a suspicion that he knows scarcely anything!

Here is one listening, with seeming lively interest, and assenting gestures, to a scientific explanation of which he comprehends nothing; but appearances must be kept up!

There is one falsely thinking himself the observed of observers; trying to look unconscious, and distinguished!

Here is one that will not see a timid poor relation, or an humble friend; as fashionable folk are near!

Yonder is a Statesman: gliding about alone: watchful: thoughtful: cautious: pondering national characters: habits: capabilities: localities: wants: superfluities: rival systems of policy, their fruits and workings: imagining new combinations: speculating on remote consequences.

Yonder walks one who has committed, or is mediating, great crime; and hoping that his heavy eye may here be attracted, and his mind dazzled into a moment's forgetfulness; but it is in vain.

There is a Philosopher, to whose attuned ear the Spectacle speaks myriad-tongued: telling of patient sagacity: long foiled, at length – or suddenly – triumphant: of centuries of mis-directed, abortive toil: of pain, suffering, privation: of one sowing, what another shall reap!

Here is a philanthropist – thinking of blood-stained Slavery:

Of millions, dealt with as though they were the very beasts that perish: bought: sold: scourged: slain: as if their Maker had not seen them, nor heard their groans, nor treasured their tears: nor set them down against the appointed Reckoning!

Here is one, little thinking that he will suddenly fall dead to-morrow: having much on hand, both of business and pleasure!

There is one tottering under the weight of ninety years:

to whom the grasshopper is a burden: leaning on the arms of dutiful and lusty youth: gazing with glazed eye: silent with wise wonder!

Here sits a laughing child, upon a gleaming cannon!

Yonder is a blind man, sightless amid surrounding splendours: but there is one telling him tenderly that he stands beside the statue of Milton!

There, in the glistening centre of the Transept, stands an aged exile: venerable: widowed: once a Queen: looking at the tranquil image of Queen Victoria: meditating, with a sigh, on the happy security of her throne!

Yonder is a musing poet: gazing silently Eastward – Westward – Northward – Southward: above – below:

Everywhere pouring a living tide of wonder – nor silent – nor noisy – a strange hum –

A radiant flood of light – many-hued objects, now glittering brightly – then glistening – fainter and fainter, till lost in distance . . .

From the epic prose-poem *The Lily and the Bee*
by Samuel Warren, 1851

The Collector Takes a Few Inventions at Random

'. . . Let me just quote at random from this catalogue of the Exhibition to which the Padre referred a moment ago, that Exhibition which I beg you to consider as a collective prayer of all the civilised nations . . . Let me see, Number 382: Instrument to teach the blind to write. Model of an aerial machine and of a navigable balloon. A fire annihilator by R. Weare of Plumstead Common. A domestic telegraph requiring only one bell for any number of rooms. An expanding pianoforte for yachts etc. Artificial teeth carved in hippopotamus ivory by Sinclair and Hockley of Soho. A universal drill for removing decay from teeth. A jaw-lever for keeping animals' mouths open. Improved double truss for hernia, invented by a labouring man . . . There seems to be no end to the ingenuity of mankind and I could continue indefinitely quoting examples of it . . .'

From *The Siege of Krishnapur* by J. G. Farrell, 1973

'Winter Afternoons in the V & A, pre-W.W. II'

Rain unslanting, unceasing,
darkening afternoon streets.

Within lofty and vast halls,
no one but I, except for

the ancient guards, survivors
of long-ago battles, dozing

under a spell, perched
on the brittle chairs of their sinecure.

My shoes made no sound. I found
everything for myself,

everything in profusion.
Lace of wrought iron,

wrought jewels, Cellini's dreams,
disappearing fore-edge paintings,
chain mail, crinolines, Hokusai, Cotman.

Here was history

as I desired it: magical, specific,
jumbled, unstinting,

a world for the mind to sift
in its hourglass – now, while I was twelve,
or forever.

Denise Levertov

A Climate of Nut Castanets

Entering
You will find yourself in a climate of nut castanets,
A musical whip
From the Torres Straits, from Mirzapur a sistrum
Called Jumka, 'used by aboriginal
Tribes to attract small game
On dark nights', a mute violin,
Whistling arrows, coolie cigarettes
And a mask of Saagga, the Devil Doctor,
The eyelids worked by strings.

From 'The Pitt-Rivers Museum, Oxford' by James Fenton

Disorder in Canterbury Museum, 1871

In the same case with these elephants' tusks are some casts of toe bones; I at
once recognised them as parts of the foot of the megatherium. I looked
about for the other bones and soon found them; the pelvis under one of the
cases, the femur in one place, the tibia in another, and some more toe bones
at the far end of the room. A cast of the armour-plated coat of the glyptodon
is leaning up against one of the cases, while the animal's head is several feet
away; close to a collection of dried cats, rats, calculi from a horse, an
armadillo's skin, wild boars' heads, sharks' teeth and backbones, the foot of
an elephant, the head of a porpoise, and other objects; all very interesting
and instructive if put in their proper places, but now exhibited without
order, label, or description.

Frank Buckland, quoted in *The Life of Frank Buckland*
by George C. Bompas, 1885

A Dealer in Marine Stores

Our readers must often have observed in some by-street, in a poor
neighbourhood, a small dirty shop, exposing for sale the most extraordinary and confused jumble of old, worn-out, wretched articles, that can well
be imagined. Our wonder at their ever having been bought, is only to be
equalled by our astonishment at the idea of their ever being sold again. On a

board, at the side of the door, are placed about twenty books – all odd volumes; and as many wine-glasses – all different patterns; several locks, an old earthenware pan, full of rusty keys; two or three gaudy chimney-ornaments – cracked, of course; the remains of a lustre, without any drops; a round frame like a capital O, which has once held a mirror; a flute, complete with the exception of the middle joint; a pair of curling-irons; and a tinder-box. In front of the shop window are ranged some half-dozen high-backed chairs, with spinal complaints and wasted legs; a corner cupboard; two or three very dark mahogany tables with flaps like mathematical problems; some pickle-jars, some surgeon's ditto, with gilt labels and without stoppers; an unframed portrait of some lady who flourished about the beginning of the thirteenth century, by an artist who never flourished at all; an incalculable host of miscellanies of every description, including bottles and cabinets, rags and bones, fenders and street-door knockers, fire-irons, wearing apparel and bedding, a hall-lamp, and a room-door. Imagine, in addition to this incongruous mass, a black doll in a white frock, with two faces – one looking up the street, and the other looking down, swinging over the door; a board with the squeezed-up inscription 'Dealer in marine stores', in lanky white letters, whose height is strangely out of proportion to their width; and you have before you precisely the kind of shop to which we wish to direct your attention.

From the essay 'Brokers' and Marine-store Shops'
by Charles Dickens (1812–70)

The Swag-Shops of the Metropolis

In one street (a thoroughfare at the east-end of London) are twenty-three of these establishments. In the windows there is little attempt at display; the design aimed at seems to be rather to *crowd* the window – as if to show the amplitude of the stores within, 'the wonderful resources of this most extensive and universal establishment' – than to tempt purchasers by exhibiting tastefully what may have been tastefully executed by the artificer, or what it is desired should be held to be so executed.

In one of these windows the daylight is almost precluded from the interior by what may be called a perfect wall of 'pots'. A street-seller who accompanied me called them merely 'pots' (the trade term), but they were all pot ornaments. Among them were great store of shepherdesses, of greyhounds of a gamboge colour, of what I heard called 'figures' (allegorical nymphs with and without birds or wreathes in their hands), very tall-looking Shaksperes (I did not see one of these windows without its

[280]

Shakspere, a sitting figure), and some 'pots' which seem to be either shepherds or musicians; from what I could learn, at the pleasure of the seller, the buyer, or the inquirer ... In another window of the same establishment was a conglomeration of pincushions, shaving-brushes, letter-stamps (all in bone), cribbage-boards and boxes (including a pack of cards), necklaces, and strings of beads.

The window of a neighbouring swag-shop presented, in the like crowding, and in greater confusion, an array of brooches (some in coloured glass to imitate rubies, topazes, &c., some containing portraits, deeply coloured, in purple attire, and red cheeks, and some being very large cameos), time-pieces (with and without glasses), French toys with moveable figures, telescopes, American clocks, musical boxes, shirt-studs, backgammon-boards, tea-trays (one with a nondescript bird of a most gorgeous green plumage forming a sort of centrepiece), razor-strops, writing-desks, sailors' knives, hairbrushes, and tobacco-boxes.

Another window presented even a more 'miscellaneous assortment'; dirks (apparently not very formidable weapons), a mess of steel pens, in brown-paper packages and cases, and of black-lead pencils, pipe-heads, cigar-cases, snuff-boxes, razors, shaving-brushes, letter-stamps, metal tea-pots, metal tea-spoons, glass globes with artificial flowers and leaves within the glass (an improvement one man thought on the old ornament of a reel in a bottle), Peel medals, Exhibition medals, roulette-boxes, scent bottles, quill pens with artificial flowers in the feathery part, fans, side-combs, glass pen-holders, and pot figures (caricatures) of Louis Philippe, carrying a very red umbrella, Marshal Haynau, with some instrument of torture in his hand, while over all boomed a huge English seaman, in yellow waistcoat and with a brick-coloured face.

From *London Labour and the London Poor* by Henry Mayhew, 1861–2

A Heterogeneous Emblem for the Nineteenth Century

But what was her surprise when, as it struck the earth, the sunbeam seemed to call forth, or to light up, a pyramid, hecatomb, or trophy (for it had something of a banquet-table air) – a conglomeration at any rate of the most heterogeneous and ill-assorted objects, piled higgledy-piggledy in a vast mound where the statue of Queen Victoria now stands! Draped about a vast cross of fretted and floriated gold were widow's weeds and bridal veils; hooked onto other excrescences were crystal palaces, basinettes, military helmets, memorial wreaths, trousers, whiskers, wedding cakes, cannon, Christmas trees, telescopes, extinct monsters, globes, maps, elephants, and mathematical instruments – the whole supported like a gigantic coat of arms on the right side by a female figure clad in flowing white; on the left by a portly gentleman wearing a frock-coat and sponge-bag trousers. The incongruity of the objects, the association of the fully clothed and the partly draped, the garishness of the different colours and their plaid-like juxtapositions afflicted Orlando with the most profound dismay. She had never, in all her life, seen anything at once so indecent, so hideous, and so monumental.

From *Orlando: A Biography* by Virginia Woolf, 1928

Encountering Strangeness

If instead of a pedagogue I were now to take a man of the world, an intelligent one, and were to transport him to a distant land, I feel sure that though his surprises on disembarkation would be great, though his process of acclimatization might be more or less long, more or less difficult, his sympathy would sooner or later become so keen, so penetrating, that it would create in him a whole new world of ideas, a world that would become part and parcel of him and accompany him as memories till his death. Those odd-shaped buildings that began by offending his academic eye (every people is academic in judging others, every people is barbaric when being judged), that vegetation so disturbing for his memory, filled with images of his own native land, those women and those men whose muscle play is unlike the classic norms in his own country, whose walk has a different rhythm from the one he is used to, whose gaze comes across with a different magnetic power, those scents that are not those of his mother's boudoir, those mysterious flowers whose deep colours strike the eye despotically, whilst their shape teases the attention, those fruits disconcerting and bewildering the senses by their different flavours, and revealing to the palate ideas belonging to the sense of smell, this whole world of new harmonies will slowly enter into him, penetrate him patiently like the steam of a scented bath house; all these unknown springs of life will be added to his own; some thousands of ideas and sensations will enrich his mortal's dictionary, and it may even happen that, overstepping the mark and transforming justice into revolt, he will do as the converted Sicambrian did, and burn what he had adored, to adore what he had burned.

Charles Baudelaire, 1855, translated from the French by P. E. Charvet

The Simple Elements of the True Poetical Effect

We shall reach, however, more immediately a distinct conception of what the true Poetry is, by mere reference to a few of the simple elements which induce in the Poet himself the true poetical effect. He recognises the ambrosia which nourishes his soul, in the bright orbs that shine in Heaven – in the volutes of the flower – in the clustering of low shrubberies – in the waving of the grain-fields – in the slanting of tall, Eastern trees – in the blue distance of mountains – in the grouping of clouds – in the twinkling of half-hidden brooks – in the gleaming of silver rivers – in the repose of sequestered lakes – in the star-mirroring depths of lonely wells. He perceives it in the songs of birds – in the harp of Æolus – in the sighing of the night-wind – in the repining voice of the forest – in the surf that complains to the shore – in the fresh breath of the woods – in the scent of the violet – in the voluptuous perfume of the hyacinth – in the suggestive odour that comes to him, at eventide, from far-distant, undiscovered islands, over dim oceans, illimitable and unexplored. He owns it in all noble thoughts – in all unworldly motives – in all holy impulses – in all chivalrous, generous, and self-sacrificing deeds. He feels it in the beauty of woman – in the grace of her step – in the lustre of her eye – in the melody of her voice – in her soft laughter – in her sigh – in the harmony of the rustling of her robes. He deeply feels it in her winning endearments – in her burning enthusiasms – in her gentle charities – in her meek and devotional endurances – but above all – ah, far above all – he kneels to it – he worships it in the faith, in the purity, in the strength, in the altogether divine majesty – of her *love*.

From the lecture 'The Poetic Principle' by Edgar Allan Poe (1809–49)

Observations

Drops of rain hanging on rails etc. seen with only the lower rim lighted like nails (of fingers). Screws of brooks and twines. Soft chalky look with more shadowy middles of the globes of cloud on a night with a not brilliant moon. Blunt buds of the ash. Pencil buds of the beech. Lobes of the trees. Cups of the eyes. Gathering back the lightly hinged eyelids. Bows of the eyelids. Pencil of eyelashes. Juices of the eyeball. Eyelids like leaves, petals, caps, tufted hats, handkerchiefs, sleeves, gloves. Also of the bones sleeved in flesh. Juices of the sunrise. Joins and veins of the same. Vermilion look of the hand held against a candle with the darker parts as the middles of the fingers and especially the knuckles covered with ash.

From the *Early Diary* of Gerard Manley Hopkins, 1866

'Poetic Subjects'

The capital city. Arrowroot. Water-bur. Colts. Hail. Bamboo grass. The round-leaved violet. Club moss. Water oats. Flat river-boats. The mandarin duck. The scattered *chigaya* reed. Lawns. The green vine. The pear tree. The jujube tree. The althea.

From *The Pillow Book of Sei Shonagon*, tenth century, translated from the Japanese by Ivan Morris

'Pied Beauty'

Glory be to God for dappled things –
   For skies of couple-colour as a brinded cow;
     For rose-moles all in stipple upon trout that swim;
Fresh-firecoal chestnut-falls; finches' wings;
   Landscape plotted and pieced – fold, farrow, and plough;
     And all trades, their gear and tackle and trim.
All things counter, original, spare, strange;
   Whatever is fickle, freckled (who knows how?)
     With swift, slow; sweet, sour; adazzle, dim;
He fathers-forth whose beauty is past change:
       Praise him.

Gerard Manley Hopkins (1844–89)

An Invocation to the Goddess of Particularities

     mother of particular perfections
     queen of otherness
     mistress of asymmetry
patroness of things counter, parti, pied, several
protectress of things known and handled
help of things familiar and small

wardress of the secret crevices
　　of things wrapped and hidden
mediatrix of all the deposits
　　margravine of the troia
empress of the labyrinth
　　receive our prayers.

From 'The Tutelar of the Place' by David Jones, 1961

Acknowledgements

There are, however, many others to whom I may be as, or more, indebted.
Who should say how much may be owing to a small textbook on botany; a
manual of seamanship; various items in the magazine *Wales* edited by Mr
Keidrych Rhys; a guide to the Isle of Wight; a child's picture-book of
prehistoric fauna; a guide-book to the parish church of Cilcain, Flintshire,
by a local antiquary, 1912; a glossy 1949 bookstall purchase on the pontifex
Isambard Kingdom Brunel; a brochure on the composition and permanence
of colours; a pamphlet on the prevention of collisions at sea; a paper read
before a London conference of psychologists; the text of a guide to a
collection of Welsh samplers and embroideries; a catalogue of English
china or plate; a neglected directive from Rome on the use of the Chant; a
reference in *The Times* to the cry of a bittern in Norfolk, or to the bloom on a
thorn-bush in Herefordshire, or to an Homeric find on Karatepe ridge?

From the Preface to *The Anathemata* by David Jones, 1952

Philately

O philately, philately, strange goddess, ga-ga muse: you lead the child by
the hand out of the enchanted forest where Tom Thumb, the Bluebird, Red
Riding-Hood and the Wolf have finally lain down together, you turn Jules
Verne to pictures, and your butterflies of colour carry across the seas the
hearts least ready for the journey. Those who, like me, have built a mental
Sudan before a little rectangle bordered with carmine where tramps across a
sepia earth a white burnous mounted on a camel, or who have been the
confidants of a Brazilian emperor trapped inside his oval office, of giraffes in
Nyasaland, of Australian swans, of Christopher Columbus as he discovered
America in violet, will take my meaning.

From *Paysan de Paris* by Louis Aragon, 1926, translated from the
French by Francis Spufford

[285]

Poems Like Old Post Cards

It is not my intention here to concern myself closely with the poetic qualities of Darmalatov, or to enter into the complex mechanism of literary fame. Nor are the poet's war adventures of any importance to this story, though I confess that certain vivid pictures from Galicia and Bukovina during Brusilov's offensive – when the cadet Darmalatov, an assistant medical officer, discovered the butchered body of his brother – are not without attraction. Nor is his Berlin excursion without charm, or his sentimental adventure, which, against the background of the starved and tragic Russia of the civil war, ended with a honeymoon in the hell of Kislovodsk. His poetry, regardless of what the critics say, offers a plenitude of empirical (poetic) facts, which, like old post cards or photographs in a shabby album, testify as much to his travels, ecstasies, and passions as to literary fashion: the beneficent influence of the wind on the marble clusters of caryatids; the Tiergarten lined with flowering linden trees; the lanterns of the Brandenburg Gate; the monstrous apparitions of the black swans; the rosy reflection of the sun on the murky waters of the Dnieper; the spell of white nights; the magical eyes of Circassian women; a knife plunged to the hilt into the ribs of a wolf of the steppes; the spin of an aeroplane propeller; the caw of the crow in the early dusk; a snapshot (from a bird's-eye view) of the terrible panorama of ravaged Povolzh; the creeping of tractors and threshers through the golden wheat of the prairies; the black shafts of Kursk coal mines; the towers of the Crimea in the ocean of air; the purple velvet of theatre boxes; the ghostly figures of bronze statues flashing amid fireworks; the sweep of ballerinas spun of foam; the splendour of the petroleum flame from the tanker in the harbour; the horrible narcosis of rhymes; the still life of a cup of tea, a silver spoon, and a drowned wasp; the violet eyes of the harnessed horse; the optimistic grinding of turbine engines; the head of the commander Frunze on an operating table amid the intoxicating smell of chloroform; the bare trees in Lubyanka's yard; the hoarse howling of village dogs; the wondrous balance of cement piles; the stalking of a cat following the trail of a winter bird in the snow; grainfields under a barrage of artillery fire; the lovers' parting in the village of the Kama; the military cemetery near Sevastopol . . .

From 'The Short Biography of A. A. Darmalatov', in *A Tomb for Boris Davidovich* by Danilo Kis, 1978

The Zahir

In Buenos Aires the Zahir is an ordinary coin worth twenty centavos. The letters NT and the number 2 are scratched as if with a razor-blade or penknife; 1929 is the date on the obverse. (In Guzerat, towards the end of the eighteenth century, the Zahir was a tiger; in Java, a blind man from the Mosque of Surakarta whom the Faithful pelted with stones; in Persia, an astrolabe which Nadir Shah caused to be sunk to the bottom of the sea; in the Mahdi's prisons, along about 1892, it was a little compass which Rudolf Carl von Slatin touched, tucked into the fold of a turban; in the Mosque of Cordova, according to Zotenberg, it was a vein in the marble of one of the twelve-hundred pillars; in the Tetuán ghetto, it was the bottom of a well.)

Jorge Luis Borges, translated from the Spanish by Dudley Fitts, 1964

The Chaos of Judaism

The chaos of Judaism showed through all the chinks of the stone-clad Petersburg apartment: in the threat of ruin, in the cap hanging in the room of the guest from the provinces, in the spiky script of the unread books of Genesis, thrown into the dust one shelf lower than Goethe and Schiller, in the shreds of the black-and-yellow ritual.

From *The Noise of Time* by Osip Mandelstam, 1928,
translated from the Russian by Clarence Brown

Everything Juts Up in Europe

          ... It was the way
Things jutted up, the way the jagged sticks,
The foul immovables, came through the clouds,
Colossal blacks that leaped across the points
Of Boucher pink, the sheens of Venetian gray.
That's what did it. Everything did it at last.
The binders did it with their armorial books.
And the cooks, the cooks, the bar-men and the maids,
The churches and their long parades, Seville
At Easter on a London screen, the seeds
Of Vilmorin, Verhaeren in his grave,

The flute on the gramophone, the Daimlers that
Dissolved the woods, war and the fatal farce
Of war, the rust on the steeples, these jutted up,
These streaked the mother-of-pearl, the lunar cress.
Everything did.

From 'The Greenest Continent' by Wallace Stevens, 1936

A Pattern Out Of This Muddle

When you come back to England from any foreign country, you have
immediately the sensation of breathing a different air. Even in the first few
minutes dozens of small things conspire to give you this feeling. The beer is
bitterer, the coins are heavier, the grass is greener, the advertisements are
more blatant. The crowds in the big towns, with their mild knobbly faces,
their bad teeth and gentle manners, are different from a European crowd.
Then the vastness of England swallows you up, and you lose for a while
your feeling that the whole nation has a single identifiable character. Are
there really such things as nations? Are we not 46 million individuals, all
different? And the diversity of it, the chaos! The clatter of clogs in the
Lancashire mill towns, the to-and-fro of the lorries on the Great North
Road, the queues outside the Labour Exchanges, the rattle of pin-tables in
the Soho pubs, the old maids biking to Holy Communion through the mists
of the autumn mornings – all these are not only fragments but *characteristic*
fragments, of the English scene. How can one make a pattern out of this
muddle?

From *England, Your England* by George Orwell (1903–50)

Culture

Taking now the point of view of identification, the reader must remind
himself as the author has constantly to do, of how much is here embraced by
the term *culture*. It includes all the characteristic activities and interests of a
people: Derby Day, Henley Regatta, Cowes, the twelfth of August, a cup
final, the dog races, the pin table, the dart board, Wensleydale cheese,
boiled cabbage cut into sections, beetroot in vinegar, nineteenth-century
Gothic churches and the music of Elgar. The reader can make his own list.

From *Notes Towards the Definition of Culture* by T. S. Eliot, 1948

An English June

The contents of an English June are, hay and ice, orange-flowers and rheumatisms!

From a letter by Horace Walpole to the Miss Berrys, 1791

The Agreeable Mixture of Constantinople

The unequal heights make it seem as large again as it is (though one of the largest cities in the world), shewing an agreeable mixture of gardens, pine and cypress-trees, palaces, mosques, and public buildings, raised one above another, with as much beauty and appearance of symmetry as your ladyship ever saw in a cabinet, adorned by the most skilful hands, jars shew themselves above jars, mixed with canisters, babies, and candlesticks. This is a very odd comparison; but it gives me an exact idea of the thing.

From a letter by Lady Mary Wortley Montagu to the Countess of Bristol, 10 April 1718

The Inventory of the Streets

January 1. They're selling New Year's boughs on the street. Passing through Strasnoi Square I saw someone holding up long saplings with green, white, blue and red paper blossoms glued onto them, every branch a different colour. I would like to write on the 'flowers' of Moscow, not dealing solely with the heroic Christmas roses but also with the huge hollyhocks on the lampshades which peddlars proudly brandish throughout the city. There are also tarts in the shape of cornucopias spilling forth cracker bonbons or pralines wrapped in different colours of paper. Cakes shaped like lyres. The 'confectioner' of old children's literature seems to have survived only in Moscow. Only here can you find pictures created out of nothing more than spun sugar, sweet icicles on which the tongue takes its revenge against the bitter cold. One might also mention what the frost inspires, the peasant shawls whose designs, stitched in blue wool, imitate ice-flowers on the windowpane. The inventory of the streets is inexhaustible. Through the optician's eyeglasses I noticed the evening sky suddenly take on a southerly tint. Then the wide sleds with three bins for peanuts, hazelnuts, and *semechki* (sunflower seeds which, following a decree by the

[289]

Soviet, are no longer allowed to be sold in public places). Then I saw a man selling small skates for dolls. Finally the tin trash cans – littering the streets is forbidden. Further notes on the shop signs: a few in Roman alphabet – Cafe, Tailleur. Every tap-room bearing the sign: *Pivnaia* – painted on a background whose upper border of drab green gradually shades off into a smudgy yellow. Many of the shop signs hang into the street at right angles.

From Walter Benjamin's *Moscow Diary*, 1927

The Palette of Blondes

So one day I was in the Opéra arcade, contemplating slow, pure python-coils of blondeness. And suddenly, for the first time in my life, I was seized with the thought that mankind has only ever found one comparison for blondeness – *corn-coloured* – and has believed that said all there was to say. Corn indeed, unfortunately: but have you never seen ferns? I've sighed for a year over fern-coloured hair. I've known hair like resin, hair like topaz, hair like hysteria. The blonde of hysteria, the blonde of the sky, the blonde of fatigue, the blonde of embraces. On the palette of blondes, I'll lay the elegance of limousines, the smell of sainfoin cut for fodder, the silence of mornings, the perplexities of hope, the ravages to the heart of casual brushes-past. How blonde is the sound of the rain, how blonde the song of mirrors! From the perfume of gloves to the screech of an owl, from the armoured heart of an assassin to the flaming flowers of a laburnum, there are as many blondes as there are sights to be seen: the blonde of roofs, the blonde of wind, the blonde of tables and palm-trees, whole days of blondeness, great shops of blondeness, galleries of desire, arsenals of powdered orangeade. Universal blondeness: and I abandon myself to this helter-skelter of the senses, to this idea of a blondeness which is not even a colour but a sort of essence of colour united with all the tones (and half-tones) of love. All the way from white to red via yellow, blonde never yields up its mystery. It resembles the stammerings of sensual passion, the piratical voyages of lips, the trembling surface of transparent waters. It escapes from definition down a capricious path where I find flowers and shells. It is a kind of reflection of a woman upon stone, a paradoxical shadow of caresses in empty air, a sigh of defeated reason. Blonde as the reign of an embrace, the hair I watched dissolved away into a shop, and I left myself for dead for a good quarter of an hour.

From *Paysan de Paris* by Louis Aragon, 1926, translated from the French by Francis Spufford

The Classifications of the Opera-House

Then two thousand hearts in the semi-darkness remembered, anticipated, travelled dark labyrinths; and Clara Durrant said farewell to Jacob Flanders, and tasted the sweetness of death in effigy; and Mrs Durrant, sitting behind her in the dark of the box, sighed her sharp sigh; and Mr Wortley, shifting his position behind the Italian Ambassador's wife, thought that Brangaena was a trifle hoarse; and suspended in the gallery many feet above their heads, Edward Whittaker surreptitiously held a torch to his miniature score; and . . . and . . .

In short, the observer is choked with observations. Only to prevent us from being submerged by chaos, nature and society between them have arranged a system of classification which is simplicity itself; stalls, boxes, amphitheatre, gallery. The moulds are filled nightly. There is no need to distinguish details. But the difficulty remains – one has to choose. For though I have no wish to be Queen of England – or only for a moment – I would willingly sit beside her; I would hear the Prime Minister's gossip; the countess whisper, and share her memories of halls and gardens; the massive fronts of the respectable conceal after all their secret code; or why so impermeable? And then, doffing one's own headpiece, how strange to assume for a moment some one's – any one's – to be a man of valour who has ruled the Empire; to refer while Brangaena sings to the fragments of Sophocles, or see in a flash, as the shepherd pipes his tune, bridges and aqueducts. But no – we must choose. Never was there a harsher necessity! or one which entails greater pain, more certain disaster; for wherever I seat myself, I die in exile: Whittaker in his lodging-house; Lady Charles at the Manor.

From *Jacob's Room* by Virginia Woolf, 1922

The Air Everywhere is Filled with Things

Laura, who loved all kinds of boxes and bottles, all objects that could keep and hold things, went gazing her fill through the store, and touching where she would. At first she thought she could find anything she wanted for a wedding present for her uncle George.

Along the tops of the counters were square glass jars with gold-topped stoppers – they held the kernels and flakes of seed – and just as likely, crusted over wine-balls, liquorice sticks, or pink-covered gingerbread stage-planks. All around, at many levels, fishing boxes all packed, china pots with dusty little lids, cake stands with the weightiest of glass covers, buckets marked like a mackerel sky, dippers, churns, bins, hampers, baby baskets, popcorn poppers, cooky jars, butter moulds, money safes, hair receivers, mouse traps, all these things held the purest enchantment for her; once, last year, she threw her arms around the pickle barrel, and seemed to feel then a heavy, briny response in its nature, unbudging though it was. The pickle barrel was the heart of the store in summer, as in winter it was the stove that stood on a square stage in the back, with a gold spittoon on each corner. The name of the stove was 'Kankakee', written in raised iron writing across its breast which was decorated with summer-cold iron flowers

The air was a kind of radiant haze, which disappeared into a dim blue among hanging boots above – a fragrant store dust that looked like gold dust in the light from the screen door. Cracker dust and flour dust and brown-sugar particles seemed to spangle the air the minute you stepped inside. (And she thought, in the Delta, all the air everywhere is filled with things – it's the shining dust that makes it look so bright.) All was warm and fragrant here, the cats smelled like ginger when you rubbed their blond foreheads and clasped their fat yellow sides. Every counter smelled different, from the ladylike smell of the dry-goods counter with its fussy revolving ball of string, to the manlike smell of coffee where it was ground in the back. There were areas of banana smell, medicine smell, rope and rubber and nail smell, bread smell, peppermint-oil smell, smells of feed, shot, cheese, tobacco, and chicory, and the smells of the old cane chairs creaking where the old fellows slept.

Objects stood in the aisle as high as the waist, so that you waded when you walked or twisted like a cat. Other things hung from the rafters, to be touched and to swing at the hand when you gave a jump. Once Laura's hand went out decisively and she almost chose something – a gold net of blue agates – for Uncle George. But she said, sighing, to Ranny running by, 'I don't see a present for Uncle George. Nothing you have is good enough!'

From *Delta Wedding* by Eudora Welty, 1946

Life, London

In people's eyes, in the swing, tramp, and trudge; in the bellow and the uproar; the carriages, motor cars, omnibuses, vans, sandwich men shuffling and swinging; brass bands; barrel organs; in the triumph and the jingle and the strange high singing of some aeroplane overhead was what she loved; life; London; this moment of June.

From *Mrs Dalloway* by Virginia Woolf, 1925

Market Research

And so for four years and maybe more they explored and interviewed and analysed. Why are pure-suction vacuum cleaners selling so poorly? What do people of modest origin think of chicory? Do you like ready-made mashed potatoes, and if so, why? Because they are light? Because they are creamy? Because they are easy to make – just open it up and there you are? Do people really reckon baby carriages are expensive? Aren't you always prepared to fork out a bit extra for the good of the kids? Which way will French women vote? Do people like cheese in squeezy tubes? Are you for or against public transport? What do you notice first when you eat yoghurt? – the colour? the texture? the taste? natural odour? Do you read a lot, a little, not at all? Do you eat out? Would you, Madam, like to rent your room to a Black? What do people think, honestly, of old-age pensions? What does the younger generation think? What do executives think? What does the woman of thirty think? What do you think of holidays? Where do you spend your holidays? Do you like frozen food? How much do you think a lighter like this one costs, eh? What do you look for in a mattress? Describe a man who likes pasta. What do you think of your washing machine? Are you satisfied with it? Doesn't it make too many suds? Does it wash properly? Does it tear the clothes? Does it dry? Would you rather have a washing machine that dries as well? And safety in coal mines, is it alright or not good enough, in your view, sir? (Make the target speak; ask him to give personal examples: things he has seen; has he been injured himself? how did it happen? And your son, sir, will he be a miner like his father? So what will he be, then?)

There was washing, drying, ironing. Gas, electricity and the telephone. Children. Clothes and underclothes. Mustard. Packet soups, tinned soups. Hair: how to wash it, how to dry it, how to make it hold a wave, how to make it shine. Students, fingernails, cough syrup, typewriters, fertilisers, tractors, leisure pursuits, presents, stationery, linen, politics, motorways, alcoholic drinks, mineral water, cheeses, jams, lamps and curtains, insurance and gardening. *Nil humani alienum* . . . Nothing that was human was outside their scope.

From *Things. A Story of the Sixties* by Georges Perec, 1965, translated from the French by David Bellos

ABC From the Store

. . . you go to the store
and you bring back:
ankles, a brain,
calves, new dentition,
elbows with new funnybones,
new gums, new hair,
new insteps, a new jaw,
new knees, new lungs,
new muscles, new nipples,
a new oesophagus, new palms,
new quick, new ribs,
new skin, new toes,
a new uvula, new veins,
a new womb, new x-
rays, and warts, and yaws,
and wrenching and vomiting,
unconsciousness, ticks,
sunburn and rhinoplasty,
quinsy, pellagra,
obesity and neuralgia,
malaria, leishmaniasis,
kidney-stones and jock-itch,
insanity, hypoglecemia,
gout, flatulence,
elephantiasis and dengue,
crabs and bursitis,
atherosclerosis –
all these real things
that don't matter,
I go to the store
and I bring back androgyny.
I go to the store
and I bring back androgyny
and a bomb. I go to the store
and I bring back androgyny,
a bomb, creams, diffidence,
Euclid and a filing-system,
Goethe, and a hat,
and ipsation, and junk,

kleenex, the *Lysistrata*
illustrated, macaroni by Marconi,
nutrients, organisms,
pills, quarterlies,
rings, sexuality, toothpicks,
Uncle Sam, vibes, wax,
Xenophon, yage, and a zipper.
The fading other
gesticulates aptly:
his gestures aren't ones I need.
His smile is small and strong,
but it's hard to determine his posture.
Or is he a woman? so silvery,
so brunette! I went, and bring back
a zest for affection and a yearning for beauty,
a xerox of concepts, the will for deliberation,
a volume of excellence, understanding for friendship,
trust in generosity (and sentiments for the hungry),
respect for intelligence, a questing for judiciousness,
passion for knowledge with an option for learning,
a need for mourning, mistrust of norms,
love of otherness, kindness towards poets,
jubilation in quirkiness, an inclination to respect,
hatred of separations, a gift for taste,
faith in unselfishness, enthusiasm for victims,
devotion to work, contempt for xenophobia,
benevolence towards youth, abnegation before zanies . . .

From *Plaque* by Harry Mathews (1930–)

Exotic Harvests

Dis, non les pampas printaniers
Noirs d'épouvantables révoltes,
Mais les tabacs, les cotonniers!
Dis les exotiques, récoltes!

Dis, front blanc que Phébus tanna,
De combien de dollars se rente
Pédro Velasquez, Habana;
Incague la mer de Sorrente

[295]

Où vont les Cygnes par milliers;
Que tes Strophes soient des réclames
Pour l'abatis des mangliers
Fouillés des hydres et des lames!

Ton quatrain plonge aux bois sanglants
Et revient proposer aux Hommes
Divers sujets de sucres blancs,
De pectoraires et de gommes!

From 'Ce qu'on dit au poëte à propos de fleurs'
by Arthur Rimbaud, 1871

'Voyelles'

A noir, E blanc, I rouge, U vert, O bleu: voyelles,
Je dirai quelque jour vos naissances latentes:
A, noir corset velu des mouches éclatantes
Qui bombinent autour des puanteurs cruelles,

Golfes d'ombre; E, candeurs des vapeurs et des tentes,
Lances des glaciers fiers, rois blancs, frissons d'ombelles;
I, pourpres, sang craché, rire des lèvres belles
Dans la colère ou les ivresses pénitentes;

U, cycles, vibrements divins des mers viride,
Paix de pâtis semés d'animaux, paix des rides
Que l'alchimie imprime aux grands fronts studieux;

O, suprême Clairon plein des strideurs étranges,
Silences traversés des Mondes et des Anges:
– O l'Oméga, rayon violet de Ses Yeux!

Arthur Rimbaud (1854–91)

Azure and Clay

Azure and clay, clay and azure,
what more do you want? Rather screw up your eyes
like a nearsighted shah at a turquoise ring,
at a book of ringing clays, at a bookish earth,
at a festering book, at a costly clay
that torments us as do music and the word.

From the 'Armenia' cycle by Osip Mandelstam, 1930,
translated from the Russian by David McDuff

'Those Various Scalpels,'

those
various sounds consistently indistinct, like intermingled echoes
   struck from thin glasses successively at random –
      the inflection disguised: your hair, the tails of two
fighting-cocks head to head in stone –
      like sculptured scimitars repeating the curve of your ears in
                        reverse order:
      your eyes, flowers of ice and snow

sown by tearing winds on the cordage of disabled ships; your
                        raised hand,
   an ambiguous signature: your cheeks, those rosettes
   of blood on the stone floors of French châteaux,
   with regard to which the guides are so affirmative –
   your other hand,

a bundle of lances all alike, partly hid by emeralds from Persia
   and the fractional magnificence of Florentine
      goldwork – a collection of little objects –
   sapphires set with emeralds, and pearls with a moonstone,
                    made fine
   with enamel in gray, yellow, and dragon-fly blue;
   a lemon, a pear

and three bunches of grapes, tied with silver: your dress, a
                                        magnificent square
        cathedral tower of uniform
        and at the same time diverse appearance – a
    species of veryical vineyard rustling in the storm
        of conventional opinion. Are they weapons or scalpels?
            Whetted to brilliance

    by the hard majesty of that sophistication which is superior to
                                        opportunity,
            these things are rich instruments with which to experiment.
        But why dissect destiny with instruments
                more highly specialized than components of destiny
                                        itself?

Marianne Moore (1887–1972)

The Ascetic Trove of Responsive Fact

            . . . I can build towers of my own,
        There to behold, there to proclaim, the grace

        And free requiting of responsive fact,
        To project the naked man in a state of fact,
        As acutest virtue and ascetic trove.

        Item: The cocks crow and the birds cry and
        The sun expands, like a repetition on
        One string, an absolute, not varying

        Toward an inaccessible, pure sound.
        Item: The wind is never rounding O
        And, imageless, it is itself the most,

        Mouthing its constant smatter throughout space.
        Item: The green fish pensive in green reeds
        Is an absolute. Item: The cataracts

        As facts fall like rejuvenating rain,
        Fall down through nakedness to nakedness,
        To the auroral creature musing in the mind.

Item: Breathe, breathe upon the centre of
The breath life's latest, thousand senses.
But let this one sense be the single main . . .

From 'Montrachet-le-Jardin' by Wallace Stevens (1878–1955)

'Écume de Mer Pain Enchanté'

Le gant rouge du crime * Le cortège du serpent * Sa tête qui est un revolver *
La gangrène * Le jeune marin qui colle un timbre * As de trèfle * Oh! mon
Dieu! que fait-il de son pouce? il se condamne à mort * Vénus, tout rose,
assise dans mille calèches démolies contre la muraille * La menthe, le bluet,
le tambour, la grenadine * Et le pain enchanté qui s'envole par-dessus le toit.

From *Vocabulaire* by Jean Cocteau, 1922

'Rose de Jéricho'

Rose de Jéricho, les clairons militaires
Mettent partout les murs, les pétales par terre;
Les hôtels, les villas, les kiosques à musique,
La carte en relief, ses cascades, ses chaînes
De montagnes, ses pics qui changent nuit et jour.

Humide est le corail, porte-chance d'amour!
Il te faut rebâtir, rose de vitres et d'arbres,
Parfois bock sur le quai, parfois cime d'un chêne,
Pommier d'Avril souvent, mais plus lourd que le marbre

On y pose dessus: quêteuses, jeux nautiques,
Le char et la déesse et le combat naval.

From *Vocabulaire* by Jean Cocteau, 1922

Too Commodious

The sea is full of fishes in shoals, the woods that let
One seed alone grow wild, the railway-stops
In Russia at which the same statue of Stalin greets
The same railway passenger, the ancient tree
In the centre of its cones, the resplendent flights
Of red facsimiles through related trees,
White houses in villages, black communicants –
The catalogue is too commodious.

From 'Mountains Covered with Cats' by Wallace Stevens (1878–1955)

Mirrors of Water, Mirrors of Ebony

Mirrors of water, mirrors of ebony,
the all-inventive mirror of our dreams,
lichens, fishes, and the riddled coral,
the clawmarks left by tortoises in time,
the fireflies of a single afternoon,
the dynasties of the Auraucarians,
the delicate shapes of letters in a volume
which night does not blot out, unquestionably
are no less personal and enigmatic
than I, who mix them up. I would not venture
to judge the lepers or Caligula.

From 'Poem of Quantity' in *El oro de los tigres* by Jorge Luis Borges, 1972,
translated from the Spanish by Alastair Reid

Chinese Scene

The old man gestures; the servant pats the dog;
The donkey ambles; the fishermen dispute;
The volcano explodes; the travellers climb;
The horses graze; the man looks out of the window.

From *A Bad Day for the Sung Dynasty* by Frank Kuppner, 1984

'A View of Things'

what I love about dormice is their size
what I hate about rain is its sneer
what I love about the Bratach Gorm is its unflappability
what I hate about scent is its smell
what I love about newspapers is their etaoin shrdl
what I hate about philosophy is its pursed lip
what I love about Rory is his old grouse
what I hate about Pam is her pinkie
what I love about semi-precious stones is their preciousness
what I hate about diamonds is their mink
what I love about poetry is its ion engine
what I hate about hogs is their setae
what I love about love is its porridge-spoon
what I hate about hate is its eyes
what I love about hate is its salts
what I hate about love is its dog
what I love about Hank is his string vest
what I hate about the twins is their three gloves
what I love about Mabel is her teeter
what I hate about gooseberries is their look, feel, smell, and taste
what I love about the world is its shape
what I hate about a gun is its lock, stock, and barrel
what I love about bacon-and-eggs is its predictability
what I hate about derelict buildings is their reluctance to
    disintegrate
what I love about a cloud is its unpredictability
what I hate about you, chum, is your china
what I love about many waters is their inability to quench love

                                             Edwin Morgan

'Approximately'

He picks up in his hands things that don't match – a stone,
a broken roof-tile, two burned matches,
the rusty nail from the wall opposite,
the leaf that came in through the window, the drops
dropping from the watered flower pots, that bit of straw

the wind blew in your hair yesterday – he takes them
and he builds, in his backyard, approximately a tree.
Poetry is in this 'approximately'. Can you see it?

From *Testimonies B* by Yannis Ritsos, 1966, translated from
the Greek by Nikos Stangos

A Hollywood Everything

Something strange is creeping across me.
La Celestina has only to warble the first few bars
Of 'I Thought About You' or something mellow from
Amadigi di Gaula for everything – a mint-condition can
Of Rumford's Baking Powder, a celluloid earring, Speedy
Gonzales, the latest from Helen Topping Miller's fertile
Escritoire, a sheaf of suggestive pix on greige, deckle-edged
Stock – to come clattering through the rainbow trellis
Where Pistachio Avenue rams the 2300 block of Highland
Fling Terrace . . .

From 'Daffy Duck in Hollywood' by John Ashbery, 1977

Entropy

The woodman weighs up the oaks; the calendar, the years; the pamphlet,
hatreds; the boxer, his teeth; the locksmith, bolts; the sweetmaker, fondant
bonbons; the jeweller, chalcedonies; the tamer, the elephants; the coiffeur,
combs; the hatter, turbans; the impresario, new prodigies; the riding-
master, white stallions; the juggler, full spheres; the conjurer, empty
spheres. The weight of things requires attention, though it may be we feel
little anxiety at the supposed law of matter's ruin, for in the end all things
re-unite: the years in the rings of the oaks, the look of hatred in the teeth, the
fondant bonbons in the cakeholes of keyholes, the precious stones in the
finery of the elephants, the combs beneath wound cloths, the hoarse
prodigies in galloping fame, and the spheres with the spheres in topological
bouquets. Now everything is clear.

From *Morale Élementaire* by Raymond Queneau, 1975, translated from the
French by Francis Spufford

Acknowledgements

Advice, luck, and secondary reading have figured largely in the making of this book. For signposting areas of literature of which I am ignorant, I am specifically indebted to Donald Davie's *Articulate Energy* (1955), Asa Briggs's *Victorian Things* (1988), Peter Conrad's *The Victorian Treasure-House* (1973), and *Kissing the Rod: Seventeenth Century Women's Verse* (1988), edited by Germaine Greer *et al.* For lists, and for suggestions that have speeded my temporary career as a list-hunter, I am grateful to Edmund Baxter, Ian Bostridge, Martin Brett, Jonathan Burnham, Simon Burt, Antonia Byatt, Edmund de Waal, Thomas de Waal, Matthew Dixon, Jennifer Doherty, Amy Erickson, David Fussner, Netta Goldsmith, Hester, Susan and Andor Gomme, Jean Gooder, Richard Gooder, Jason Goodwin, Kate Hardy, Kate Harris, Andrew Holgate, Kate Horgan, Garry Kelly, Robert Lacey, Anthony Lane, Athena Leoussi, Julian Loose, Alasdair Mackinnon, Bernice Martin, Jessica Martin, Shawn Maurer, Andrew Motion, Bridget Spufford (1967–89), Margaret Spufford, Kate Teltscher, Jenny Uglow, John Vallance, David Whiting, Hamish Whyte and Kathy Zuckerman. Jennifer Ramkalawon provided lists too; but also disorganised domestic pleasures, kind diversions, and a usefully eccentric collection of books. Ian Hunt helped me through numerous difficulties in the writing of the introduction, and remained miraculously enthusiastic. Andrew Motion read the introduction at a later stage and suggested improvements. At Chatto & Windus Robert Lacey edited me with zeal and patience, and was resolutely nice about the shortcomings of my card-index.

Finally – if an editor is allowed to make a dedication – this book is for my father, because he may be surprised to hear it and ought not to be.

The editor and publishers gratefully acknowledge permission to reprint copyright material as follows:
The British Library for 'The Shires', from BMMS Harley 7371; Jonathan Cape Ltd for the excerpts from *Paris Peasant* by Louis Aragon (a translation by Simon Watson Taylor is published by Picador); 'Into the Dusk-Charged Air' and the excerpt from 'Daffy Duck in Hollywood', from *Selected Poems* by John Ashbery, reprinted by permission of the author and Carcanet Press Ltd; 'As the poets have mournfully sung' reprinted by permission of Faber & Faber Ltd from *Collected Poems* by W. H. Auden; two extracts from *The*

permission of The Bodleian Library, Oxford; the excerpt from Bruce
Chatwin's Introduction to *The Road to Oxiana* reprinted by permission of
the Legal Personal Representatives of C. B. Chatwin; the poems 'Écume de
mer pain enchanté' and 'Rose de Jéricho' from *Vocabulaire, Plain-chant et
autres poèmes* (1983) by Jean Cocteau, © Éditions Gallimard, reprinted by
permission of Éditions Gallimard; the excerpt from *57 Views of Fujiyama*, by
Guy Davenport, originally published in *Granta* and reprinted in *Apples &
Pears*, is reproduced by permission of the author and North Point Press; the
excerpt from *Notes Towards the Definition of Culture* by T. S. Eliot reprinted by
permission of Faber & Faber Ltd; the excerpt from *The Siege of Krishnapur* by
J. G. Farrell reprinted by permission of Weidenfeld & Nicolson Ltd; the
excerpt from 'The Pitt-Rivers Museum, Oxford', from *The Memory of War*
by James Fenton, reprinted by permission of the Peters Fraser & Dunlop
Group Ltd; the excerpts from *The Violins of St Jacques* and *Mani* by Patrick
Leigh Fermor reprinted by permission of John Murray (Publishers) Ltd; the
Estate of F. Scott Fitzgerald and The Bodley Head for the excerpt from *The
Crack-Up*, from *The Bodley Head F. Scott Fitzgerald*, Volume 3; Lescher &
Lescher, Ltd and Pan Books Ltd for the excerpt from *Cities on a Hill*,
copyright © 1981, 1983, 1986 by Frances Fitzgerald, published by Simon
& Schuster and Picador; the author and Jonathan Cape Ltd for the excerpt
from *1982, Janine* by Alasdair Gray; the excerpt from *Death in the Afternoon*
by Ernest Hemingway, copyright 1932 by Charles Scribner's Sons, renewal
copyright © 1960 Ernest Hemingway, is reprinted with permission of
Charles Scribner's Sons, an imprint of Macmillan Publishing Company; the
illustration from *The Crab With the Golden Claws*, © Hergé 1953, published
by Methuen & Co. Ltd, is reproduced by kind permission of Sundancer Ltd;
the excerpt from the 'Night Letters' of Roger Hilton reprinted by kind
permission of Mrs Rosemary Hilton; the excerpt from the *Early Diary* of
Gerard Manley Hopkins reprinted by permission of Oxford University
Press on behalf of The Society of Jesus; the excerpts from *Anathemata* and
the excerpt from *The Sleeping Lord and Other Fragments* by David Jones
reprinted by permission of Faber & Faber Ltd; The Society of Authors as
the literary representative of James Joyce for the excerpts from *Finnegans
Wake*; the excerpt from 'The Short Biography of A. A. Darmalatov', from *A
Tomb for Boris Davidovich* by Danilo Kis, reprinted by permission of Faber &
Faber Ltd; 'What to Say When You Talk to Yourself' by Stephen Knight
reproduced by kind permission of the author and *New Statesman & Society*;
the excerpts from *A Bad Day for the Sung Dynasty* by Frank Kuppner
reprinted by permission of Carcanet Press Ltd; the excerpt from *The Leopard*
by Giuseppi di Lampedusa, translated by Archibald Colquhoun, reprinted
by permission of William Collins Sons & Co Ltd; 'A Hunger', from Denise
Levertov, *Poems 1968–1972*, copyright © 1970 by Denise Levertov Good-

Index of Authors

Thus I conclude with this chance-medley Parenthesis ...
THOMAS NASHE